Monograph 53

THE AMERICAN ETHNOLOGICAL SOCIETY

Robert F. Spencer, Editor

The Mound Builders

Agricultural Practices, Environment, and Society

in the Central Highlands of New Guinea

ERIC WADDELL

UNIVERSITY OF WASHINGTON PRESS

Seattle and London

Library of Congress Cataloging in Publication Data

Waddell, Eric W   1939–
  The mound builders.

  (American Ethnological Society. Monograph 53)
  A revision of the author's thesis, Australian
National University, 1969.
  Bibliography: p. 239
  1. Enga (New Guinea people)   2. Agriculture,
Primitive.   3. Anthropo-geography—New Guinea (Ter.)
I. Title.   II. Series.
GN425.W33   1972   309.1'95'5   70–159437
ISBN 0–295–95169–9

To those of us who seek to live

in harmony with nature

Preface

THE identification and successful execution of a program of field research is determined by a variety of considerations—intellectual, emotional, and circumstantial. In my own case I would be hard put to segregate these out. Certainly as a student of human geography I have always been concerned with the relationships between man and nature, and intuitively I "knew" these could be defined and structured in a precise way. However, I found little in my early professional training to give substance to these convictions. Then in late 1963, while in the employ of the New Guinea Research Unit of the Australian National University, I had the good fortune to visit the Western Highlands District of Australian New Guinea. I was immediately struck by the carefully worked sweet potato mounds that characterize Enga agriculture, and I could not help but feel that in interpreting so distinctive a practice lay the key to providing a functional explanation of the total adaptation. An exceptional situation such as this, where tropical food plants are cultivated in a tropically marginal environment, and where adaptive stresses are accentuated by dense, geographically confined, subsistence populations, could only serve to bring into focus the interrelationships between society, technology, resources, and environment.

The project lay dormant for several years, nourished occasionally by a growing familiarity with Highlands ethnography and conversations with Pim Straatmans, a New Guinea Research Unit colleague with a fascination for "agro-dynamics." But in December 1965 plans came to fruition when I assumed tenure of a Ph.D. scholarship at the Australian National University. There followed thirteen months of fieldwork, from January 1966 to February 1967, in the Wabag Subdistrict, and it is to this period that the study explicitly refers. Most of that time I spent at Sabakamádá, a clan territory located on the southern slopes of the Lai Valley near Wapenamanda. From my house I could look across the Lai gorge and the patrol post to Mount Hagen, and it was this breathtaking view, together with the vitality of Raiapu Enga society surrounding me, that made my stay as rewarding an experience emotionally as it was intellectually.

The initial version of the manuscript was submitted as a Ph.D. thesis to the Australian National University in December 1968 and the degree was conferred in September 1969. Since that date various revisions have been made to accommodate the criticisms of colleagues and written communications from a number of individuals resident in the Highlands, but no further fieldwork has been undertaken in the area. The present book is thus the product of a series of essentially minor modifications to the thesis.

It is well known that field research in the social sciences involves the cooperation of a large number of people if it is to be successful. Mine is no exception. First and foremost I am indebted to those Enga who welcomed me into their territory, their houses, and their gardens, who bore with my initial ignorance of language and customs, who suffered many impositions on their time and generosity, and who in the final analysis benefited little, except from the novel experience of knowing a European who did not come to judge their ways and who sought to share their lives with them. The burden of my inquiry fell heavily on the shoulders of ten families, and from among them I must single out one man in particular, Wajó, as a friend who unceasingly shared his knowledge, food, and hospitality. In addition there was Pidú, an everwilling helper, always eager either to fetch water, light my fire, show the way to a garden, hold the end of a measuring tape, or simply provide company. Bae Rakayati, my field assistant, successfully filled a role that was essential to effective prosecution of the research.

The New Guinea Lutheran Mission (Missouri Synod) demonstrated a keen interest in my work from the outset, and they made many services available to me. Edmund Bloos, Elizabeth Banke, Edward Dicke, Roland Freund, and Ted Westermann were particularly helpful, while William and Ruth Wagner extended many kindnesses to my family during our two-month stay at Sirunki. The assistant district commissioner at Wabag, David Hook, also provided assistance wherever possible, and various other Administration officials gave freely of their knowledge.

Analysis of the material and preparation of the dissertation and its revision for publication have involved assistance drawn from a variety of sources. The principal chemist at DASF, Konedobu, kindly arranged for the soil samples to be analyzed in his laboratory. John Flenley and Jocelyn Powell identified the botanical specimens. Ken Barnes of the Division of Computing Science, CSIRO, Canberra, wrote the program for handling the data on sweet potato mounds. The figures were drawn by Keith Mitchell and Leo Pancino, and the preparation of photographic plates for publication was made possible by a grant from the Social Sciences Research Fund at McGill. The original manuscript was typed by Ann Newsome, while Lee Carter and Barbara Forbes handled the revisions. Such are some of the parts; the whole is essentially the product of the stimulating intellectual environment provided by the Research School of Pacific Studies, the Australian National University. A great many individuals commented on my ideas and drafts, and aided in the interpretation of my results. Most important among these were Ann Chowning, Robert Ho, Peter Rimmer, Ric Shand, and Lyle Steadman. Roland Freund and Peter Holland have played similar roles in the preparation of the revised version of the manuscript. But my greatest debt is undoubtedly to Harold Brookfield, my supervisor at the ANU, who gave direction to my inquiry as well as the encouragement and criticism one seeks but so seldom receives. Only my wife and children have given more, in sharing with me an experience of which this book is but one manifestation. I am indebted to all of these people, Enga, expatriates, colleagues, friends, and family alike, that the work should have proceeded so smoothly and that the experience should have been so rewarding.

McGill University
Montréal
February 1971

Contents

Illustrations

FIGURES

PHOTOGRAPHS   *Following page* 80

Modópa: *looking southeast across the terrace section*

Modópa: *broken mound containing mulch of sweet potato vines
and* Setaria palmaefolia *leaves; closing a mound*

Modópa: *view from the terrace section; clearing regrowth
to establish a mixed garden*

Modópa: *planting yams; inside a mixed garden*

Modópa: *kitchen garden; group of men preparing the site
of a new woman's house*

Modópa: *"emergence festival"; small feast
and distribution of pigmeat*

Modópa: *"making business" with pigmeat; mixed gardens
on a dissected valley slope*

Sirunki: *cabbage and "chinese cabbage" interplanted with sweet
potato on* modó; *frost damaged sweet potatoes; establishing* modó

Conventions

Orthography

GENERALLY speaking the orthography advocated by the New Guinea Lutheran Mission (Missouri Synod) during the time of my research has been followed in the use of Enga terms. Tonal stresses are indicated; voiced stops and the voiced affricate *j* have a prenasal and are rendered as follows:

> *d* is pronounced *nd* (as in end)
> *g* is pronounced *ng* (as in English)
> *b* is pronounced *mb* (as in bombastic)
> *j* is pronounced *nj* (as in sponge)

All final vowels are voiceless.

Although the Administration is not directly concerned with the Enga language a few terms, primarily place names, are commonly used. Officials transliterate these and in such cases their rendering has been adopted. The most important of these terms are: Enga, Lai, Mae, Minyamp, Raiapu, Sirunki, Tchak, Wabag, and Wapenamanda.

Neo-Melanesian terms and expressions, unless specifically identified, have been anglicized and are indicated by quotation marks.

Abbreviations

ANGAU   Australian New Guinea Administrative Unit
BP   before present
CSIRO   Commonwealth Scientific and Industrial Research Organization
DASF   Department of Agriculture, Stock, and Fisheries

DDA	Department of District Administration (formerly DNA)
df	degrees of freedom
DNA	Department of Native Affairs
FAO	Food and Agriculture Organization
ha	hectare
kg	kilogram
m	meter
MSL	mean sea level
N-M	Neo-Melanesian
sd	standard deviation
sp	species
t	ton
TPNG	Territory of Papua and New Guinea

THE MOUND BUILDERS

Agricultural Practices, Environment, and Society

in the Central Highlands of New Guinea

1. Introduction

Tropical Agricultural Systems

THE more exotic agricultural practices of preindustrial societies have long attracted the attention of both anthropologists and geographers, reflecting in the case of the former one dimension of their ethnographic investigations, and for the latter an aspect of their concern to identify distinctive patterns of man-land relationships. Further to this anthropologists have produced a number of agriculturally focused monographs, of which the most important are perhaps Conklin (1957), Geertz (1963), and Rappaport (1967). Similarly geographers have synthesized much of the material in order to provide general surveys of such common variants as shifting cultivation (Watters, 1960; Spencer, 1966) and agricultural terracing (Spencer and Hale, 1961). In spite of these facts theoretical statements regarding the structure, function, and evolution of agricultural adaptations generally have been remarkably slow in appearing. This is all the more surprising in light of the obvious importance of agriculture to the evolution of complex societies. Explanations for this omission lie in part in the restricted objectives of many of the ethnographers and geographers, to describe and to classify, respectively. More important, perhaps, was the failure of the one to deal effectively with the environment and the other with society, in an area where the two fields of study so obviously converge.

A unifying conceptual framework only followed the formal adoption of an ecological approach incorporating the ecosystem as its basic unit of analysis. Geertz was probably the first to make effective use of it, but others have been quick to adopt a strategy

3

which provided for an essentially dynamic and at the same time rigorous treatment of man-environment relationships. The ecosystem concept essentially "emphasizes the material interdependencies among the group of organisms which form a community and the relevant physical features of the setting in which they are found" (Geertz, 1963:3). Furthermore, it focuses attention on the properties such ecological systems share with all other systems—of structure, function, equilibrium, and change. In this context agriculture emerges as a distinctive type of man-modified system to be evaluated in the light of such questions as how it functions, how stable it is, and how it evolves through time.

A number of statements outlining the methodology and theoretical potential of research into agricultural systems have followed. Brookfield (1968), for instance, discusses the ways in which meaningful crosscultural comparison and hence major theoretical advances are possible. Essentially, he argues for a "precise description of the structure and content" of the systems, and for an "appreciation" of them through the "essentially agronomic considerations of farming technique and management." He also stresses that this can only be achieved by limiting the scale of description to "a particular tract of land used in a particular way," and by utilizing the more rigorous research generated by a variety of disciplines ranging from botany to economics. Elsewhere Harris (1969) urges the comparison of agricultural and natural ecosystems "as a prelude to deductions about the ecological and cultural conditions most likely to give rise to domestication and the initiation of agriculture."

Finally, growing concern with the study of change in agricultural systems has followed from the recent expansion of commercial cropping and a monetary economy among many primitive and peasant societies in the tropics. In an attempt to elucidate the circumstances of such change Boserup (1965) put forward a very simple, but attractive, theory of agricultural evolution that has served to give direction to many of the studies of local ecosystems subsequently published. Her thesis is that "primitive" (or preindustrial) agriculture is a dynamic adaptation wherein a series of successive stages are identifiable, each characterized by varying intensities of land use. These stages are, in order of increasing intensity, forest-tallow cultivation, bush-fallow cultivation, short-fallow cultivation, annual cropping, and multicropping. The intensification process, she argues, occurs only in response to increasing population pressure, because the more intensive systems require larger capital investments and yield lower output per man-hour. That is, without demographic growth no incentive to intensify exists.

Together these various developments have served to provide the student of tropical agricultural systems with a clear focus to his inquiries, with concepts capable of synthesizing a whole range of cultural, biological, and physical variables, and with general hypotheses to lead him beyond local study to structured, cross-cultural inquiry. At the same time substantive information is lacking at almost all levels: there have been few serious attempts to apply ecological principles to the analysis of traditional agricultural systems, detailed knowledge of agricultural techniques and management is limited, and there has been little real progress made in crosscultural inquiry. Finally, Boserup's evolutionary thesis remains an appealing hypothesis clouded by conflicting evidence.

The Central Highlands of New Guinea have played an important role in these methodological developments of the last decade or so. They have provided the setting for a number of the more rigorous investigations of agricultural systems that draw on ecological concepts, among them being Brookfield's and Brown's (1963) Chimbu and Rappaport's (1967) Tsembaga studies. They have also provided the locus for an early crosscultural evaluation of agricultural methods (Brookfield, 1962), and for a minor controversy over the origins and development of intensive agriculture (Watson, 1965a, b; Brookfield and White, 1968; Clarke, 1966, 1968) where two of the protagonists make implicit or explicit reference to Boserup's thesis in accounting for variations in intensity of cultivation. Such inquiries continue, in large part because of the obvious importance of interpreting agricultural practices as a prerequisite to explaining societal variables. As Newman (1965:75) has so aptly observed of the Gururumba, they are overwhelmingly concerned with "technical mastery of the physical world and mastery of affairs in the social world"; thus where the former is a prerequisite for the latter, an arbitrary division between society and environment can scarcely be maintained.

The present study stands, in both a methodological and a regional sense, squarely within this developing tradition. Using as its point of departure the highly distinctive agricultural mounding practices of the central Enga, an attempt is made to isolate the regularities characterizing a single local ecological system. Thus the objective is to demonstrate the links between the various agricultural practices observed and a specific set of environmental variables. The interconnections between the spatial, social, and political organization of the population and these same practices are in turn indicated. In outlining the structure of the ecosystem emphasis is placed on the dynamic relationships between the elements in order to suggest the manner in which changes, both historic and modern, are wrought. These latter are shown to be initiated in response to a variety of phenomena—expectations, population, technology, and resources—with the effects being felt throughout the system. Finally the significance of internal diversity within the system to individual control and manipulation of the overall adaptation is demonstrated.

More significant from a theoretical point of view, the local study serves as a basis for generalization, at one level in accounting for the basic features of Enga agriculture and observed variations in practices, and at another level for attempting crosscultural analysis throughout the Central Highlands region. In the latter case it serves as an attempt to identify and account for the processes of agricultural intensification, and incidentally to serve as a commentary on Boserup's hypothesis.

The whole forms part of the necessary "tooling-up" process in cultural ecological research, where an attempt is made at rigorous inquiry, and some of the more productive lines of theoretical progress are indicated. The Raiapu Enga themselves have provided the opportunity and stimulus for such a study by virtue of the fact of their having achieved a remarkably sophisticated and stable adaptation with a simple technology and under high population densities. Indeed it is similar such populations in New Guinea and elsewhere in the world that have contributed largely to advancing the study of tropical agricultural systems and cultural ecology generally in recent years.

The New Guinea Highlands

The New Guinea Highlands (Fig. 1) offer a particularly rich field for research into agricultural systems. Their societies provide, as a number of observers have noted:

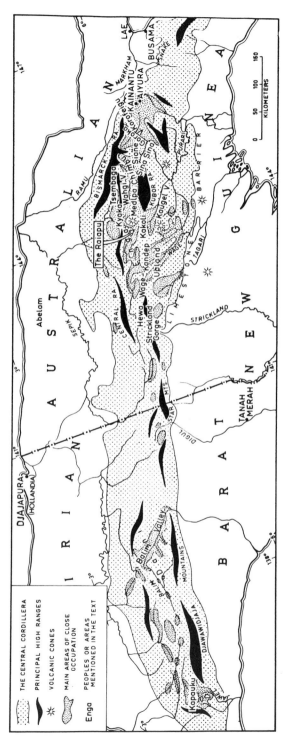

Figure 1. The New Guinea Highlands

. . . to some extent a natural experimental situation. They are set in an external environment that is in many important respects relatively uniform, and there are significant correspondences among what might be called their cultural contexts. The people all make their living in much the same ways and on much the same scale, utilising a common range of techniques, crops, and livestock. Their material conditions of residence are similar in that villages are either absent or very small, households are limited in size, and men and women generally dwell apart. Present information suggests that patrilineality everywhere receives some sort of recognition. There are characteristic and pervasive constellations of social attitudes concerning such matters as the importance of material possessions, the opposition of the sexes, the value of aggression, the qualities of the supernatural world and their effects on human activities, and so forth. But, at the same time, the various groups differ markedly with regard to the density of population and supplies of arable land [Meggitt, 1965a: 267–68].

The differences extend equally to a diversity of responses in terms of agricultural techniques, responses that range from simple dibbling to swamp drainage and mulched mounds. Indeed Brookfield (1962:246) suggests that agricultural methods, categorized as utilizing grasslands by means of tillage, provide the principal criteria for defining a Central Highlands region spanning both Australian New Guinea and West Irian. In attempting this he has sought to place the observations of the early explorers, all of whom were struck by the orderliness and scale of agricultural activities, into a scientific framework, and the theme has been developed by Watson in a series of speculative papers dealing with agricultural evolution in the Highlands (especially 1965a, b, 1967). Although I have suggested elsewhere (cited in Brookfield and White, 1968: 49–50) that agricultural contrasts between Highland and lowland New Guinea may well be overstressed and even misleading, what is undoubtedly important is the fact that:

Central Highlands peoples live in a profoundly horticultural world. They are consummate gardeners in the proportion of their food derived from crops and the relative insignificance of other present food-getting, in the amount of time they spend in gardens, and the extent to which negotiations, disputes, and strife among them involve garden land, the depredation of gardens by pigs, or the gift or theft of crops [Watson, 1967:81].

Agricultural practices are brought into sharper focus in the Highlands by the existence of two major constraints: climatic marginality and demographic pressure. The first, concerning the fact that the people "practice a tropical adaptation at its ultimate limit of altitude and temperature" (Watson, 1964:4), has been given some consideration by Brookfield (1964), but the second, that intensification is linked with pressure on resources, awaits detailed treatment on a regional basis.

Coupled with these constraints is the fact that, generally speaking, Highlands social structure and kinship systems are perceived in terms of man-land relationships. Although anthropologists sought for a number of years to consider structures in terms of lineal-segmentary models drawn from Africa, and one—Meggitt (1965a)—has persisted in this, they failed thereby to handle the obvious discrepancies between ideology and reality. Progress has been achieved only through giving much greater attention to the local as distinct from the descent group (Langness, 1964; de Lepervanche, 1967–68). This revised approach recognizes that kinship can be achieved on the basis of locality, and that the dimensions and size of the "effective, autonomous unit" or clan (generally of 200–300 persons and rarely above 400; de Lepervanche, 1967:143) can be accounted for in terms of ecology, agricultural requirements, and defense.

Highland societies are characterized by as pragmatic a view of religion as they are of kinship. In the case of the latter, membership can readily be achieved in the interest of group viability. As to the former, the societies are essentially secular, and leadership is achieved basically through the successful manipulation of the flow of goods produced within the agricultural system. "The ability to promote socio-economic welfare is the essential qualification for leadership," and religion is geared to this general requirement in its primary concern with such matters as the fertility of crops and animals (Lawrence and Meggitt, 1965:5, 13).

This whole must be set within a dynamic perspective where agricultural practices appear as the major instrument of change. The grasslands, where most Highlanders dwell, are almost certainly the product of continued cultivation and burning (Robbins, 1963a, b). The ongoing process of forest recession and replacement by grassland associations has been investigated in one locality (Bowers, 1965b, 1968). Watson (1965a, b) has proposed that agricultural practices were revolutionized by the introduction of the sweet potato (*Ipomoea batatas*) to the Highlands less than three hundred years ago on the grounds that this crop is the principal source of subsistence and it also permits the support of very large pig populations, while the special techniques of cultivation occur only in strict association with it. As has been noted, Clarke (1966) argues not for an agricultural "revolution" but rather for an "evolution" toward intensive cultivation in response to increasing population pressures. Whatever the merits of their respective theses, and the former has attracted considerable criticism (Brookfield and White, 1968), Watson (1967) is certainly correct in asserting the rapidity with which cropping innovations, both pre- and post-contact, are integrated into the system. To date, however, only Brown and Brookfield (1967) have considered in any serious way exactly how they are integrated.

Given the stresses to which Highland agricultural systems are now exposed as a result of commercial cropping, the predominance of agricultural production within the economic systems, and the considerable diversity of local responses within a broadly uniform cultural and ecological area, their investigation in dynamic terms provides both an amenable and a stimulating proposition.

Area, Method, and Objectives

A variety of considerations influenced the selection of the Raiapu Enga for this intensive analysis of an agricultural system. Through the writings of Mervyn Meggitt the language group as a whole has "won . . . a salient position in the ethnography of the highlands" (Barnes, 1967:33). Meggitt's view of Enga society is most clearly formulated in *The Lineage System of the Mae-Enga of New Guinea* (1965a). While maintaining a rigidly structural approach he has sought to account for the stress on agnation in terms of the limited availability of agricultural land, illustrating his argument by contrasting central with fringe Enga groups. According to Meggitt (pp. 45–48) the Mae explicitly refer to land shortage and account for their reluctance to admit outsiders to clan territories in these terms. On the grounds that all the major Highlands societies are sedentary horticulturalists recognizing the principle of patrilineality, he concludes (pp. 260–82) by proposing that the association is of general applicability.

In developing his thesis Meggitt fails to provide any quantified agricultural or ecological information and ignores the technological means by which the Enga exploit their resource system. Yet their agricultural system is, superficially at least, a unique one where sweet potatoes, their staple, are grown in large, plano-convex mounds 3.0m or more in diameter and 0.5m high. These are mulched and cultivated on a semipermanent basis. The Enga ecosystem is characterized by two other distinctive attributes: population densities of about 96/km² that are widely exceeded only by the Chimbu, but a mean level of settlement located at a somewhat higher altitude—1900m MSL compared with about 1700m among the Chimbu.

The Enga-speaking peoples number over 140,000 and inhabit a series of valleys to the west of the Mount Hagen range in the Western Highlands District of Australian New Guinea. Their central axis, in both a cultural and a demographic sense, is the Lai and its tributary valleys, the Ambum, Tchak, and Minyamp. Here about half the population live at an altitude ranging between 1500 and 2700m MSL within a *paysage humanisé* where forest is restricted primarily to the ridge-tops and the rest of the terrain is covered by secondary regrowth, grassland, or simply extensive cultivated areas. The Enga themselves distinguish two distinct subcultures within this central group, the Mae (to whom Meggitt directed most of his attention) and the Raiapu. The former occupy the western half centering on Wabag station, number about 37,000, and everywhere live at altitudes in excess of about 1950m MSL. The latter occupy the eastern half centering on Wapenamanda patrol post, number about 30,000, and mostly live below 1950m MSL. In consequence the Raiapu are able to cultivate a greater range of crops within a somewhat more diversified system, while possessing an analogous social structure to that of the Mae (Meggitt, 1965a:268–69).

In approaching the Raiapu agricultural system I directed considerable thought to the scale and method of inquiry. Since the primary objective was to establish how the system operates—the sorts of processes involved in terms of relations between the cultural, biological, and physical elements in the ecosystem—attention was focused on a series of individual economic units or farmsteads. For most purposes these comprised no more than ten households, all located in a named and topographically distinct locality. More general inquiries were conducted over the whole of the clan, or group, territory. It is at this group level that the Raiapu most obviously seek to resolve the opposing forces of locality and descent, and I felt that some general principles covering the relations of culture to environment as manifested in Raiapu technology might emerge from a consideration of the group territory. In both topographic and demographic terms each local group tends to replicate the other: each possesses a high degree of internal solidarity, but a variety of rules of residence, marriage, and participation in communal affairs apply, and result in it standing in clear contradistinction to other such groups. While it is possible to generalize from these data to the Raiapu as a whole, on the basis of cultural uniformity, no such assumption could legitimately be made for the ecological material. These investigations were, therefore, much more widely based, extending through the whole of the central Enga culture area from Sirunki in the west to Wapenamanda in the east—a linear distance of about 45km.

The study is approached through a consideration of the Raiapu garden typology. From a range of diagnostic criteria extending from tenurial status to soil type a number of attributes are linked with each cultivation unit. On this basis a distinction is drawn between two major types, the "open fields" and the "mixed gardens," and this provides the major analytical device around which this study is built. By means of this distinction household composition, the distribution of residences in relation to gardens, adjustments to pressure on resources and to environmental constraints, the notional stress on agnation, and the means by which leaders (or "big-men") emerge in an acephalous society are all considered, and the regularities that characterize the ecosystem are identified.

The study is structured in such a way as to make a clear distinction between description and explanation. The division is, of course, artificial: both are essentially cognitive processes, the difference is one of degree, and I have aimed to describe only those aspects of the Raiapu system which I consider to be relevant to my analysis. But in making this decision I have borne in mind two important considerations: first, that in a number of areas I have proceeded far beyond my own field of competence and, second, that there are important strategic objections to elaborate hypothesizing. By incorporating my data wholly within the frame-work of an involved argument on the operation of a Highlands ecosystem I am likely not only to conceal inherent weaknesses from the reader, but to risk rejection of the whole material when that argument is refuted. Theories are notoriously short-lived, and as yet there is a serious lack of material on tropical agricultural systems that reveals some of the means whereby information on the processes and concepts involved can be acquired. The study is designed to stand as much by the methods it demonstrates as by its findings, and it is hoped the utility of the data will outlast the conceptual framework within which they are elaborated.

2. Organization of Space

Aruní Group Territory: The Land and the People

THE Aruní are one of an estimated 176 Raiapu-Syáka clans (Meggitt, 1958a:263). Their territory, known as Sabakamádá after the name of the group's main ceremonial ground, is situated on the southwest side of the Lai Valley overlooking Wapenamanda patrol post (Fig. 2). It comprises a single strip of land, about 2.7km broad at its widest point, extending from the Lai River to the crest of a ridge overlooking the Tchak Valley, a distance of about 3.3km. The topographic form is characteristic of most central Enga group territories and it has the merit of providing their residents with equal access to several types of terrain and therefore resources.

At Sabakamádá three major terrain types are identifiable on the basis of the classification of land systems proposed by Perry et al. (1965): the deeply dissected Lai gorge and its tributaries (Lai system), the level or gently sloping terrace sections (Wabag system), and the steeper slopes of the main range (Ambum system). This whole area of only 6.5km² falls within an altitudinal range of 1650 to 2440m MSL, with the terrace sections themselves located at about 1740–1780m. Yet in spite of the variation in terrain the territory is, floristically, relatively impoverished. It lacks the swampy flats along its river frontage that are characteristic of other parts of the Lai Valley, and only a little over 5 percent (c. 35ha) of the total area is forested, this confined to the crest of the main range and maintained as a "sanctuary" where the nut-bearing *Pandanus* sp. grow and the greater part of the ritual associated

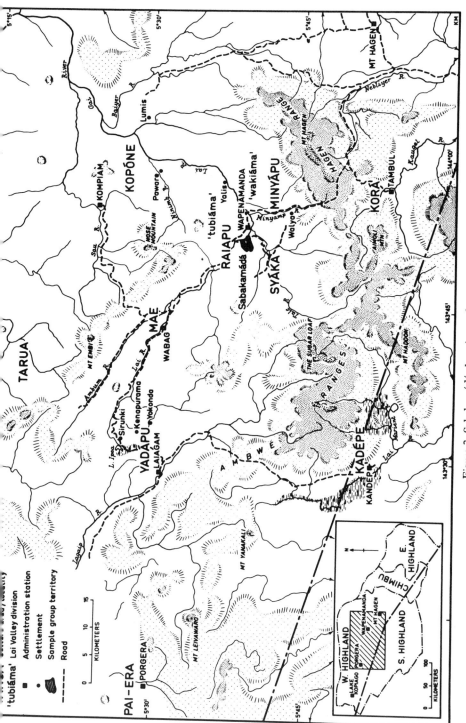

Figure 2. Sabakamádá: location and *oecumene*

with the periodic *sadárú*[1] ceremonies is carried out. Instead the bulk of the territory is covered, variously, by *Imperata cylindrica* and *Miscanthus floridus* grasslands with shrubby regrowth restricted largely to the slopes of the Lai and its tributary streams. The terrace sections are largely under continuous cultivation.

Consequently, in terms of resources, the Aruní lack an extensive area to harbor game, provide building timber, and serve as an agricultural frontier or as foraging for their pigs. Further the Lai River is too fast-flowing and liable to flash floods for the people to be interested in the eel-trapping that is apparently practiced in other parts of the valley (Meggitt, 1958a:284). In theory this situation is ameliorated by hunting and *Pandanus* rights clansmen exercise over an uninhabited section of the uplands between the Tchak and Marient valleys, about one and a half days' walk away, but in fact visits are so infrequent as to preclude any real advantage being derived from their claim.

Like most Raiapu clans the Aruní are, perforce, agriculturalists dependent primarily on the sweet potato to support both themselves and their pigs. Production is facilitated by a relatively benign climate with little seasonality or threat of ground frosts. Data for Wapenamanda patrol post, situated at an altitude of 1745m MSL and 1.6km from the Aruní terrace sections, reveal a mean annual precipitation of 2459mm (for the period 1956 and 1958–66) with a coefficient of seasonal variation of 0.30 indicative of a moderately seasonal climate.[2] Estimated mean maximum and minimum temperatures for the same place are 23.7 and 12.5°C respectively.[3]

These mild conditions, associated at Sabakamádá with "deep, productive soils" (Rutherford and Perry, 1965:137), enable the Aruní to grow a wide range of subsidiary crops, the most important of which are yam, banana, sugarcane, several varieties of beans, Highland pitpit, and peanuts. Although extensively cultivated elsewhere in the middle Lai Valley, these crops are of little or no importance among adjacent groups in the Tchak and upper

1. The ritual seclusion of bachelors. See p. 87.
2. This is a measure of total rainfall variability which can be applied to areas not experiencing a marked dry season. For an elaboration of this measure and some comparisons with other parts of the Highlands see Brookfield and Brown (1963:20–22).
3. These figures represent the means of the monthly means and are derived from readings at Wabag (2001m MSL) for the years 1957–66, adjusted on the basis of an estimated lapse rate of 5.58°C per 1000m.

Lai valleys. This fact largely compensates for the Aruní's locational disadvantages vis-à-vis other groups with their more abundant forest, pig-grazing, and *Pandanus* resources and their more immediate access to supplies of tree-oil, salt, and, formerly, stone axes.

In terms both of area (6.5km^2) and of the population it supports (460 persons) Aruní group territory considerably exceeds Meggitt's (1958a:263–64) central Enga modal size of 2.59km^2 and Raiapu-Syáka mean population of 270 persons. However, the resultant density of 71/km^2 is in no way exceptional, lying between Meggitt's (1965a:268) estimate of 46.3/km^2 and McAlpine's (1966:4) estimate of 84.2/km^2 on land used in the Tchak census division (within which Sabakamádá falls). Assuming the latter's definition of "land used" to exclude only the forested area at Sabakamádá, a figure of 77.2/km^2 is derived, thus approximating closely to his Tchak mean. This high Aruní density is in part a response to their having been dispossessed of an area equivalent to 45 percent of their present territory by two neighboring clans (one of them related patrilineally) during the 1930s—an imbalance which has not been restored through subsequent litigation. If this area were reincorporated the overall density would be reduced to only 49.4/km^2.

In most aspects of social and territorial organization the Aruní conform to Meggitt's (1958a:263–83, 1965a) general description of the central Enga and, more particularly, of the Raiapu. The structure and composition of the Aruní's particular segmentary hierarchy is outlined in Figure 3. The phratry, the largest recognized patrilineal group, in this case incorporates only two clans (or subphratries, depending on the perspective) compared with Meggitt's (1958a:265) Raiapu-Syáka mean of 5.1; however, the estimated total population of 1,072 persons (including absentees) in 1965 differs little from his mean of 1,020. The two clan territories are adjacent and the phratry theoretically exercises residual interests in both; consequently a union incorporates obligations of mutual defense against invasion. Propinquity also results, among the Mae, in a high rate of intraphratry marriages (Meggitt, 1965a:103). In the case of the Aruní, however, the agnatic link has little substance, this being forcibly demonstrated in Waiminaugína's conquest and occupation of a large section of their territory c. 1938 and subsequent revision of the segmentary hierarchy. Both developments reflect an increasing divergence in the clans' respective interests, with the intraphratry fight itself having demanded significant and continuing readjustments of population to resources at Sabakamádá.

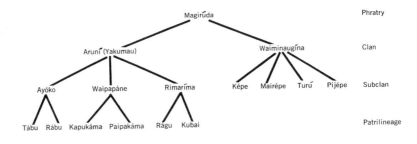

a. As perceived by members of Aruní

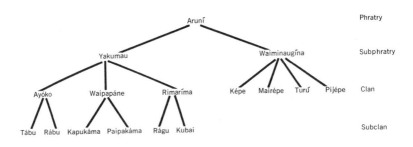

b. As perceived by members of Waiminaugína (Westermann, 1968)

Figure 3. Aruní clan: the segmentary structure

Within the hierarchy political organization centers variously at the clan and subclan levels, where each is identified with discrete territories and specific ceremonial grounds. The clan, with its ceremonial ground close to the ridge-top and on the site first occupied by the eponymous ancestor, is the largest unit to form a corporation with effective residual rights in all the land within its territory. At each level within the hierarchy, however, subclans, patrilineages, and families exercise full title to their respective blocks. None can alienate land without the consent of the super-ordinate category, although usufructuary rights are granted and alienation (or assimilation within the group) may eventuate from these.

Aruní clan conforms to the Raiapu ideal of an exogamous group, but not all its members are recruited agnatically. Table 1 outlines the proportions of natal to immigrant members where 7 percent of the males (wedded or otherwise) were born elsewhere but subsequently were accommodated, mostly as sons of female agnates, and 7 percent of wedded women (mostly divorcees and widows) reside among their natal clan.

TABLE 1

SABAKAMÁDÁ: NATAL CLAN OF RESIDENTS

	Aruní Clan		Other Clans		Total	
	No.	%	No.	%	No.	%
All						
Males	236	93	18	7	254	100
Females	85	41	121	59	206	100
Wedded						
Males	100	93	8	7	108	100
Females	9	7	115	93	124	100

While the clan bachelors (unmarried adult residents) all go into seclusion together, the associated "emergence festivals" are frequently held on the appropriate subclan ceremonial grounds; individuals are commonly spoken of by reference to their subclan rather than clan affiliation; and each of the three subclans holds its own *tée* ceremony. At Sabakamádá their territories, like that of the clan, extend from the Lai gorge to the ridge-top.[4] Not only does this provide each subclan with equal access to resources but a concentration of population on the terrace sections is facilitated. There, in association with the dissected valley slopes that are also exploited by residents of these sections, densities approach

4. One of the subclans, Waipapáne, was however displaced from the lower part of its territory as a result of the intraphratry fight and many of its members have since been accommodated on land belonging to the others.

130/km².⁵ Thus, although the settlement pattern is nominally a dispersed one with dwellings scattered through the cultivated areas and concealed behind small stands of trees and *Cordyline* sp. fences, the actual distribution assumes a markedly uneven form.

The proliferation of categories within the segmentary system, in particular the presence and role of the patrilineage, seems to bear some relationship to population density. Many residents of the upper slopes of the main range either claim not to know their patrilineage or consider it unimportant to them in view of their small numbers and an abundance of land. However, in this area mobility across slope is of little importance compared with that downslope in the direction of the fertile terrace sections.

Within the subclan territory, family holdings (and those of the patrilineage where identifiable) are intermingled. This reflects the process of inheritance—where land is divided among all male heirs—and the limited practices of granting usufructuary rights and effecting long-term transfers at these levels. Although the patrilineage may assume an explicit role in ceremonial affairs, informal and sustained contact takes place within the context of a "locality group," the co-residents of a named area. Since such named localities do not normally transgress subclan boundaries these groupings do not influence loyalties at or above that level in the lineage system.

The primary social and economic unit is normally the elementary or composite family, often with other individuals attached to it. Throughout the succeeding discussion it will be termed the "household." Each is associated with a territory or "residence," comprising one or more houses, and a number of fragmented holdings, referred to as the "farmstead." Male and female members of a household generally occupy separate but adjacent houses. However, the association between household and farmstead is not a strict one for, in the case of polygynous families, individual wives and their children may live some distance apart, producing and consuming much of their food separately. Similarly there are considerable variations in the degree to which the activities and interests of attached members are integrated. Nevertheless all activities

---

5. Furthermore people living on the slopes of the main range also exploit the resources of these areas—for mixed gardens and pig-grazing—although the reverse does not apply to any significant degree.

are characterized by the fact that ultimate authority in matters of food production, consumption, and distribution and in membership of the household is vested in a single person, the husband or "household head."

Modópa sample community

Within the group territory one locality, a terrace section, was selected as the focus for detailed investigations into the nature of the agricultural system. A terrace section was chosen because this is the terrain unit which the Raiapu acknowledge as having the most favored soils and climate for cultivation. Consequently the terraces carry the highest population densities. It was presumed that under such conditions agricultural patterns would be the most highly elaborated. Modópa was selected in preference to the other two occupied sections because settlement patterns and farm organization were felt to be less "disturbed" there: the establishment of a church and school at Ráku in 1957 had led to an influx of christians (and catechumens) but without any real rationalization in the distribution of their agricultural holdings, while Rimádá had been depopulated during the intraphratry fight and many of the landowners had not returned there since.[6]

The recent history of Modópa is not characterized by such radical events. Of a total population of seventy persons only three, recently moved from Ráku, live in a nontraditional house, while all household heads claim affiliation to Ayóko subclan with which the locality is identified. Ten households with a total of forty-five members (at the beginning of the survey) were investigated, nine being all those residents attached to one of the patrilineages and the tenth to a second. The intention was to restrict the sample to a distinct social unit, the patrilineage, but proximity to the researcher's house also proved to be an influential consideration.[7] The group is a relatively stable one in which only one youth left in search of wage employment during the study, and it comprises a diversity of household types ranging from divorcees to polygynous families with attached adults. Each household averaged 4.5 members, or 2.9 labor units, and all par-

---

6. These differences are borne out by the data where occupation densities are estimated to be 4.2 on the Modópa, 6.9 on the Ráku, and 1.7/ha on the Rimádá terrace sections, respectively.

7. The main characteristics of the sample group are detailed in Appendix 1.

ticipated to varying degrees in the traditional social and economic life and in commercial production. The investigation of Raiapu agricultural practices that follows is founded on a thorough analysis of the farm organization and activity patterns of these households, with the broader, regional variations considered essentially in terms of the particular adaptations that the Raiapu have made.

Population, Household, Residence, and the Pattern of Settlement

It is generally recognized that settlement pattern represents a concrete ". . . and obvious expression of the relationship between social institutions and the use and allocation of productive resources" (Brown and Brookfield, 1967:119). However, the exact, causal, nature of this relationship is seldom the subject of detailed investigation. Among the Raiapu there are certain striking regularities in the stability, composition, and distribution of residences. These regularities reflect, on the one hand, social patterns of marriage and divorce frequencies and male-female relationships generally, and on the other, the very close association between residence and garden. It is pertinent to the study that both, in turn, be given detailed consideration in order to segregate the independent from the dependent variables.

Population, household, and residence

Of all aspects of the demographic and social structure of the population it is those that bear directly upon male-female relationships which are particularly relevant to agricultural organization. Relations between the sexes are characterized by a marked ambivalence reflecting both a fear of female pollution and a necessary cooperation in agricultural matters founded on the conventional division of labor, where women are wholly responsible for sweet potato cultivation and pig husbandry, and men are responsible for the subsidiary crops. The household is the context in which this conflict is enacted.

The commonest residential unit at Sabakamádá is the elementary family where the husband and boys over the age of c. 5–10 years live in one house, while the wife plus all other children live in a separate but adjacent house. However, there are a large number of variations around this norm (Table 2). Most of these variations can be viewed as a direct expression of the preponderance of males over females in the population, and the frequency of divorce and polygyny and, conversely, of bach-

TABLE 2

SABAKAMÁDÁ: COMPOSITION AND FORM OF RESIDENCES

Composition	No. of Houses in Residence				Total Households	
	1	2	3	4	No.	%
Incomplete family*	5	5	...	...	10	10
ditto + dependents† (same sex)	3	2	...	...	5	5
ditto + dependents (different sex)	6	1	...	...	7	7
Elementary family	15	26	...	..	41	39
ditto + attached adults	3	7	3	...	13	12
ditto + dependents	4	7	...	1	12	11
ditto + both		2	...	...	2	2
Composite family						
Polygynous	1	2	1	...	4	4
ditto + attached adults	...	1		2	3	3
ditto + dependents	...		2	...	2	2
Two elementary families sharing houses	...	3	2	...	5	5
ditto + attached adults	1	...	...	...	1	1
Total Residences No.	38	56	8	3	105	
%	36	53	8	3		100/101

* Bachelor, widow, etc.: one or more persons of same sex, no offspring.
† Dependent defined as including orphans, divorced offspring and their progeny, aged parents, and, in the case of incomplete families only, immediate offspring.

elorhood. Thus, while 39 percent of the households comprise elementary families without additional members, 40 percent comprise incomplete families or families with attached adults. In addition 15 percent of the adult male population (over the age of 25 years) are bachelors and marriages are relatively unstable, leaving a number of people temporarily, at least, without a spouse.

Bowers (1965a) discusses the high incidence of "permanent bachelors" among the Kakoli of the upper Kaugel Valley, and accounts for the phenomenon primarily in terms of an unbalanced male-female ratio and a high incidence of polygyny: there are 81 females per 100 males, and 24 percent of wedded males claim to have been polygynous at some stage. Almost 16 percent of the Kakoli males who are over the age of 25 years are bachelors.

At Sabakamádá there are 81.1 females per 100 males. Although the difference is not statistically significant at the 1 percent level for a population of 460 persons, the imbalance is characteristic of the Tchak census division as a whole. Here, according to Administration census figures for 1966, there are 86.2 females per 100 males in a population of 10,729.[8] The disparity at Sabakamádá would appear to be a function of differential birth and survival rates where, out of 430 births recorded by the present female population, there were 95 female per 100 male births. Of these, 65 percent of the latter are surviving but only 56 percent of the former—a differential survival rate of 82 females per 100 males.

However, in spite of the high masculinity ratio, differences in age at first marriage result in there being an excess of women available. Customarily men do not marry until they are 25 to 30 years old whereas women marry between 15 and 20 years and, excluding absentees, there are 122 men over 25 years and 141 women over 15 years at Sabakamádá. This differential may in turn make polygyny possible and thereby effectively restore the imbalance.

As indicated in Table 3, there are substantial differences in the present marital status of the sexes. Of the wedded men 9 percent are polygynous (and 22 percent have been at some stage), but 19 percent of the men have never been married. The divorced men are of all ages whereas the five divorced women are all under 35 years and the widows all over 50 years, suggesting that

8. High masculinity ratios have also been reported in other parts of New Guinea, for example the Tor (Oosterwal, 1961:37–40) and the Gazelle peninsula (Epstein, 1962:77).

TABLE 3

SABAKAMÁDÁ: PRESENT MARITAL STATUS OF THE POPULATION

	Un-wedded	Wedded (No. of spouses)						Total Wedded	Total
		0							
		Di-vorced	Wid-owed	1	2	3	4		
Men (aged 20+)	25	9	3	84	8	1	1	106	131
Women (aged 20+)	1	5	11	102	...	...	...	118	119

women readily remarry (unless they are past child-bearing age) but men find it more difficult.

Marriage appears to be a relatively unstable institution among the Raiapu. Although only nine men and five women were divorced at the time of the survey, the data on individual marital experience given in Table 4 reveal a high divorce frequency, which is emphasized by the following figures: The ratio of marriages ending in divorce to all marriages was 92:358 (25.5 percent); to completed marriages, 92:156 (59 percent); and to all marriages except those ended by death, 92:294 (31.3 percent).

In the absence of direct information on the duration of unions it is noteworthy that, of the 92 marriages terminated through divorce, 52 were childless and a further 28 had resulted in only one child. It may be postulated on this basis that divorces occur most commonly in the early years of marriage when women still profess considerable loyalty to their natal clans, but the unions assume greater stability through time.[9]

9. See Westermann, 1968:64–65. He states, "The wife's shifting of loyalty to her husband's clan appears to be more a function of the fact that her children are members of his clan than of her marriage," implying a clear causal relationship between the birth of offspring and marital stability. Elsewhere he suggests that marital stability has decreased sharply in recent years, noting, "In most cases examined, women left their husbands for reasons which would not have been sanctioned ten to fifteen years ago. Freedom from the fear of harsh punishment and reprisal and the failure of groups to insist on the wife's returning to her husband have established a new climate of liberality among the Laiapu" (p. 192). My own data do not support this contention.

TABLE 4

SABAKAMÁDÁ: CUMULATIVE MARITAL EXPERIENCE

	All Males	Males over 45 Years	All Females	Total Both Sexes
Number of wedded persons	106	35	124	230
Number of divorces experienced:				
0	76	19	89	165
1	19	8	31	50
2	5	2	3	8
3	2	2	1	3
4	. . .	. . .	. . .	. . .
5	2	2	. . .	2
6	. . .	. . .	. . .	. . .
7	1	1	. . .	1
(?	1	1	. . .	1)
Mean number of divorces per head of population	0.49	0.91	0.32	0.40
Number of persons divorced at least once	29	15	35	64
Percent of wedded population divorced at least once	27.4	42.9	28.2	27.8

The general picture that emerges from the Sabakamádá data is one of a few men experiencing a succession of wives but of a significant number remaining bachelors throughout their lives. Marriages more commonly terminate in divorce than in death and, while women remarry fairly quickly, many of the men simply revert to the status of a bachelor. This situation contrasts markedly with that reported for the Mae with respect to both the incidence of bachelors and the frequency of divorces. Concerning the former Meggitt (1965a:85) states: "Of the hundreds of adults that I encountered who were more than ten or fifteen years past the usual age for marriage, only seven men and three women had never married. One of the men was an achondroplasic, another a deaf-mute, and the rest appeared to be mentally unstable or deficient." Of the latter, he reports a mean number of only 0.76 divorces per head of population and only 17.3 percent of completed marriages terminating in divorce (pp. 149–50). Male-female relationships may, consequently, be interpreted somewhat differently at Sabakamádá—in terms of agricultural organization.

Apart from the widespread fear of female pollution, newly married Raiapu men feel constantly threatened by the precariousness of their union in a situation where there is an effective scarcity of women and where rules concerning the sexual division of labor are strictly adhered to. The presence of females in any production unit is vital. In terms of economic organization it is only after several years of marriage that the men can claim to "have won their battle and have relegated women to an inferior position" (Meggitt, 1964:220). Women clearly recognize the crucial importance of their role and pose a constant threat to the poorer husband.[10] Not only do wives facilitate participation in ceremonial activities and exchanges but, without one, a man alone cannot even achieve subsistence, except in the face of public ridicule. The diverse composition of households reflects this situation where bachelors and divorced men must, perforce, attach themselves to other families. Even those bachelors residing apart, in houses designated as *patáge áda*, frequently attach themselves to others for the purposes of food production, general domestic tasks, and meals.

Various social processes evident among the Sabakamádá population are modifying it in ways which have a direct bearing on economic organization and activity. Some are implicit in the data, as in the changing form of residences. Traditionally each comprised two buildings, but, as Table 2 indicates, 36 percent now have only one, and the trend continues. Most are in response to the establishment of a nexus between Raiapu and European society through, in particular, the commencement of missionary activity.

The establishment of a Lutheran church within the group territory, in association with intensive work by Enga evangelists, has resulted in a marked concentration of population on one of the terrace sections, Ráku,[11] while radical changes are also being

10. Some of the dilemmas faced by Enga husbands are revealed in the records of Supreme Court cases heard at Wabag. See Appendix 2.
11. Similar developments have occurred elsewhere in response to evangelical work. Westermann (1968:91), writing of a locality in Waiminaugína territory, states: "As he [the evangelist] began to instruct prospective candidates

effected in the form and composition of residences. Both developments are in response to the identification of "christians," who comprise 50 percent of the population, as a distinct interest group in opposition to the "heathens" among whom they live.

TABLE 5

SABAKAMÁDÁ: CHRISTIANITY AND PLACE OF RESIDENCE

Locality*	Total Population	Christians						Natal Members		
		Lutherans		Catholics		Both			Residing in Locality of Birth	
		No.	%	No.	%	No.	%	Total	No.	%
Modópa	71	22	31	2	3	24	34	48	45	94
Ráku	99	94	95	...	...	94	95	71	28	39
Rimádá	67	7	10	8	12	15	22	50	48	96
Kuilyakáma	23	1	4	8	35	9	39	17	15	88
Keamádá	73	46	63	...	...	46	63	49	33	67
Kosepósa	29	6	21	...	...	6	21	20	19	95
Poralyamádá } Remása } Sabakamádá }	61	17	28	3	5	20	33	40	36	90
Lyokapósa } Gimalúsa } Kobaginapósa } Yokamádá } Waipuráma }	37	9	24	8	22	17	46	24	14	58
Totals	460	201		29		230		319	233	
% of total population			43.7		6.3		50.0			73.0

* See Figure 4 for their relative locations.

Table 5 demonstrates the relationship between religious affiliation and place of residence within the group territory. There is a concentration of christians at Ráku (around a church and vernacular school) and at nearby Keamádá, and natal members

for baptism, it was decided that the people who lived at the extremes of Maitépe territory should come and build houses close to Talyakósa, thereby facilitating their attendance at the daily worship services and instruction periods."

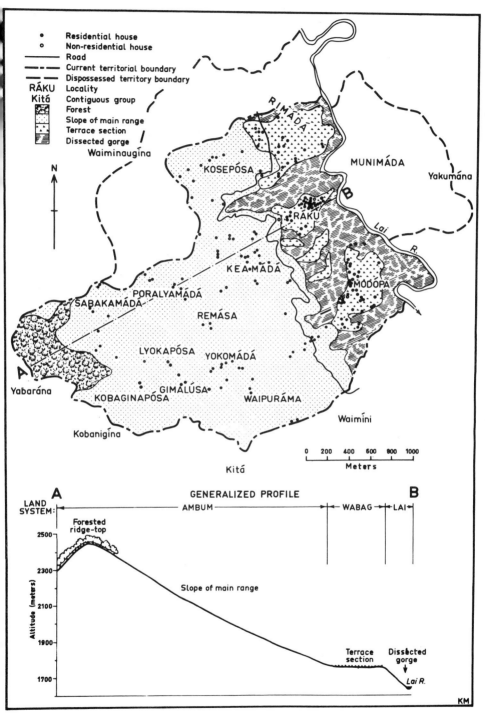

Figure 4. Sabakamádá: terrain, locality, and settlement (aerial photography, QUASCO, Dec. 1967)

have moved to these localities from other parts of Sabakamádá. While the relative instability of the Ráku and Keamádá populations is a direct product of missionary activity, that of Lyokapósa and other localities exists because the subclan was displaced from much of its territory in the intraphratry fight and its members had to seek refuge in the remaining part higher up on the range.

Lutheran evangelists encourage individual christians and christian families to live together in single houses, known as *kitisenáda*, rather than separate the sexes. By tradition men live either in circular houses, about 5.0m in diameter and 3.4m high, or in rectangular houses, about 6.7m long, 3.4m wide, and 2.4m high, which are similar to those of the Mae but smaller and without a pitched ridge-pole. Both are termed *akáryáda*. Women's houses (*édáda*), incorporating pig stalls, are much larger—about 10.7m long, 3.8m wide, and 2.7m high. While the majority of houses at Sabakamádá are of these types, increasingly modifications are being made in the uses to which they are put. Either the whole family occupies the woman's house, leaving the man's to fall into disrepair, or, more commonly, they move into the man's house while continuing to use the other for the preparation of meals and accommodation of pigs.

The erection of *kitisenáda* represents a more radical departure from tradition. These are of two types, one replicating the *akáryáda* and the other the Administration rest house with its high roof and walls made of woven *Miscanthus floridus*, sometimes referred to as *nai áda* (new house). In both cases the residence consists of a single house and, when a site is selected, consideration is given to proximity to the church or a chapel.

Table 6 outlines the frequency with which each type of house occurs and the characteristics of its occupants. While family houses are located with less consideration for economic activities they are also significantly more crowded than those utilized in the traditional manner, yet they are no bigger. The trend towards this type of residence is revealed by its frequency and the fact that only 58 percent of adult males live apart from women.

The pattern of settlement: form, distribution, and change

In spite of the immediate relevance of settlement patterns to aspects of social organization, economic activity, and population movement little serious consideration has been given to them in

TABLE 6

SABAKAMÁDÁ: HOUSES BY FUNCTIONAL CLASS AND NUMBER OF OCCUPANTS

Type	Utilization	Houses			Occupants (Males over 19 Years)	
		No.	%	Mean No.	No.	%
Akáryáda/kitisenáda	Men only	51	27	2.0	73	56
	Men and aged widows	5	3	2.8	8	6
	Families	21	11	4.6	25	19
Édáda	Women and children	62	33	2.4	. . .	. . .
	Families	8	4	3.6	8	6
	Unoccupied*	27	15	. . .	. . .	. . .
Nai áda	Men only	2	1	1.5	3	2
	Families	10	5	6.1	14	11
Totals		186	99		131	100
Means				2.5 per utilized house 2.9 per occupied house		

* Used for pigs and food preparation.

New Guinea until recently,[12] beyond the recognition of a simple dispersed-nucleated dichotomy in the Highlands and the identification of a few distinctive forms as the "line village," the "ridge-top settlement," and the less tangible "locality group." Furthermore, evaluations of pattern and morphology have been made primarily in terms of strategic considerations and innovations inspired by missions and the Administration.

The customary Highlands dichotomy requires that the Raiapu be typed as "dispersed" along with all other groups between the Chimbu and the Strickland Gorge, in contrast to "nucleated" groups in the area lying to the east of the central Chimbu (Brown and Brookfield, 1967:121). However, reference has already been made to the clearly defined tendency within Aruní group territory

12. Brown and Brookfield's (1967) treatment of Chimbu settlement and residence represents a significant step in the direction of more rigorous description and analysis.

toward a concentration of settlement on the terrace sections, a concentration which is primarily in response to ecological variations and only secondarily to mission activity. Thus not only may the "either/or" distinction be imprecise but it can be particularly misleading in overriding such important considerations as, first, the stability of settlement, second, patterns of house relocation, and third, differences in the distribution of males and females. Of the first Salisbury (1962:12) remarks that while Siane settlement is ostensibly nucleated, with villages averaging two hundred persons each, it is relatively unstable and at any one time about 30 percent of the population is residing in pig houses dispersed through the group territory. As regards mobility, Brown and Brookfield (1967:140–41) have noted that over the period 1958–65 only 11 percent of Chimbu resident at Mintima remained on a single site, while 60 percent made at least one move outside their subclan territory involving a mean distance in excess of 1.83km. Finally, the same authors (p. 131) note a striking, although declining, difference in the distribution of men as opposed to women where each is residentially separate: "The men are concentrated on the higher points towards the centre of an enclosed block of group territory, while the women and pigs are mostly housed on the fringes of the cultivated area, often on lower ground." In effect to introduce the dichotomy in this last case would be to suggest that the men are nucleated and the women dispersed!

In the light of these apparently considerable variations in the character of Highlands settlement patterns a precise description of Raiapu settlement is obviously an essential preliminary to any investigation of its rationale or to any comparative discussion. Following in part on Brown and Brookfield's analysis attention is focused on five main aspects within Aruní group territory: first, a mathematical expression of the total distribution of houses; second, the relation of male to female residences; third, the form assumed by individual aggregations; fourth, stability in the location of houses; and fifth, the course and extent of postcontact changes.

The technique of nearest neighbor analysis, used to provide a quantified expression of the spacing of plant populations in terms of degree of departure from random expectation, was first described by Clark and Evans (1954). A number of geographers have since, with varying success, applied it to urban studies (for example, King, 1962; Getis, 1964). The measure (R) is derived from the ratio of the observed mean distance to nearest neighbor in a given population ($\bar{r}_A$) to the expected mean distance ($\bar{r}_E$) if the same individuals were randomly distributed. The value, R, has a limited range from 0.0 through 1.0 to 2.15 indicative, respectively, of completely aggregated, random, and perfectly uniform patterns of distribution. The reliability of the measure can also be derived from the same data.

Because "randomness as here employed is a spatial concept, intimately dependent upon the boundaries of the space chosen by the investigator" (Clark and Evans, 1954:446), care must be exercised in the selection of an area for investigation if meaningful results are to be obtained. In the Raiapu case the group territory would appear to be the most legitimate unit, on the grounds that the agnatic idiom facilitates freedom of movement within its boundaries but not beyond them. A modification (proposed by Clark and Evans, 1954:450) was introduced at Sabakamádá to overcome distortion arising from the frequent association of men's and women's houses in a single residence. This involved treating each individual selected as a center of measurement surrounded by a circle, of infinite radius, divided into two sectors with a variable orientation to the diameter. Two measures were then obtained, one to the absolute nearest neighbor and the other to the nearest neighbor located within the second sector. In cases where one sector was found to be empty no measurements were taken from that center; thus, of the 188 houses identified from aerial photographs,[13] measures were made from 185.

Data presented in Table 7, where $R = 0.74$ and $c = -9.79$, confirm the impression gained from Figure 4 that although the settlement pattern does not assume the structural form of a village there is a marked and highly significant (at the 0.1 percent level) tendency toward aggregation. Further, this tendency applies equally to both sexes. Not only is the mean population of the men's houses slightly less than that of the women's (Table 6), reflecting both the sexual imbalance in the population and the fact that

13. These photographs were taken in December 1967, approximately 11 months after completion of the field survey in which 186 houses were recorded.

TABLE 7

SABAKAMÁDÁ: DISTRIBUTION OF HOUSES, MEASURED IN TERMS
OF NEAREST NEIGHBOR ANALYSIS
(Following Clark and Evans, 1954)

Symbol	Concept	Statistic Obtained
N	the number of measurements of distance taken in the observed population	370
k	the number of sectors in a circle of infinite radius about each individual used as a center of measurement	2
p	the density of the observed distribution expressed as the number of individuals per square yard	0.00002446
$\sqrt{p}$		0.004946
Σr	the summation of the measurements of distance to nearest neighbor, in yards	39070.9
$\bar{r}_A = \dfrac{\Sigma r}{N}$	the mean of the series of distances to nearest neighbor	105.6
$\bar{r}_E = \dfrac{\sqrt{k}}{2\sqrt{p}}$	the mean distance to nearest neighbor in a randomly distributed population of density p	142.9
$R = \dfrac{\bar{r}_A}{\bar{r}_E}$	the measure of the degree to which the observed distribution departs from random expectation	0.74
$\sigma \bar{r}_E = \dfrac{0.26136\sqrt{k}}{\sqrt{Np}}$	the standard error of the mean distance to nearest neighbor in a randomly distributed population of density p	3.81
$c = \dfrac{\bar{r}_A - \bar{r}_E}{\sigma \bar{r}_E}$	the standard variate of the normal curve	-9.79

male offspring spend their early years with their mothers, but the widespread tendency toward "pairing" precludes a different distribution. In no sense do men's houses conform to the Mae ideal of patrilineage dwellings (Meggitt, 1965a:20–22). Instead the typical Raiapu residence comprises a man's and a woman's house spaced about 14m apart, although in polygynous families the head generally lives close to only one of his wives, and the houses of the others may be 185m or more away.

While the marked concentration of settlement on the terrace sections is primarily in response to such ecological considerations as climatic equability and stability, depth and fertility of soils, the

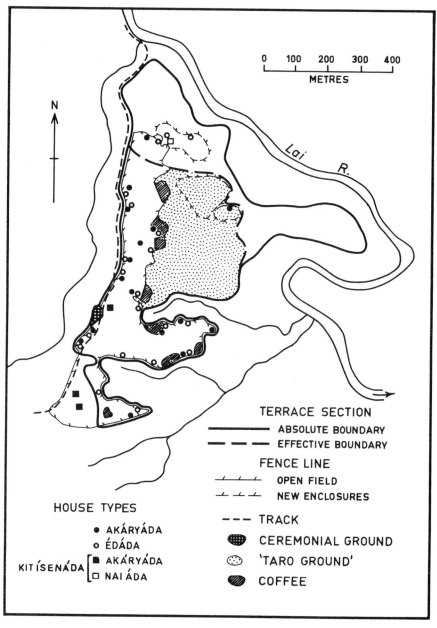

0 100 200 300 400
METRES

N

Lai R.

TERRACE SECTION
——————— ABSOLUTE BOUNDARY
– – – EFFECTIVE BOUNDARY

FENCE LINE
⊢⊣⊢ OPEN FIELD
⊣ ⊢ ⊣ NEW ENCLOSURES

– – – TRACK

⬤ CEREMONIAL GROUND

◌ 'TARO GROUND'

◨ COFFEE

HOUSE TYPES
● AKÁRYÁDA
○ ÉDÁDA
KITÍSENÁDA [■ AKÁRYÁDA
            [□ NAIÁDA

Figure 5. Modópa: land and settlement (aerial photography, QUASCO, Dec. 1967)

actual form assumed, both there and elsewhere within the group territory, reflects the dominant pattern of resource exploitation where houses are distributed around the periphery of extensive open field areas. These areas are devoted to the intensive cultivation of the staple food, sweet potato, and the boundary of each is sharply delimited by a pig-proof barrier, comprising variously a fence, ditch and embankment, or dense *Miscanthus* "hedgerow." Figure 5 depicts the pattern at Modópa where the open field area covers much of the terrace section and where the houses are, almost without exception, located at its margins.

The concept of the "distorted lattice" (Haggett, 1965:94–95) provides a useful framework for explaining the various agglomerations at Sabakamádá. This accounts for departure from a uniform distribution of settlement (or "triangular lattice") in terms of a response to the localization of resources, where in this case a major resource, the open fields, assumes a distinctly *zonal* form. "On the assumption that all settlements must have access to this resource, but that they will move as short a distance as possible from their lattice positions, a set of new locations is assumed (with appropriate changes in their territories determined by Thiessen analysis . . .)" (p. 95). Haggett's simulation of the resultant pattern is reproduced in Figure 6. In the present case the problem is complicated to the extent that direct access to the unenclosed area is also axiomatic (see below, pp. 62–63), and this demands that all residences be located at the margins of the major resource. Vindication of the assumption of minimum energy location, on which the concept is based, will be attempted in Chapter 5 (see "The Economics of Location"); but it can be stated here that the general similarity of the model to the prevailing situation at Sabakamádá is undeniable.

The open field areas are both clearly delimited and, because of the associated system of continuous cultivation, they are very stable phenomena. Consequently there is little shifting of houses. Although the mechanics of house-building (where some materials from the old house are used again) require some relocation, this seldom involves a move of more than a few meters. In fact houses tend to be resited within the grove of trees and shrubs surrounding each residence and the abandoned site is utilized as a kitchen garden. The total absence of any stands of trees within the open field areas bears witness to the fact that houses are never located there, while the dissected valley slopes, for obvious reasons, contain few suitable sites.

Apart from moves which are in response to a *force majeure*—for example territorial conquest or mission activity—longer shifts generally reflect changes in the dimensions of individual open field areas or the acquisition of rights to extensive areas of such

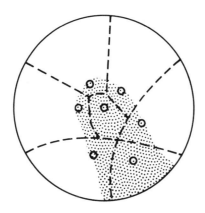

Source: HAGGETT, 1965:95

Figure 6. Assumed location of settlement in response to a zonal resource

land in other parts of the group territory. Thus, at Modópa, the recently abandoned taro area is being gradually encroached on and during 1966 alone four houses were established at that "frontier," in association with small enclosures which are likely to be incorporated within the main open field block.

In the past, warfare frequently resulted in either the temporary or permanent displacement of large numbers of people, and the effects of the intraphratry fight are still reflected in the low density of settlement at Rimádá. Nevertheless, in such cases, the form of the agglomeration persists. It is only since the advent of missionary activity that radical departures from the traditional norm have occurred. The concentration of settlement around a "point" resource (the church and school) at Ráku has led to the fragmentation and occupation of a significant part of the original open field area. Both there and elsewhere in the group territory the advent of *kitisenáda* occupied by whole families have likewise obviated the immediate need to locate at the margins of the open field areas, because their pigs no longer require direct access to the houses from the unenclosed land. Already at Modópa three such houses have been established well within the boundary fence, admittedly on land not previously used for intensive sweet potato cultivation.

These latter developments are potentially disruptive of the orderly system of land use evolved by the Raiapu, yet there is little to suggest that they are only of a temporary nature. The increasing trend toward family dwellings is evident elsewhere among the Enga and in the Highlands generally, while one can only presume a stigma will develop about living with pigs ultimately resulting in their being housed elsewhere. Thus Brown and Brookfield (1967:142) remark, of the Chimbu, "The most significant trends in residence have been the growing tendency of men to live separately, or with their families, and for women to sleep most nights in houses separate from their pigs."

Referring to a "village situation" which has developed around the Lutheran church and school in a neighboring group territory Westermann (1968:92) states, somewhat optimistically, "The situation may reflect a temporary arrangement. People at Talyakósa have discussed the matter and it appears that many of the houses will not be rebuilt when they fall into disrepair." Yet during his eighteen-month stay there he witnessed a net decline of only one house (from nineteen to eighteen), although the church has been on that site for at least a decade.

A rigorous treatment of settlement immediately points to the diversity of patterns within the Highlands—patterns which, it will be demonstrated later, bear a close relationship to systems of land use. Where changes in the former take place independently of the latter, problems can be expected. Among the Chimbu these are reflected in the constant change and neglect of fence-lines, their increased breaching by pigs, and the abandonment of some garden areas (Brown and Brookfield, 1967:145). No such developments are identifiable at Sabakamádá, partly because of the greater permanency of the open fields and partly because active christians still tend to be the poorer people, monogamous and with few pigs, but primarily because there has been less time for the consequences of these as yet limited settlement changes to manifest themselves.

The System of Land Use

The Aruní associate five main crops and one domestic animal with their putative ancestor, Magilúda, whose two sons, Yakumau and Waiminau, took up residence at Sabakamádá. The crops are sweet potato (*Ipomoea batatas*), yam (*Dioscorea* spp.), banana (*Musa* spp.), taro (*Colocasia esculenta*), and sugarcane (*Saccharum officinarum*), while the domestic animal is the pig. Whatever the frailties of oral tradition may have done to obscure the degree of antiquity of these food resources the Enga typology of gardens is clearly framed in terms of them, while the network linking an individual residence and its scattered holdings, together with the broad patterns of land use, can only be understood with reference to them.

In the immediate precontact period there were three major garden types, the sweet potato garden (*mapú eé*), the yam garden (*amú eé*), and the taro garden (*máa eé*), while a scattering of food crops were planted around the houses, sometimes in formal "kitchen gardens." The sweet potato gardens were of two types, *yukúsi* and *modó*, each characterized by radically different technologies and intensities of cultivation. In both cases the sweet potato was grown under a system of monoculture with, perhaps, a few small sections devoted to stands of sugarcane. Virtually all subsidiary crops were intercultivated in the yam gardens, the dominant ones in terms of yield being yam (*Dioscorea alata*), sugarcane, banana, highland pitpit (*Setaria palmaefolia*), and winged bean (*Psophocarpus tetragonobulus*). (See Appendix 3 for a list of principal Raiapu cultigens.)

In terms of total cultivated area sweet potato gardens were predominant, but elderly informants claim the taro gardens to have been more extensive than the yam, with taro itself ranking second to sweet potato as a food source. The winged bean, sugarcane, ginger (*Zingiber* sp.), highland pitpit, and yam (*D. bulbifera*) were all grown in association with it. The food plants scattered around the houses largely duplicated those found in the yam and taro gardens—sugarcane, taro, banana—but a number were unique to these sites, for example, tobacco (*Nicotiana tabacum*) and sweet flag (*Acorus calamus*).[14] More recent introductions such as pawpaw (*Carica papaya*), cassava (*Manihot dulcis*), taro (*Xanthosoma sagittifolium*), agave (*Marayllipaceae*), and, locally, exotic varieties of bananas and the nut pandanus (*Pandanus jiulianettii* & *P. brosimos*) are also largely confined to the surrounds of residences. Preferentially either the embankment raised from earth removed in leveling the house site and amply watered by run-off from the roof, or old house sites (noted for their great fertility) were utilized. Formal gardens did not necessarily occur and the evidence points to these areas having usually been selected for the first attempts at cultivating new introductions.

Scattered through these cultivated areas were a variety of other plants and trees which played an important part in the Raiapu economy, some of them associated with the fallow and others purposefully planted. *Casuarina oligodon*, *Bambusa* sp., *Ficus dammaropsis*, and *Cordyline* sp. were planted around the houses, the first two valued as building materials and the bamboo also used as a sharp-edged tool, the leaves of *Ficus* for lining the earth ovens used to cook pigmeat in and those of the *Cordyline* as clothing. *Casuarina* also dominated the yam garden fallows and were always left at clearing and pollarded to promote straight growth. *Acalypha* sp., the timber of which is used for building and for making bows and tongs for the fire and the leaves for wrapping tobacco, was also associated with abandoned yam gardens. The taro garden fallows were dominated by *Trema amboinensis*, like *Casuarina* an important building and fencing timber and one whose bark is used as a binding. Finally the small creeks were dammed and ponds, about 3m in diameter, were established by each household for planting *Eleocharis sphacelata*, a reed from which the women's aprons are made. While these plants and trees represent but a fraction of those playing a useful role in the traditional Raiapu economy, they are all cultigens or closely associated with garden fallows and therefore of immediate relevance to agricultural practices.

14. Primarily of ritual significance, being fed to pigs to fatten them, and planted by the bachelors at their *sadáru* ceremonies for use in association with spells which "ensure their physical development and good looks, avert the danger of sexual pollution and draw pigs to their houses" (Meggitt, 1965b:124).

Within the past ten to fifteen years the traditional system has undergone certain modifications associated with the introduction of a range of commercial crops and the apparent ending of extensive taro cultivation. Among the former the Raiapu make a clear distinction between coffee and *Pyrethrum* on the one hand and "business" crops on the other. All the "business" crops are annuals, readily integrated into the traditional system and also consumed to varying degrees within the subsistence sector. The majority of these comprise such temperate vegetables as lettuce, carrots, tomatoes, beans, peas, and cucumbers, for which there is a ready market among the expatriate population. Coffee and *Pyrethrum* are perennials that require special cultivation techniques and whose only utility follows from the conversion of the products into cash. Therefore the agricultural system as modified comprises distinctive sweet potato and yam gardens, monocultural holdings of coffee and *Pyrethrum*, and a broad but fragmented complex of kitchen and "business" plots. The general distribution of other economic plants and trees still assumes the traditional form with the *Casuarina* also often planted as a shade tree for coffee. The taro area, although still readily identifiable by its *Trema* dominated fallow, is being progressively resumed for incorporation within the sweet potato and coffee areas.

The following discussion of Raiapu agricultural practices focuses on the distinctive characteristics of site, technology, cultivation cycle, tenurial status, size, and spatial distribution of each of these garden types, or subsystems. The names that are attributed to each reflect this concern with the ". . . essentially agronomic considerations of farming technique and management" (Brookfield, 1968:417), rather than with the crops as such. Although individual crops are in fact largely specific to one or other of the garden types and the Raiapu do identify their gardens with reference to the principal crops, it is considered that the distinction will better facilitate the identification of the character and dynamics of the total system. Thus the sweet potato gardens are termed "open fields" and the yam become "mixed gardens"; the less important "kitchen gardens" persist as such but encompass the "business" crops, while the fourth subsystem, "cash-crop gardens," represent the most recent, major innovation which has as yet established no clearly defined niche.

A detailed survey of the holdings of the ten households making up the Modópa sample community revealed a total of 7.2ha under cultivation, or 0.16ha per head of population, during March–April 1966 (Table 8). Of this some 66 percent comprised open fields, 19 percent mixed gardens, 10 percent cash-crop gardens, and 5 percent kitchen gardens. The mixed gardens were resurveyed during November–December to take into account a new planting cycle and, if areas under the other subsystems are assumed to have remained constant,[15] the total cultivated area was found to have increased to 7.8ha, or 0.19ha per head of population. The cash-crop holdings apart, these figures are still well above the level considered by Barrau (1958:31) to be the subsistence requirement for human consumption or the pattern generally found through Melanesia. However, as Brookfield and Brown (1963:115) have already indicated, wide variations are evident within the Highlands, and the Modópa figures compare with those for the Kyaka, 0.15ha per head of population (Bulmer, 1960a:79), and for the Korofeigu, 0.16ha per head under subsistence crops (Howlett, 1962:174).

Open fields

Sweet potato gardens cover almost two-thirds of the total cultivated area and are primarily of the *modó* type—large plano-convex mounds averaging 3.8m in diameter and 0.6m high. However, about 6 percent are *yukúsi*—gardens of small mounds about 0.45m in diameter and 0.23m high which can be considered as bearing some genetic relationship to the *modó* in that they reflect an "initial" as opposed to an "established" stage of development. Apart from a few corn or *Colocasia* in the *yukúsi* gardens and an occasional sugarcane cutting or Irish potato plant (*Solanum tuberosum*) in a mound, no crops are intercultivated with the sweet potatoes. A few sections are given over to other crops, principally peanuts and sugarcane, and to plots of *yukúsi* within the larger *modó* gardens. Thus, of the total open field area, 83 percent comprises *modó*, 15 percent *yukúsi*, and 2 percent other crops.

The *modó* areas are restricted, almost entirely, to the Modópa terrace section where the general slope of the ground surface averages only five to ten degrees (Table 9). Here the humic

15. In fact the area under cash-crops declined slightly. See Table 8 and pp. 58–59.

TABLE 8

Modópa Sample Community: Area under Cultivation

	Mar./Apr. 1966*		Nov./Dec. 1966†	
	ha	%	ha	%
By subsystem				
Open field				
modó	4.49	62.5	...‡	57.9
yukúsi	0.26	3.6	...‡	3.4
Mixed garden	1.39	19.4	2.00	25.8
Kitchen garden	0.34	4.7	...‡	4.4
Cash-crop garden	0.70	9.8	0.66	8.5
Total	7.18	100.0	7.76	100.0
By crop				
Sweet potato				
modó	3.93	54.7	...‡	50.6
yukúsi	0.89	12.4	0.97	12.5
Yam and associated crops	1.28	17.8	1.81	23.3
Kitchen garden subsistence crops	0.09	1.2	...‡	1.2
Coffee	0.53	7.4	...‡	6.8
Pyrethrum	0.13	1.8	0.08	1.0
Peanuts	0.16	2.2	...‡	2.1
Other "business" crops	0.18	2.5	0.19	2.4
Total	7.18	100.0	7.76	99.9
Mean areas				
Per head of population				
subsistence	0.14		0.17	
commercial	0.02		0.02	
Total	0.16		0.19	
Per able-bodied person				
subsistence	0.19		0.22	
commercial	0.02		0.02	
Total	0.21		0.25	
Per household				
subsistence	0.64		0.70	
commercial	0.08		0.08	
Total	0.72		0.78	

* 45 persons (all 15 years plus), 10 households.
† 42 persons (all 15 years plus), 10 households.
‡ No measurements taken but area assumed to be unchanged.

TABLE 9

Modópa Sample Community: Percentage of Open
Field (modó) Area within Each Slope Category

| Slope (°) | ha | % | Cumulative | |
			ha	%
0–4.9	0.74	16.5	0.74	16.5
5–9.9	3.38	75.3	4.12	91.8
10–14.9	0.37	8.2	4.49	100.0
Total	4.49	100.0		

brown clay soils, occurring extensively through the Lai and Tchak
valleys, are well drained, stable, and characterized by "strongly
developed black to very dark grey-brown A_1 horizons, which
abruptly or clearly over-lie dark brown, yellow-brown, or strong
brown subsoils" (Rutherford and Haantjens, 1965:88). Mounds
are prepared strictly from this topsoil and it is only on the terrace
sections that the depth is sufficient to establish gardens with the
appropriate density, about 840 mounds/ha at a 0.3m spacing.

Basic to any understanding of the mounding system is the fact
that it is designed to permit continuous cultivation of the soil.
Inquiries as to cropping practices were invariably met with amusement and the assurance that "we do not fallow this ground."
Informants claimed that 88 percent of the modó area had been
under continuous cultivation, at least since the intraphratry fight
disrupted activities around 1938. The only other instances of
fallowing or of incorporating new areas into the open field subsystem were in response to changing household requirements
brought about through death or population increase. So 8 percent
of the current area under modó had been resumed from the taro
area within the past ten years.

The cultivation cycle is a continuous one in which, at the final
harvest, the mound is broken open and the earth piled in a ridge
at the perimeter. The weeds which have colonized it, together
with the unwanted sweet potato vines, are thrown to the center
and, over a period of about ten weeks, S. palmaefolia and sugarcane leaves may be introduced. A survey of the vegetable matter
incorporated into ten mounds with dimensions averaging 3.1m in
diameter and 0.6m high revealed a mean of 20.2kg per mound, of

which 63 percent were sweet potato vines, 20 percent a variety of ruderals and forbs (in particular *Polygonum nepalense, Erigeron sumatrensis, Bidens pilosa, Arthraxon hispidus, Commelina* sp., *Imperata cylindrica, Setaria pallide-fusca,* plus *Crassocephalum crepidiodes, Oenanthe javanica,* and *Drymaria cordata*), 10 percent leaves of the *S. palmaefolia,* and 3 percent sugarcane leaves. The remaining 4 percent consisted of a banana leaf and a quantity of *Pyrethrum* plants, reflecting the lack of any apparent selectivity in mulching material.

When the vegetable matter has started to decompose the mound is closed, preferably on a dry day. Traditionally the only tool used in this and other sweet potato gardening activities was a wooden stick (*yáti*) about 0.75m long, shaped like a paddle at one end and pointed at the other. Nowadays a small metal spade is used, either in association with a simple digging stick or with the handle pointed so that it can be reversed and double as a stick. The soil is shoveled from the rim to the center of the crater to cover the mulch and establish the general form of the mound; then, as the profile break between the topsoil and lower horizon is approached, the edge of the mound is delineated by horizontal movements with the spade. The mound is then smoothed into shape, large clods are broken up, any stones or exposed vegetable matter removed, and, finally, the surface compacted slightly—all with the hands.

The sweet potato is propagated vegetatively, with about eighteen plants spaced at about 0.45m intervals over the surface of the mound to within 0.21m of the base. Each plant consists of three to five cuttings of a single variety about 0.45m long and consisting of the growing ends of young, healthy vines. The cuttings are held together in the hands and the broken ends pushed beneath the surface of the soil. A little earth is then heaped over, leaving about half the total length of the vines exposed. These exposed ends may be oriented in any direction.

The mounds are clean-weeded until the the first harvest which follows about twenty-four weeks after planting; thereafter little weeding is done. A system of progressive harvesting is practiced, extending over a further period of thirty weeks or more, in which only mature tubers are removed from the vines until the final harvest when the mound is broken open. This is achieved by probing the mound with a digging stick, lifting the vine, removing the selected tubers, and replacing the soil. Generally two or three harvests are effected in this manner. The final one only takes place when the mound is required for replanting, as much as a year or more after the initial harvest. By this stage grasses such as *S. pallide-fusca* and *I. cylindrica* are colonizing the mound and few of the remaining tubers are considered suitable for human consumption. Thus, when the mound is finally opened, a small pig is frequently tethered nearby to root out any edible material and assist in breaking up the soil.

Each household operates an average of 4.7 *modó* gardens of a mean size of 0.10ha each.[16] However, the plots are not obviously demarcated and the general impression obtained is one of a continuously mounded area, interspersed with a few small patches of *Imperata*, extending across the whole terrace surface. The area is free of any woody vegetation, *Casuarina* being conspicuously absent, while the particular character of the cultivation cycle gives rise to a seemingly random interspersal of mounds at all stages of development. Dispersed around the periphery of this area, sheltering beneath towering *Casuarina* and concealed behind hedges of *Cordyline*, are the residences; and an important feature of the spatial distribution of these is their close proximity to the *modó* gardens.

Table 10 reveals over half the *modó* area to be within a two-minute walk of the cultivators' residences.[17] Special circumstances apply in the case of the two plots greater than twenty minutes distance away; one involves permissive rights only, in the territory of a neighboring clan, while the other comprises a block of land 245m higher up the range above Modópa to which primary rights had only recently been acquired. In the case of the former the operator is frequently involved in pig exchanges and, rather than bring the animals across the Lai gorge, keeps some with a sister who is married into the clan. Also, he spends a great deal of time supervising the sale of "business" crops to a company based in that group.[18] A readily available supply of sweet potatoes is there-

16. One household possessed eighteen separate plots, divided among three resident wives and a dependent spinster.
17. For conversion to linear distance a walking speed of 3.2km per hour, or 530m in 10 minutes, may be assumed (Brown and Brookfield, 1967:134).
18. The company, Waso Ltd, is a largely indigenous-financed but Lutheran

TABLE 10

MODÓPA SAMPLE COMMUNITY: PERCENTAGE OF OPEN
FIELD (MODÓ) AREA DISTANT FROM RESIDENCES

Traveling Time from Residence (mins.)	ha	%	Cumulative	
			ha	%
0–1.9	2.64	58.8	2.64	58.8
2–4.9	1.26	28.1	3.90	86.9
5–9.9	0.53	11.8	4.43	98.7
10–19.9	. . .	. . .	. . .	. . .
20 +	0.06	1.3	4.49	100.0
Total	4.49	100.0		

fore invaluable on both accounts. With the latter the rightholder
has inherited no suitable land at Modópa through the direct
patrilineal line and has only permissive rights over 60 percent of
the area he is presently cultivating; he is therefore concerned to
obtain sole rights to *modó* land wherever possible, so that he may
have sufficient to transmit to his two sons.

Related to the distinctive characteristics of spatial organization
and technological sophistication are others of availability of land
and tenurial status. Only two of the ten households claimed to
have substantial areas suitable for *modó* lying fallow at Modópa
and both had granted permissive rights over some surplus ground
to other households. As a corollary of this most are primary rightholders over the land they cultivate, this being the case in thirty-
five of the forty-seven gardens surveyed. In only seven were permissive rights being exercised, while in the others claims were
being asserted following the death without male offspring or the
out-migration of the prior rightholder.

Yukúsi gardens are very restricted in number and size—seven
households possessed ten plots, each averaging 0.02ha—and lack
the clearly recognizable site characteristics associated with *modó*.
Like the latter, they are located relatively close to the residences

---

mission–directed enterprise based at Kumbasakama, near Wapenamanda. It
purchases all the locally grown coffee and "business" crops and has a
variety of other commercial interests (Fairbairn, 1967).

but on somewhat steeper sloping ground; however, considerable
variations are evident (Tables 11 and 12). Generally speaking
they are distributed around the periphery of the terrace section
(and *modó* area)—on the steeper slopes at the foot of the main

TABLE 11

Modópa Sample Community: Percentage of Open
Field (yukúsi) Area Distant from Residences

| Traveling Time from Residence (mins.) | ha | % | Cumulative | |
			ha	%
0–1.9	0.08	30.8	0.08	30.8
2–4.9	0.03	11.5	0.11	42.3
5–9.9	0.10	38.5	0.21	80.8
10+	0.05	19.2	0.26	100.0
Total	0.26	100.0		

TABLE 12

Modópa Sample Community: Percentage of Open
Field (yukúsi) Area within Each Slope Category

| Slope (°) | ha | % | Cumulative | |
			ha	%
0–4.9	0.10	38.5	0.10	38.5
5–9.9	0.04	15.4	0.14	53.9
10–19.9	0.04	15.4	0.18	68.3
20+	0.08	30.7	0.26	100.0
Total	0.26	100.0		

range, the edge of the dissected tributary valleys, and encroaching
on to the ceremonial ground.

Six of the ten *yukúsi* holdings had no previous owner and
claims were being asserted through cultivation. In the other cases
the operator was exploiting his own ground or had been granted
permissive rights to that of another. Related to this are the very
different cultivation histories of the gardens, where seven were
being planted for only the first or second time following clearing

from a grass fallow. In terms of a cultivation sequence *yukúsi* represents (1) an initial stage prior to the establishment of *modó*, (2) a situation where sweet potato is being rotated with other crops, particularly peanuts, or (3) a simple rotational fallow crop where one or two successive plantings are followed by lengthy fallows.

Like *modó*, *yukúsi* involves complete tillage of the soil, but without mulching. In the case of clearing from a grass fallow, the vegetation is first removed by "cutting" with a spade at ground level, and left to dry for six to eight weeks. It is then heaped and burned and the beds of ashes (*abí*) are commonly used as seed beds for establishing various greens, lettuce, and tomatoes. After burning, the ground is broken to a depth of about 0.1m with a spade, sweet potato cuttings are selected as for *modó*, and the mounds formed by placing individual plants on the ground and sweeping the soil up around them, again leaving the growing end exposed. The mounds average 0.45m in diameter and 0.23m high and are spaced about 0.6 to 0.9m apart but, since the intervening soil has been broken up without exposing the underlying clay, the whole surface is available for sweet potato development. This contrasts with *modó* where the vines seldom "take" to the exposed clay.

Tubers are harvested progressively but appear to take a little longer to mature than when planted in mounds—about twenty-eight weeks from planting to the initial harvest and a minimum of sixty weeks to the final one. Again gardens are only weeded in the early stages.

Where the sweet potato is rotated with a second crop, or individual plantings are separated by lengthy fallows, the dimensions of the small mounds remain constant and each carries only one plant. However, where new ground is being incorporated into the open field system a progressive increase in mound size is apparent at each successive planting, and there is a commensurate increase in the worked depth of the soil. So, at the second or third planting, the mounds may be 0.9 to 1.2m in diameter and 0.4 to 0.6m high with as many as three plants established in each.

The many patches of *yukúsi* within the extensive *modó* areas reflect both marginal extensions to the cultivated area and rotational cropping. Alternatively, where the earth has become compacted, as with mounds which have been left for long periods before opening, the ground may be leveled and *yukúsi* established. The object of this is to rework the soil and develop the texture appropriate for *modó*. Only rarely is the sweet potato planted in association with long fallows; in most respects the *yukúsi* areas are integral parts of the open field subsystem, designed specifically to prepare the ground for the establishment of *modó*. Finally, none of the thirty-five varieties of sweet potato known to the Aruní are specific to one or other of the garden types. The six which are planted extensively through all the gardens, *kelyópu*, *koroká*, *burú*, *konemá*, *síbi*, and *kopé*, are all recent introductions, preferred to the traditional varieties because they are higher yielding and have a sweeter taste.

Mixed gardens

During early 1966 the sample had 1.39ha under mixed gardens but by the end of the year this had risen to 2.00ha, an increase from 19 percent to 26 percent of the total cultivated area. The gardens are established annually, during the dry season when clearing of secondary growth and movement to and from the sites are relatively easy tasks, and their effective life does not exceed fifteen months. Consequently, by the time of the second survey all the gardens established during the previous year had been abandoned to the pigs and encroaching regrowth. Variations in the area cleared from year to year relate, in part at least, to the supply of yam cuttings, and the increase in 1966 was paralleled by a decline in the length of the fallow period from a mean of 14.2 years (sd 4.1) to 10.7 years (sd 2.4) per garden.

Like the open fields, mixed gardens are specific to a particular terrain unit—the slopes of the Lai gorge and its tributaries abutting on the terrace sections. Within this broad area any largely boulder-free sites with a covering of black topsoil and with slopes not exceeding 45 degrees are considered suitable. Since the gardens are established on relatively steep slopes (Table 13) soil stability is a problem and slips are a constant hazard during the wet season. This factor is an added consideration in restricting clearing and planting to the dry season, in the sense that the practice ensures that an adequate plant cover is achieved before the wet.

Gardens are cleared by the customary "slash-and-burn" method of felling the trees and clearing the undergrowth, fencing with strong pig-proof barricades, and burning off. Apart from small

TABLE 13

Modópa Sample Community: Percentage of Mixed Garden
Area within Each Slope Category (Mar./Apr. 1966)

| Slope (°) | ha | % | Cumulative | |
			ha	%
0–4.9	0.06	4.3	0.06	4.3
5–9.9	0.18	12.9	0.24	17.2
10–19.9	0.14	10.1	0.38	27.3
20–29.9	0.53	38.1	0.91	65.4
30–39.9	0.41	29.5	1.32	94.9
40+	0.07	5.0	1.39	100.0
Total	1.39	99.9		

ditches dug in particularly wet sections to channel run-off down-slope, no erosional control devices are used, and once the surface has been swept clean the garden is ready for planting. Table 14 details the crops most commonly planted in the mixed gardens and the frequency with which they occur. Except for minor concentrations of taro in the ditches and poorly drained depressions, sweet potato on shallow stony ground,[19] and lettuce in patches where ash remains from burning off, all are closely intercultivated. Three of the principal crops, yam (D. alata), sugarcane, and banana, are designated as strictly "male" crops to be planted and tended only by the men. The other subsistence crops are all considered "female" crops, while the "business" crops are also generally their responsibility (although this is as yet in no way sanctioned). Moreover the gardens as a whole are considered "male," in contrast to the "female" open fields, and menstruating women are not allowed to enter them for fear of polluting the "male" yams. These sexual distinctions reflect something of the different values attached to the several crops where the "male" ones, in particular the yams, are of considerable social significance, cooked in earth ovens and consumed primarily when exchange partners visit or at the food distributions associated with life crises. So, while within an individual's garden there is a reasonably high degree of freedom with which members of other households

19. It is considered that sweet potatoes help to "break the ground" for subsequent yam plantings.

TABLE 14

Modópa Sample Community: Extent and Frequency of
Individual Crops in the Mixed Gardens (Nov./Dec. 1966)*

	Crop	Percent of Sample Plots in Which Crop Was Located†	Mean Frequency with Which Crops Occurred through All Plots
Crops occurring in more than 50% of the plots	Yam (D. alata)	100	29.1 plants
	Banana	100	5.8
	Psophocarpus tetragonobulus	95	66.5
	Amaranthus tricolor	95	numerous
	Setaria palmaefolia	84	16.2
	Tomato	79	8.1
	Zingiber sp.	79	5.6
	Sugarcane	74	3.8
	Corn	63	23.7
	(?) Ricinus communis	63	3.3
	Saccharum edule	63	3.0
	Bean	58	9.7
	Cucumber	53	5.7
	Rungia klossii	53	2.3
Crops occurring in less than 50% of the plots but with an overall frequency of greater than 1.0 per plot	Lettuce	47	15.6
	Pea	47	13.4
	Gourd (Lagenaria sp.)	42	2.6
	Irish potato	21	2.8
	Taro (Colocasia esculenta)	5	4.4
	Sweet potato	5	3.3

* In addition the following crops were found in small numbers: *Dioscorea bulbifera, Dolichos lablab,* Brassicaceae, *Oenanthe javanica, Xanthosoma sagittifolium,* peanut, soya bean, cabbage, pumpkin, and coffee.

† A total of 67 plots, each of 25m², in 19 gardens were sampled. The plots were located by (1) determining the most northerly point of the garden, (2) using a random numbers table to determine a bearing from that point along which one or more 25m² quadrats fell entirely within the garden, (3) counting by species all the individuals in each plot.

can remove a few lengths of S. *palmaefolia* and other minor crops, such liberties most definitely do not extend to the "male" crops.

Most of the crops are planted by a simple dibbling procedure, using the short digging stick associated with sweet potato cultivation. However, for yams the actual sites are tilled, using two stakes of differing lengths. First a hole about 0.7m deep is made by driving a 10cm wide (and 1.8m long) stake into the ground at an angle of about 60 degrees to the surface. The stake is then rotated to widen the hole to a diameter of about 0.3m. It is then discarded for a shorter stake which is used to break the ground at the back of the hole and form a layer of loose earth at the bottom. This earth is worked with the hands and stick into a bed of finely textured soil—similar to that in the *modó*—about 0.3m deep, and on it are placed one or two yam tops. Finally, these are covered with additional loose earth to fill the hole.

Crops are, variously, propagated vegetatively and by seed reproduction. Yam, banana, sugarcane, *Zingiber* sp., *S. palmaefolia*, *Saccharum edule*, and taro fall within the first category, as do the potato and sweet potato, while the others fall within the second. When a considerable interval elapses between harvesting and replanting a crop (as with the several greens, corn, *P. tetragonobulus*, *Dolichos lablab*, cucumber, and gourd) the seeds are dried under the roof of the house and stored in gourds until required. Seeds of the greens, lettuce, and tomato are by preference planted in *abí* and may be transplanted later. With the yam (*D. bulbifera*) debris is swept into small piles about 0.4m in diameter and the aerial tubers are planted in them.

In the early weeks after planting gardens require considerable attention in staking out the yams, *P. tetragonobulus* and *D. lablab*, and training the vines up them. The gardens are also clean weeded until a good cover of crops has been established. Thereafter weeding is largely incidental to harvesting. Otherwise the fences require maintaining throughout the life of the garden. Although crops are closely interplanted, their maturation periods vary considerably and most are in production for only a few weeks; there is therefore little competition between the plants. Within six to eight weeks such greens as *Amaranthus tricolor* and Brassicaceae are harvested, followed by cucumber at ten weeks, corn at twelve to fifteen, the beans of *D. lablab* and *P. tetragonobulus* at twenty-two and the tubers of the latter at about twenty-six weeks. *S.*

palmaefolia and *S. edule* are in production for several months, commencing about thirty weeks after planting. The first yams are ready at about the same time, but of the eleven or so varieties of *D. alata* grown the two principal ones, *korá* and *lakápu*, which together account for about 80 percent of the total, only mature at ten or twelve months. Within three or four months of the final yam harvest the fences are broken, with only the sugarcane and bananas left. The clumps of sugarcane are generally ringed with stakes from the old fence to protect them from the pigs. Alternatively they may not be left to mature but are consumed before abandonment of the gardens.

Nine varieties of banana are grown at Modópa, three of them recent introductions from the lower Lai Valley, but only one, *uakápa*, is planted extensively in the yam gardens. From 3.7 to 4.6m high when mature, it carries a bunch of from four to seven hands of small fruit, and a second sucker generally bears before being destroyed by pigs and secondary growth in the abandoned garden. The plants seldom survive more than two years after the initial planting. The immature bunches are tightly wrapped in banana leaves to protect them from flying fox and, supposedly, to encourage the development of large fruit with "plenty of meat inside." (It is not known whether this theory has any foundation in fact.)

Abandoned gardens are readily identifiable by the tall, pollarded *Casuarina* which have been planted or allowed to grow on them. These mixed gardens are scattered throughout the slopes of the Lai gorge and its tributaries, ranging up to an altitude of about 1830m MSL. This scattering is indicative of the practice of bush-fallowing. Because of it the gardens are at a variable distance from the residences and, on average, substantially further than the open fields (Table 15). However, the distribution is not entirely random in any one year, for there is a tendency to focus activity in particular localities. Of the gardens established during 1965, 29 percent were grouped with others belonging to individuals from outside the sample in an area about a ten-minute walk from Modópa ceremonial ground. Nevertheless households have an average of 2.5 plots,[20] of a mean size of 0.06ha, with each in a different locality.

20. Only one, consisting of a divorced man, had none in 1965 but he established a garden the following year.

There is considered to be abundant land available for mixed gardens and no one household has insufficient; nevertheless individuals tend to garden together and temporary transfers of rights are common. Sixteen of the twenty-five plots surveyed in early 1966 comprised sections within larger gardens. In six of these sixteen cases individuals had been invited to plant sections on

TABLE 15

MODÓPA SAMPLE COMMUNITY: PERCENTAGE OF MIXED GARDEN AREA DISTANT FROM RESIDENCES (Mar./Apr. 1966)

Traveling Time from Residence (mins.)	ha	%	Cumulative	
			ha	%
0–1.9	0.23	16.5	0.23	16.5
2–4.9	0.13	9.4	0.36	25.9
5–9.9	0.40	28.8	0.76	54.7
10–19.9	0.30	21.6	1.06	76.3
20–29.9	0.01	0.7	1.07	77.0
30–45	0.32	23.0	1.39	100.0
Total	1.39	100.0		

another's land, while in the others individuals were working their own ground but sharing common fences. Various motives appear to underlie these practices: first, to economize on effort, especially by minimizing the extent of fencing and facilitating efficient clearing, second, to provide access to suitable land for kinsmen living at higher altitudes, and third, to provide a mechanism whereby incomplete families and aged people are able to cultivate for themselves the crops associated with mixed gardens. Gardens are occasionally identified with specific lineages, with as many as ten or fifteen households clearing, fencing, and subdividing the ground together. In other cases, where individuals have worked adjacent plots over a period of time, they may decide regardless of affiliation to carry out the initial clearing and fencing together, or at least to agree upon the location of a single bounding fence. Affines are commonly invited to plant sections and the invitation may involve assistance in the preparatory work or it may only follow this. Finally, in the case of widowed and divorced or unmarried adults, the "male" and "female" crops within a single section may be the property of different households. So it is not only in technology but equally in the mode of exploitation that the characteristics associated with mixed gardens differ widely from those of the open fields.

Kitchen gardens

Both "kitchen" and "business" crops largely duplicate those found in the mixed gardens. Like the mixed gardens, both are intercultivated but these sites are distinguished by the small size of plots, their proximity to the residences, and their extended periods of cultivation. Although covering only 0.34ha there were fifteen separate plots of a mean size of 0.02ha in March–April 1966, with at least one per household. Eleven of them were immediately adjacent to the residence of the operator or on old house sites a short distance away, and therefore on the level or gently sloping ground of the terrace sections (Table 16). However, with the in-

TABLE 16

Modópa Sample Community: Percentage of Kitchen Garden Area within Each Slope Category

Slope (°)	ha	%	Cumulative ha	Cumulative %
0–4.9	0.17	50.0	0.17	50.0
5–9.9	0.15	44.1	0.32	94.1
10+	0.02	5.9	0.34	100.0
Total	0.34	100.0		

troduction of the "business" crops, this garden type is beginning to occur more widely and small plots have been established in previously unutilized areas, as on the ceremonial ground, or in association with yukúsi holdings (Table 17). In these latter areas the plots are established specifically to grow "business" crops—in particular lettuce and tomatoes, but also peanuts—and these are rotated with sweet potatoes for short periods, prior to probable fallowing. Ground preparation is similar to that for the sweet potatoes, with the earth broken to a depth of a few centimeters and turned, while shallow trenches may be dug to improve drainage.

TABLE 17

MODÓPA SAMPLE COMMUNITY: PERCENTAGE OF KITCHEN
GARDEN AREA DISTANT FROM RESIDENCES

Traveling Time from Residence (mins.)	ha	%	Cumulative	
			ha	%
0–1.9	0.17	50.0	0.17	50.0
2–4.9	0.15	44.1	0.32	94.1
30	0.02	5.9	0.34	100.0
Total	0.34	100.0		

Old house sites are particularly fertile as their soils contain the dung of pigs and fowl and the rotting fibers of sugarcane previously strewn over the floor. Also the house structure itself has served to reduce the leaching effect of heavy rainfall, thus improving the nutrient status of the soil beneath.

After a house has been demolished the debris is left to dry, burned off, and turned into the soil. Once the site has been planted, litter from the occupied house may be added, and in this way it is cultivated for several years until it is resumed for building purposes. Crops most commonly found at these locations are sugarcane, taro (*Colocasia* and *Xanthosoma*), pumpkin, corn, yams, carrots, peas, lettuce, and the more exotic varieties of banana, although the numbers and extent of intercultivation varies considerably from plot to plot.

On account of the particular value placed on old house sites and their proximity to the residences they are invariably exploited by the primary rightholders, while the further plots are characterized by a diversity of tenurial statuses more typical of the mixed gardens.

Cash-crop holdings

The two cash-crops which have been the subject of active extension work by DASF, coffee (*Coffea arabica*) and *Pyrethrum cinerarifolium*, are grown in discrete holdings, in the latter case actually delimited and planted by agricultural extension workers. Together they cover 0.70ha or 10 percent of the cultivated area. However, the imminent abandonment of *Pyrethrum* cultivation

and the considerable differences between gardens in their general
condition, types of land which have been utilized, and patterns of
exploitation all point to these gardens not yet having established
a clearly defined niche within the wider agricultural system. The
readiness with which individual households have turned over open
fields to cash-crops and the equal speed with which they have
abandoned the holdings reflect on the one hand a certain ambivalence where expectations have not been realized, and on the other
the greater problems involved in accommodating perennial crops
within the existing agricultural system.

As with the open fields, a primary consideration in siting cash-
crop gardens is proximity to the residence (Table 18). All the

TABLE 18

MODÓPA SAMPLE COMMUNITY: PERCENTAGE OF CASH-CROP
AREA DISTANT FROM RESIDENCES

Traveling Time from Residence (mins.)	ha	%	Cumulative ha	%
0–1.9	0.32	45.7	0.32	45.7
2–4.9	0.33	47.1	0.65	92.8
5–9.9	0.05	7.2	0.70	100.0
Total	0.70	100.0		

Pyrethrum gardens are in fact on ground previously incorporated
in the open field system, while 43 percent of the area under coffee
comprises old house sites and their adjacent kitchen gardens. However, another 35 percent of the coffee acreage is located in abandoned mixed gardens at the periphery of the Modópa terrace section and, consequently, this crop is established under variable slope
conditions (Table 19).

Pyrethrum has had a brief and checkered history below 2000m
MSL in the Wapenamanda area. DASF established nurseries early
in 1963 and by the end of the year the first indigenous holdings
were being established. Each was required to be of a minimum of
0.04ha and sited on "deep, free-draining soils," and consequently
on well-cultivated ground. Inevitably open field locations were
considered the most suitable. In May 1964, six of the ten Modópa

TABLE 19

MODÓPA SAMPLE COMMUNITY: PERCENTAGE OF CASH-CROP
AREA WITHIN EACH SLOPE CATEGORY

| Slope (°) | ha | % | Cumulative | |
			ha	%
0–4.9	0.13	18.6	0.13	18.6
5–9.9	0.36	51.4	0.49	70.0
10–19.9	0.09	12.9	0.58	82.9
20+	0.12	17.1	0.70	100.0
Total	0.70	100.0		

households established plots, yet by the end of 1965, disenchanted by low returns, most had ceased to harvest their crops. Twelve months later only three, badly overgrown, plots remained. The other households, complaining of land shortages, had returned the ground to subsistence food production.

Planting was at a density of 64,246/ha, on beds 1.8m wide separated by 0.3m drains. Harvesting commenced within six months, with the flowers generally picked low on the stalk by one hand and gathered in the other. Afterwards the heads were removed and sun-dried for a period of five to ten days outside the houses on mats, pieces of cardboard, or any movable surface. The dried flowers were then sold in 0.5 to 2.0kg lots directed to DASF at Wapenamanda.

Coffee planting commenced in 1959, purely on indigenous initiative with individuals buying and selling seedlings. By 1962 DASF had begun patrolling through the area, to advise on the layout and operation of holdings and distribute seedlings. In that year they established a seed bed at Modópa, the seedlings to be distributed to whoever required them. Statements about the crop are invariably enthusiastic—"this business yields good money"—and, although now officially discouraged, planting still continues. This is in part because, in the initial stages, coffee appears easier to integrate into the existing system in the sense that its ecological requirements are similar to those of the principal food crops. Plots are small, averaging only 0.05ha each, but seedlings are planted wherever possible, preferably in kitchen or mixed gardens, and are often intercultivated with the other crops. Alternatively they may be planted when a mixed garden is about to be abandoned. Nine of the ten households have holdings, with a total of 1,234 trees on 0.56ha: 10 percent of them mature, 54 percent starting to bear, and 36 percent immature. The condition of individual holdings varies enormously, with trees spaced rectangularly, triangularly, and randomly, from 1.1 to 2.7m apart; some are clean-weeded while others appear to have been abandoned to the encroaching regrowth; some of the owners have secateurs to prune their trees and one has even made a ladder to reach the higher branches. The techniques of processing are invariably primitive with the cherries often picked while still partly green, split between the thumb and forefinger or between the teeth, and the bean placed in a cooking pot. The pot is then filled with water, the beans soaked, "washed," and then laid out to dry, much like *Pyrethrum*. A sackful of parchment weighing as much as 25kg may be accumulated before it is sold to Waso Ltd.

Apart from two cases in which households established common holdings and agreed to share the proceeds from them, apparently because of a shortage of available land, cash-crops have been established on land over which the operator is the primary rightholder. This tendency probably reflects an early stage of development where cash-cropping has assumed no distinctive organizational pattern within the agricultural system rather than a specific concern for security of tenure. Certainly holdings do not yet assume a readily identifiable entity within the landscape for, although close to the houses, plots are small and scattered through a variety of garden and terrain types.

Animal husbandry: the place of pigs

Pigs, fowls, dogs, and, rarely, cassowaries are kept by the Raiapu. A few men (four of the ten householders at Modópa) own dogs, but they are considered purely as pets, invariably undernourished and fed only on food scraps at meal times. Two or three fowls are kept by most households but are likewise only fed on food scraps. Their eggs are seldom gathered, but the birds do feature to a limited degree in ceremonial transactions and even, in recent years, in the *tée*. Small hutches or pens are erected for them adjacent to the residences for protection against the dogs. Wild cassowaries are not found locally and the two held by individual Aruní clansmen during 1966 had both been received in *tée* exchanges. They are extremely dangerous birds, quite capable of doing serious injury to an adult person and therefore requiring considerable attention.[21] Strongly made enclosures are built for them, and they are fed all the fluids and solids they require through a small aperture large enough only to admit their heads. The cassowaries are held primarily for their exchange value, which is at least equivalent to that of a large pig. But their claws, plumage, and bones are also greatly sought after for decorative use and as spear tips.

Of all the livestock only the pigs assume an important role within the Raiapu agricultural system; indeed, they can almost be considered an integral part of it. Much has been written on the place of pigs in Highlands economic systems, particularly in "financial" terms of "currency," "credit," and "wealth." This is because of their critical role in determining the frequency, form, and course of the ubiquitous festivals. The implications of the possession of pigs for enhancing individual prestige and social status are clearly recognized and many of the details of their rearing are known, but less is understood about their place in the wider agricultural system.[22] Brookfield and Brown (1963:59) state, "Though Chimbu pig husbandry is to some degree integrated with cultivation, the system cannot be termed mixed farming"; while Vayda, Leeds, and Smith (1961:69, 72) have argued cogently "that pigs are, in fact, vitally important to the management of subsistence by Melanesian populations. . . . The massive slaughters at the festivals help to maintain a long-term ecological balance between Melanesian man and the crops and fauna from which he draws his sustenance."

The pig population among a number of Highlands groups has been estimated to exceed the human, at least in the months preceding a major festival. Brookfield and Brown (1963:59) assume 1.5 adult pigs per head of population as a maximum for the Chimbu; Bulmer's (1960a:95) Kyaka figures suggest a ratio approaching 1.6:1 only a year after "a large number of pigs had been slaughtered and given away in the Moka." The 69 residents of Modópa were responsible, in April 1966, for 158 pigs—a ratio of

21. The Raiapu invariably refer to a "strong" man as *raimá*, or cassowary, meaning essentially "the most" and used as an expression of admiration.
22. For detailed discussion of pigs, with particular reference to their ceremonial contexts and to breeding practices, see Brookfield and Brown (1963), Bulmer (1960a), Meggitt (1958a), and Salisbury (1962).

2.3:1. These were all either their own animals or ones that had been agisted with them and were accommodated in the women's houses or slept in the bush nearby. The figures probably reflect above average numbers for this was a time when the *tée* festival was suffering from severe organizational set-backs that had resulted in some people participating the previous year while others were to wait until March 1967 before they took part. The group as a whole had last participated in an exchange in 1960–61.

Pig raising is complicated by the almost complete absence of river flats for foraging, and the animals are dependent to a very considerable degree on cultivated produce. About 80 percent of them sleep in stalls inside the women's houses and the remainder out in the bush, but even the latter are fed daily and small shelters may be erected for them. During the day they roam the slopes of the Lai and its tributaries foraging for insects, roots, and grass through the abandoned mixed gardens and regrowth. As a by-product of their foraging, the soil is broken up and fertilized with dung. In the evening the pigs return voluntarily to the women's houses where they are fed large quantities of sweet potato tubers and leaves and other food scraps. Most of the tubers are of inferior quality removed in the later harvestings of the sweet potato mounds, but, as the pig population increases, their owners are obliged to feed them ones of better quality. During May 1966 it was estimated that almost two-thirds of the harvested sweet potatoes were fed to them (see Table 28). The practice of agisting, frequently carried out by large owners, is motivated partly by a need to overcome the problem of food supply by placing pigs with kinsmen who have few animals of their own or who live near good foraging areas. However, it is also a matter of risk-spreading, designed to protect the pigs from sickness and other types of disaster. Although small pigs are occasionally tethered in the open fields, to assist in the breaking of *modó* and *yukúsi*, their movements are generally restricted to the slopes around the terrace sections. The open field areas are bounded by extensive fences through which the animals can only obtain access to the houses.

The behavior pattern of pigs differs little from that associated with less intensive agricultural systems in the sense that they forage through the day and return to the residences at night. But their extreme dependence on cultivated produce bears upon the system to the extent that foraging is restricted to the areas cultivated under the mixed garden subsystem, while their staple food is cultivated intensively in open fields; and it is to the residences adjacent to these fields that the pigs find their way to eat and sleep.

Processes of change within the agricultural system

By identifying a series of agricultural subsystems on the basis of crops and associated technologies and considering the internal consistency of each in terms of such criteria as terrain types, size of holdings, tenurial status, mode of exploitation, and distance from residence, some illuminating data on the broad processes of change are provided. The dynamic characteristics of the Modópa situation follow the introduction of commercial cropping and the end of extensive taro cultivation. The open fields and mixed gardens can be seen as essentially stable elements, fluctuating marginally from year to year in response to food requirements and availability of planting materials, and readily accommodating minor innovations such as the cultivation of peanuts and inter-cultivation of "business" crops.

The kitchen gardens appear to have been the traditional focus for testing new crops and they have greatly increased in size and altered in character with the diversity of recent introductions. The "business" crops in particular appear to be well suited to them. The two cash-crops, whose modes of cultivation have been dictated primarily by DASF, have assumed less characteristic or stable forms although many kitchen gardens are being transformed into small stands of coffee.

Taro (*Colocasia*) is no longer extensively cultivated although a large area of fallow land on the terrace section dominated by *Trema* bears witness to recent holdings. Informants claim that only three generations ago the crop was "always" planted and, as with the mixed gardens, sections were frequently offered to affines. They are able to name some twenty-three varieties all of which were apparently planted. The last gardens were established about fifteen years ago and, although individuals claim they will try the crop "once more," this appears unlikely because the land is already being resumed for other purposes. Of the 8.9ha still identified as "taro ground" 1.7ha have recently been cleared or planted with other crops; the open field area has made an important inroad into it, while the boundary between the two is strung with a series of coffee gardens. Reasons for the abandonment of taro are obscure—disease and declining yields associated with shorter fallow periods and reduced soil fertility are often spoken of—but, whatever the case, the steadily increasing land requirements for commercial and subsistence crops will not permit the area to lie unnecessarily idle.

The Range of Human Interaction

In traditional Raiapu society there were considerable restrictions on individual mobility beyond the group territory. The much-quoted Highlands dictum that "we marry the people we fight" (Meggitt, 1958a:278) evokes the basic ambivalence of interclan relations. Temporary alliances and ties of descent and affinity linked each group with a number of neighbors; however, none of these links were considered binding. Faced by the constant threat of attack and usurpation of rights to land, each group stood in potential or actual opposition to the others. Meggitt (p. 264) describes the result in terms of the communications network: "Each house is connected by a narrow muddy path to one of three or four main paths that meander through the territory to link with paths in friendly neighbouring clan territories. The main paths are open to all clan and parish members, as well as to friendly relatives, but not to other people."

These traditional political and ideological restrictions on mobility both reflect and are accentuated by a subsistence economy founded almost entirely on agricultural production and a tenurial situation characterized by a marked fixity of interest in land. Data presented in Chapter 3 on activity patterns reveal an almost exclusive concern with food gardening and pig-husbandry—activities demanding intensive utilization of the ecosystem—as opposed to hunting, foraging, and fishing. Pigs are, admittedly, marginally dependent on the resources of the unenclosed area, but even the materials used in building, in the preparation of tools and clothing, and for firewood are largely derived from the enclosed land, or have been spared in the course of clearing regrowth to establish mixed gardens.

Most land is individually owned and inherited, although transfers outside the patrilineage can theoretically only be effected with the consent of the appropriate superordinate group and extra-clan transfers are inconceivable. Land suitable for incorporation within the open field system is very limited and mounding requires a considerable investment of labor. The end product of this is a close relationship, in both time and space, between residence and open field in which even members of adjacent farmsteads do not normally enter one another's ground. Any land suitable for cultivation or residential use that is not individually owned can legitimately be claimed by a member of the subclan within which the ground falls. In its unenclosed state all members of the group have equal rights of access to territorial land for the purposes of hunting, foraging, and grazing their pigs but not for the indiscriminate felling of trees. Other areas held in common include the ceremonial grounds, springs and watercourses, and that forest tract normally located in the highest parts of the group territory and above the upper limits of cultivation. However, the Raiapu make only occasional visits to most areas where individual rights are not being exercised, to search for timber, *Pandanus* nuts, or game, or to attend ceremonial events.

Finally there are the extensive forested uplands, termed "public domain" by Meggitt (1965a:224), which are "too high for successful cultivation and settlement and too far from habitation to be visited often by hunters." Such for the Raiapu is the area lying between the Tchak and Marient valleys and the upper slopes of the Mount Hagen range. In theory anyone can travel or forage without hindrance in the public domain but in fact groups whose territories abut on it frequently claim rights over sections and attack "any solitary travellers they encounter" (Meggitt, p. 224). Aruni's claim to a section of the Marient-Tchak divide has little substance because of its relative inaccessibility. Only during the *Pandanus* season do clansmen visit the area in any number.

The terms of recruitment of nonagnates to full membership of a group also serve to promote the concentration of economic activity within a restricted area. Meggitt (1965a:46) states that the agnatic ideology incorporates "the explicit rule that a person may inherit unqualified land rights in one clan only, in return for which he is bound to give undivided allegiance to that group." Agnatic status is required for security of tenure, and this status requires in turn that the individual relinquish all economic, ceremonial, and social ties with his true agnates. In the circumstances the idiom of descent is invoked as a lasting and secure basis on which loyalties are founded and territorial integrity is maintained. While usufructuary rights, for a single planting in the mixed gardens, are commonly granted to nonkinsmen, the areas involved are insignificant, exploitation does not require the continuity of effort characteristic of the open fields, and the practice provides no basis for asserting exclusive claim to the land.

This relative immobility of the Raiapu population thus reflects basic features of social and economic organization, and the situation has been little modified by developments following European contact. While land alienated by the external agencies (roads, Administration and mission stations) has become part of the "public domain" and increasing use is made of some of the pathways traversing group territories the fact remains, as the Aruní data demonstrate, that most Raiapu have neither the means nor the cause to move far beyond the confines of their respective territories.

The Aruní *oecumene* bears little relationship to the realities of physical space. Shrouded in obscurity are the places of origin of the majority of expatriates who live among the Raiapu—America, Australia, and England. Similarly Japan, the enemy in the early contact period, and Indonesia, which some say provides a threat to their present security, are countries known by name alone. The Highlands are dimly conceived as bounded by the "coast" (N-M: *nambis*), now known to be the source of shells and the home of the *pubúti* ("black men," or inhabitants of the New Guinea islands) and the Papuans, who are largely employed by the expatriates. A few coastal localities where individual kinsmen have worked as contracted laborers are identified—principally Port Moresby, Lae, Madang, Rabaul, and New Ireland. Other places within New Guinea are known of largely through contact with individual members of the constabulary stationed locally.

Only within the Western Highlands District does the *oecumene* assume comprehensible dimensions, and this largely within the Enga culture area itself (see Fig. 2). Widespread familiarity is largely restricted to those groups participating in the *tée*, which are categorized either with reference to the axis formed by the River Lai or according to locality and cultural distinctiveness. In the case of the former the left bank area is designated *tubiáma* and the right *wakiáma*, while the principal sub-culture-areas are Kopóne (located in the Sau and Ninimb valleys), Korá (the Kaugel Valley in the vicinity of Tambul), Minyápu (Minyamp), Syáka

(Tchak), Raiapu (middle Lai), and Mae (upper Lai). "Big-men" can readily enumerate the sequence of clans through which the *tée* passes, from Kopóne through the Lai and Tchak valleys, but the extremities of the system are only vaguely understood. Similarly little is known of nonparticipating Enga groups or of adjoining cultures except for those few with whom specific trading links, and consequently some marital ones, are maintained. Of these, the only important groups are the Kadépe of the Marient Valley and the Yadápu around Yokonda.

Contact has done little but add a few areas, such as the Tarua River, Pai-era, and Kopiago, where members of the New Guinea Lutheran Mission and their Raiapu evangelists are active. All the expatriate centers with which the Aruní have dealings—Pausa, Syaka-Raiakama, Mukuramanda, Kumbasakama, Wapenamanda, Mambisanda, and Yaramanda—are located within a very restricted zone of much the same dimensions as that over which most agnatic and affinal ties are operative, namely within a radial distance of about 8km of Sabakamádá. Only Mount Hagen disrupts this pattern. This is the administrative center for the Western Highlands District, two days' walk from Sabakamádá across a 2750m MSL pass, and among a culture group with which no traditional ties existed. The town is however linked by road to Wapenamanda and people travel by vehicle to visit relatives employed there or attend the biennial agricultural show.

Two types of mobility can usefully be distinguished within this Aruní *oecumene:* first, short-term movements involving absences from the residence of anything from a few minutes to a few weeks where there is no change in the location of agricultural activity or of residence, and second, long-term movements involving an explicit relocation of interests outside the group territory.

Figure 7 depicts the pattern of short-term movements effected by members of the Modópa sample community in connection with the activities discussed in Chapter 3. A total of 3,385 such moves were made by 36 adults on 2,615 man-days within the periods of 8 March to 18 April and 25 May to 5 July 1966.[23] Of these 83 percent were restricted to Aruní group territory (Sabaka-

23. A movement being defined as a return trip from the place of residence.

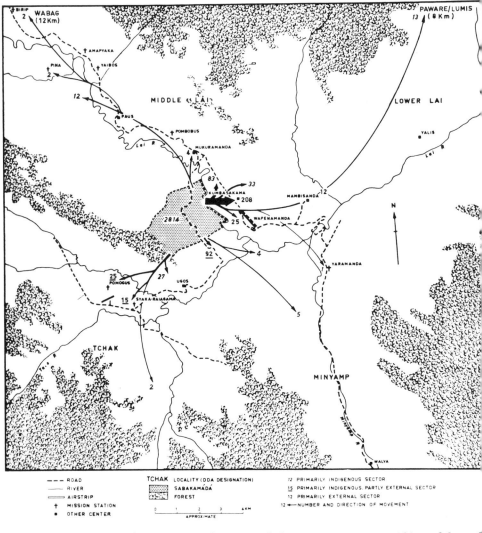

Figure 7. Modópa sample community: frequency of short-term movements within and beyond the group territory

mádá) while 78 percent were actually within the confines of the subclan section. All but 15 of the outstanding 571 moves were to points not more than 7.2km from Sabakamádá.

At least half of the extraterritorial movements are connected with the external agencies, mission and Administration stations, hospitals, trade stores, and Waso Ltd's buying center, which are all located well within the 7.2km zone.[24] Of these Kumbasakama attracts by far the greatest number (208 visits), primarily to market "business" crops and parchment coffee. Other movements largely reflect the intensity of agnatic and affinal ties, where physical proximity facilitates frequent contact. Aside from the visits to Kumbasakama and Wapenamanda, 261 movements were made between Aruní and adjacent group territories. Mobility here assumes the form of casual visiting and exchanges of food but is also connected with the practice of inviting kinsmen to cultivate mixed garden sections. This latter operates primarily in the direction of Sabakamádá for the strictly ecological reason that, unlike territories in the Tchak, it has a considerable amount of agricultural land lying below 1850m MSL which is suitable for yam cultivation. Thus, during 1966, nine sections from gardens in which members of the sample community participated had been granted to residents of other group territories. Most of these sections went to daughters' husbands, but two were granted to male agnates and one to the wife of a male agnate residing elsewhere. By contrast only one member of the sample was cultivating a section in an adjacent territory.

The further journeys are of a more exceptional nature—to solicit loans of pigs for use in the *tée*, to witness the progress of the festivals, or to participate in such ritual activities as mourning the death of a female agnate. Since exchange partnerships are largely restricted to the network of kin it is the circumstances of the festivals themselves which precipitate the longest journeys, in this case of 1–1½ days to Lumis and Paware.

The data conform closely with impressions gained of other journeys made by Aruní. Since the 1950s many have visited such distant localities as Walyá, Korá, and Kopóne in connection with the *tée* (see, e.g., pp. 86–87 below). In the early years of Administra-

<hr>

24. The two journeys to Wabag were purely incidental to my own activities and were made in my company.

tion and mission contact a few individuals traveled widely—one to jail in Wau, another to hospital in Goroka, and a third to witness a baptism in Kerowagi. A few evangelists and their friends have visited Porgera, Tarua, and Laiagam in connection with Lutheran mission activities, and one even went to the Sepik and Madang. Others have worked briefly in Wabag and Wapenamanda as laborers for the Administration and servants for policemen. Nevertheless the vast majority have no cause to travel far, particularly as expatriate activity becomes more intensified. Despite many references, by Administration observers and in published materials on the Enga, to increased mobility in association with the *tée* since pacification it is unlikely that the geographical range of interaction has expanded greatly, although the frequency of contacts most certainly has. Even today many, including youths, profess to be afraid to walk along roads through unfamiliar territories while, perhaps for different reasons, few visits are made to Aruní hunting grounds on the Marient-Tchak divide.

Long journeys were certainly made prior to contact, most of them facilitated by affinal links in the Tchak Valley where group territories abut directly on the "public domain." These affines permitted safe passage to the hunting territory, particularly on the occasion of the nut *Pandanus* harvests. By virtue of the marital ties existing between Kadépe and Syáka clans, at least two men and a woman have visited the Marient in connection with bride-wealth payments and to obtain tree-oil.[25] A number of others have visited the salt springs at Yokonda and Kenapurama to obtain *aipí* (native salt). Such journeys were admittedly undertaken only by large groups of people, but they were nevertheless possible. Similarly the practice of inviting nonresidents to cultivate mixed garden sections is long standing, and extended to the now forsaken taro gardens. In both cases it is claimed that "friends" and "affines" not only from neighboring clans but also from the Tchak and Minyamp valleys were invited. In every instance these short-term movements are closely linked with the network of affinal ties, being facilitated by and adding substance to them; furthermore these moves maintain the avenues whereby new ties can readily be established—axioms which hold as much for the contemporary as the traditional society.

---

25. Derived from *Campnosperma* sp., found in the Lake Kutubu area.

Changes of residence are made both within the Raiapu cultural context and between it and the external sector. The former are associated primarily with changes in marital status but some result from the recruitment of nonagnates and individuals seeking refuge from sorcery and, formerly, military conquest, others from reinvoking claims to land from which the group had previously been displaced.

Although land is no longer acquired through warfare, pressures persist and litigation plus gradual infiltration have become the means for effecting expansion. Thus the motives, if not all the mechanisms, for such long-term movements apply as much today as they did prior to pacification. Movements into the external sector are, by contrast, a recent innovation dating only from about 1958, when the Highland Labour Scheme was extended to the area and opportunities for recruitment into the police and DASF (as farmer trainees) were provided.[26] Given the type of opportunities available for their level of education, few individuals are away for longer than two years at a time, the duration of a plantation laborer's contract.

Comprehensive genealogical data were not gathered for the whole of Aruní clan and the current place of residence of all agnates is not therefore known. However, the main features of the pattern are clear. Because of the rules of clan exogamy and patrivirilocal residence, women invariably change their domicile at least once in their lives and some several times. Of the 184 marriages contracted by the present male population of Sabakamádá, 104 (56 percent) were with women from adjacent clans but a few were from places a full day's walk away. Three women were from Ulidáne, a Syáka clan situated at the furthest settled point along the Tale River and astride the route to the Aruní hunting ground and the Marient; and two were from Yadamáne at Yalis, about 12km down the Lai Valley in the direction of Kopóne. In fact 38 percent of all marriages by males were with Syáka clans, an orientation which is to their mutual advantage. For the Aruní it provides more effective access to supplies of tree-oil, salt, and, traditionally, stone axes, while the Syáka receive yams and other locally unavailable "luxury" foods, or even invita-

26. However, some men were co-opted for short periods by the Administration as early as 1947, to work as laborers in improving the Wabag airstrip.

tions to cultivate mixed garden sections. More limited data on marriages by female natal members confirm this general pattern in which contracts are predominantly with neighboring clans but a significant number are spread among distant and seemingly strategically located groups in the Tchak, lower Lai, and Minyamp valleys (Fig. 8). An unquestionable innovation has been the acquisition of Mae wives by two men, in each case the consequence of having been employed in the area as either an evangelist or a servant.

When a marriage ends, through either divorce or death, the woman and any young children often return to her natal group. Older women may spend extended periods living with different offspring: one widow from the sample community moved between the homes of her son at Modópa and her daughter married into a neighboring clan. Of the ten wedded female natal members of Aruní clan now living at Sabakamádá, five were divorced, three were widowed, and two were married to immigrants.

Other moves largely involve issues of rights to land and concern men as much as women. Traditionally, when people were displaced through military conquest, individuals sought refuge with relatives, or whole groups were granted temporary sanctuary by friendly clans. In one case, when Sabakamádá was temporarily overrun in an intraphratry dispute, many sought refuge elsewhere and one male agnate and his wife have remained with the host clan. The man has, admittedly, no son, but his brother, who has since returned to the Aruní side of the common boundary, continues to maintain a sweet potato garden in the host clan's territory.

In the absence of warfare as a means for reasserting claim to areas from which they have been displaced, some Aruní are attempting gradual resettlement. Two families have recently returned to an area across the Lai gorge, alienated in the 1930s and now occupied by fourteen families from the controlling clan. In both cases affinal connections (in the form of a wife and a daughter's husband, respectively) give added substance to their claims, yet neither householder has transferred allegiance to that group. In another case a wife and daughter of a polygynous householder from Modópa have taken up residence on ground permanently alienated following the intraphratry fight with Waiminaugína that

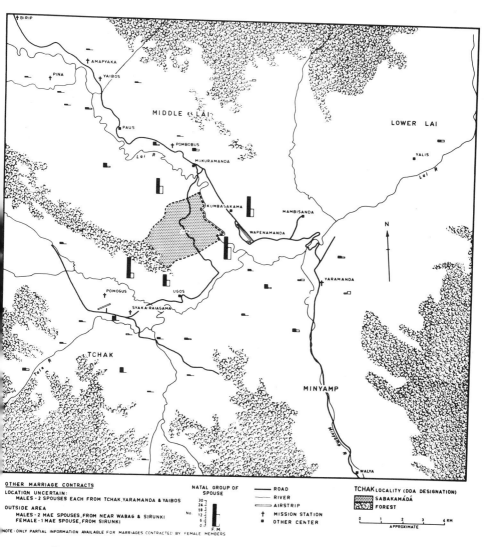

Figure 8. Aruní clan: distribution of marriages contracted by natal members

occurred c. 1938. Although the woman is not a member of that clan her husband's father was, but had sought refuge among the Aruní. In settling one of his wives there the householder is therefore not only reasserting his claim as an Aruní clansman but also invoking some residual rights as his father's son. He uses both claims to extend his influence beyond his natal group.

Such cases can, however, be viewed simply as peripheral incursions across territorial boundaries, and a change of residence is not a necessary corollary of them. Other clans are encroaching on Aruní territory and in most cases, where no serious threat is posed, tacit approval is given on account of support they have rendered in the past. Thus the Yabárane, a Syáka clan, claim a large number of nut *Pandanus* in the Aruní forest sanctuary, most of which they planted themselves. Their presence is tolerated only because of assistance rendered in the intraphratry fight.

At least four other male agnates have joined their mothers' natal groups, three to avoid threats of sorcery and internal friction and the fourth to share, and ultimately assume, rights to his mother's brother's land.

The relative mobility of the sexes between the agnatically defined groups is clearly reflected in Table 1 where 59 percent of the females resident at Sabakamádá are shown to be immigrants but only 7 percent of the males. The interterritorial links are established through marriage, and these provide the framework on which other moves are made. The dimensions of this system are extremely restricted, as most marriages and all other known moves are made to neighboring clans. Although interaction over a wide area is not necessary for the operation of the economic system it does serve to increase an individual's power and also his control over certain scarce resources, by increasing the number of his potential creditors and supporters and providing entry to completely new kinship networks (see pp. 190–91). In the case of some of the Syáka clans these networks provide direct access to the Kadépe and to those Yadápu who control the salt springs. Thus individuals do aspire to have distant connections.

Movements into the external sector involve similar motives: to acquire cash and a whole range of material goods not readily available to the residents of the group territory, and to undergo a variety of novel experiences not the least of which is a regular diet of "European foods." [27] However, the number of such movements and the distances involved are quite different.

Only about eighteen male natal members are currently absent in wage employment, one accompanied by his wife and daughter. Fifteen of them are serving two-year contracts under the Highland Labour Scheme, working on coastal plantations. Of the others, two are employed by the New Guinea Lutheran Mission, one as a carpenter moving from one station to another and the other as a medical orderly based in the Minyamp Valley; the third is in the constabulary, and currently stationed at Kandep. Most of the absentees are in the 19–24 years age bracket, single, and in close contact with their kinsmen at home. The policeman maintains a house at Sabakamádá and spends all his leaves at it, the two mission employees make regular visits at weekends, and few of the plantation laborers serve more than one contract on the coast.

In the absence of any general increase in educational standards this pattern of limited movement into the external sector is likely to persist for some years.[28] Increasing difficulty is being experienced within New Guinea in meeting the demand for plantation laborers but the Enga are unlikely to profit by it. Many requests for labor that are received by the Administration in the Western Highlands District specify "definitely no Wabagas or Wapenamandas" on account of their notoriety for "clannishness," arrogance, and violence while working on coastal plantations.[29]

Although one Sabakamádá resident is employed as a driver at

27. See Salisbury (1962:126–35) for a description of the effects of returned laborers on traditional Siane economy and society.

28. Only two Aruní boys have completed standard five to date, while about 10 percent of students proceed beyond the vernacular schools. Standard five is the penultimate year in a primary school system using a syllabus which concentrates on the teaching of English as a foreign language.

29. Meggitt (personal communication to Director, DNA, 1963) offers the following explanation for their unpopularity: "While there are probably many factors, including those of past history, determining their apparent arrogance vis à vis other natives, I think one of the most important conditions is the continuing and increasing shortage of arable land. . . . Those who sign on the Highland Labour Scheme are not, in my opinion, really whole-hearted about it; if they had enough land at home, together with some kind of cash employment or cash cropping, they would certainly not go. In short, these people are true peasants with all the peasant's grasping love of land, and distrust of potential despoilers of his land."

Kumbasakama, wage labor normally requires that men move into the external sector, an act that can threaten their successful participation in the Raiapu social and economic system in the long term. With the alternatives of a low level of participation in the external sector and independent cash-cropping at home, the former is now viewed largely as a youthful experience prior to marriage, and the latter increasingly as an effective means of acquiring the goods previously only obtainable through wage employment. In effect cash-producing activities are considered subordinate to subsistence interests, hence the need to evaluate the implications of long-term moves. Similarly interterritorial changes of residence by males require careful consideration since they can prejudice individual standing in both the natal and host groups. It is nevertheless possible to turn them to real advantage, as in substantially extending one's network of exchange partners (*káita minígi*) and so permitting more successful participation in the *tée*. By contrast short-term moves and the establishment of marital ties over a wide area are favored because they clearly enhance individual prestige. However, as has been shown, political, social, and economic considerations restrict such mobility to a very small area for the great majority of individuals. These considerations apply as much to the traditional as to the postcontact society.

3. Organization of Time

Raiapu Concepts of Time and Labor

ACCORDING to Meggitt (1958b:74) the Mae Enga, and likewise the Raiapu, have devised accurate means for marking the passage of time and co-ordinating such activities as "tilling their gardens and . . . organizing inter- and intra-clan gatherings for magico-religious rituals, funerary and other distributions and exchanges of wealth, and house-building." Briefly, this is achieved through a "luni-solar calendar in which the sequence of synodic months is correlated with seasonal activities by adjustment to observed variations of the ecliptic." The pattern assumed by such activities is dictated primarily by rainfall, which in effect determines the availability of various foods and the ease with which tasks like house construction and clearing can be prosecuted. Other long-term calculations are made with reference to the growth-rate of the *Casuarina*, which may be used to determine the duration of a fallow period, and the breeding cycle of the pig, which dictates the intervals at which the *tée* festivals can be held.

References to shorter intervals of time were made, traditionally, not in terms of weeks but of days preceding or following the present; for example *arébo* (the day before yesterday) and *taitá* (tomorrow). Meggitt (1958b:75) states that such terms "enable Mae to indicate up to six days hence, or back to seven nights ago." It is now also customary to speak in terms of days of the week, expressed in Neo-Melanesian, and of numbers of weeks, using the Neo-Melanesian "sunday" (hence "week") with Enga numerals, thus *sadé ráma* (two weeks).

Finally the day (*kóte*) itself is divided into a number of periods

77

determined by the movements of the sun; for example *yogáma* (morning—to midday) and *kúka* (night—dusk to dawn) with, more recently, *beró* (from the Neo-Melanesian for midday) as a reference point. However, shorter periods are not identified and the expatriate's concern with time as dictated by the twenty-four-hour clock serves only as a source of some amusement.[1]

The terms in which the temporal dimension is expressed relate strictly to the general rhythm of life, and it is only in the more detailed allocation of time among individual tasks that the requirements of the agricultural system and the place of that system within the broader cultural context can be understood.

Broadly speaking, tropical and subsistence economies are characterized by only a moderate level of general activity. A range of tasks is pursued concurrently and there is little specialization of labor on other than a sexual basis. Periodic variations in the amount of work done reflect both the controls that climate exercises over certain tasks and changes in the availability of staple foods. Finally there is a broad interweaving of what the economist considers productive and nonproductive enterprise,[2] in which the routine food producing tasks may involve ritual practices and incorporate social elements (as in the feasting and good-natured rivalry involved in house construction or clearing new garden sites) and in which ceremonial activities provide the mechanism for the flow of goods and services that is central to the acquisition of power and prestige and to the establishment of credit which may be drawn upon in times of economic stress.

While the Aruní conform to this pattern in most respects, the dominance of intensive agricultural production and associated pig husbandry in their economy does influence their attitudes to labor, and distinctions are drawn between at least two types. On the one hand are those essentially uneventful tasks directly concerned with the achievement of individual subsistence, categorized as "work" or "manual labor" (*karai*), for example, the several gardening and household tasks, the collection of firewood, and

---

1. For an extended discussion of Mae Enga time-reckoning, upon which the preceding discussion is partially based, see Meggitt (1958b).
2. Or economic and leisure activity, the one concerned with the production of goods to meet normal, immediate consumption and the other with the social and ceremonial life which appears as an important dimension of these cultures. See, for instance, Fisk (1962).

the preparation of tools and equipment. More recently the term has been extended to commercial crop production and to council and Administration work. These tasks are commonly pursued alone, and no great pleasure is derived from them. Either no tangible benefits are seen to accrue from them (as in work for the external agencies), or those that do accrue apply only to the appropriate household. In effect they are not the focus of a great deal of interest.

On the other hand there are those activities whose actual prosecution places the individual clearly within a societal context because they expressly confer prestige and power and enhance group solidarity. Such were the traditional preoccupations of Raiapu males, fighting and "making *tée*," together with the complex of smaller-scale ritual and ceremonial activities and, currently, the work of the local government councillor and his committee member (or "committee").

These two types of activity represent poles in a continuum rather than sharply defined categories, and there are several activities which incorporate features of both. House-building is one. Some extrahousehold assistance is sought throughout construction, but the final task of gathering the *Imperata cylindrica* grass and thatching the roof generally involves the cooperation of ten or more adults plus children and the presence of several women to prepare food for consumption when the task is completed.[3] The people work energetically, in good spirits and with much talking. A few days later several bundles of sugarcane are collected and a large number of people gather in the house to eat it and spread the debris over the floor as covering.

Reasons for this distinctive approach to what is essentially a domestic task are obscure, but several may be postulated. Meggitt (1957:174) considers large work groups to be necessary because thatching "should be completed in one day. Otherwise evening showers will spoil the *Imperata* sp. grass collected for the job." Some assistance is certainly valuable in gathering and throwing

3. Meggitt (1957:174) states that among the Mae, "Thatching employs up to 20 men and 30 children." The degree of cooperation does not appear to vary among the Mae and Raiapu and it is likely that this figure represents a pre- or early stage of contact standard. Several Enga remarked to this writer on the decreasing level of cooperation in house-building, explaining that, with pacification and opportunities for employment, smaller numbers of kinsmen are available at any given time to render labor services.

up the grass to those actually tying the bundles to the eaves, but the fact that it is only the act of completing a house which attracts such numbers of people may be related to nonmaterial considerations. The extent of assistance the householder can solicit may serve as public affirmation of his influence. Thatching provides a convenient opportunity for an informal social gathering since it is one of the few subsistence tasks where a large number of individuals can effectively work closely together, and it enables the householder to inform friends and relatives of the location of his new residence. Finally there are psychological considerations which may precipitate the gathering—the establishment of a home to accommodate a member family of the group, where group solidarity is reaffirmed and recognition given to the critical stages in the human life cycle.

Mixed gardens, perceived primarily as being for the cultivation of yams, are likewise the subject of considerable interest. Up to fifteen households may cooperate in clearing and fencing an area for subdivision into individual plots prior to planting. In addition, unlike the open fields, householders frequently boast about the size and number of their holdings. While the large work groups may be related to the high labor requirements in clearing regrowth, the difference in attitude is founded largely on the use to which the main products of these gardens are put. Yams are invariably cooked in earth ovens and eaten at feasts or distributed ceremonially on such occasions as the termination of a *sadáru* ceremony. They are in fact a luxury crop, the supply of which is severely restricted by low yields and the need to set aside a substantial proportion of the total harvest as cuttings for replanting.

In many respects the distinctions drawn by the Raiapu accord with the Siane's "three nexuses of activity"—subsistence, luxury, and *gima*—described by Salisbury (1962: chap. 3). The first involves "the routine daily tasks apparently performed to keep alive"; the second, "the production, distribution, and consumption of certain luxury commodities," most commonly "tobacco, *roi* palm-oil, pandanus nuts, and salt—pleasant but inessential commodities, mainly consumed in the entertainment of visitors"; the third, "public events, involving the handing over in a ritual way of commodities termed *neta* or 'things' that are owned as personalty by individuals." The first nexus is associated primarily with the

Modópa: looking southeast across the terrace section to the Lai Gorge and Mount Hagen

Modópa. (*Top*) a broken mound containing a mulch of sweet potato vines and *Setaria palmaefolia* leaves; *yukúsi* in the background. (*Bottom*) closing a mound. Soil is thrown from the periphery to the center to cover the mulch; the edge of the mound, and the soil profile break, are delineated by horizontal movements with the spade

Modópa. (*Top*) view from the terrace section toward the main range, showing the sequence from *modó* to *yukúsi* to unenclosed grassland; (*bottom*) clearing regrowth from a 45° slope to establish a mixed garden

Modópa. (*Top*) planting yams—the first stage of site preparation. (*Bottom*) inside a mixed garden c. five months after establishment. *Psophocarpus tetragonobulus* beans have been harvested, and a gourd (*Lagenaria* sp.) is being scraped prior to hardening over a fire and use as a water container; *Setaria palmaefolia* (the linear leaves in the foreground) and *Dioscorea alata* (the cordate leaves on the central vine) are also identifiable

Modópa. (*Top*) à kitchen garden. Coffee seedlings, each protected by a "tripod" of stakes, have been planted; subsistence crops include taro (*Colocasia*) in the drainage ditch, banana, yam, and *Zingiber* sp. (*Bottom*) a group of men preparing the site of a new woman's house for the son of an influential member of Ayóko subclan

Modópa. (*Top*) "emergence festival" terminating Aruní clan's *sadárú* ceremony; a large number of spectators are present at the return of the bachelors. (*Bottom*) small feast and distribution of pigmeat following the mourning of a male agnate's death

Modópa. (*Top*) "making business" with pigmeat. (*Bottom*) mixed gardens on a dissected valley slope; the frequency of *Casuarina* (indicative of a "controlled" fallow) varies from nil in the foreground to a relatively dense cover in the distance

Sirunki. (*Top*) cabbage and "chinese cabbage" interplanted with sweet potato on *modó*; (*middle*) frost damaged sweet potatoes; (*bottom*) establishing *modó*

execution of agricultural activities and the second and third with village-based activities, or at least with those which operate independently of the agricultural system. Thus particular commodities tend to be associated with each although, more generally, it is the circumstances in which the commodity is used which define the nexus: intraclan help, exchange between friends, and interclan prestation (pp. 102–3).

Among the Raiapu the circulation of luxury commodities is closely integrated into their ceremonial exchange system and consequently there is no exact parallel with the Siane's luxury nexus. They do however draw distinctions between the production, distribution, and consumption of certain cultivated foods and the execution of a range of subsistence tasks, and it is here that analogies are to be found. These distinctions between types of activity find expression in the ensuing discussion of work organization: through the sexual division of labor, the size and composition of work groups, and the variations in labor supply between the households, and also, ultimately, in the substantial differences in "returns" or "benefits" derived from the labor invested in each.

Patterns of Activity

Methods adopted and characteristics of the samples

The activity patterns of all resident adult members (those aged fifteen years or more) of the ten Modópa households were recorded during two six-week periods, 8 March to 18 April and 25 May to 5 July 1966.[4] The periods were selected to cover differences associated with climatic seasonality, the first being characteristically "wet" and the second "dry." March, with a mean monthly precipitation of 295.4mm, is the wettest month at Wapenamanda and June and July are the driest, with monthly means of 117.9 and 103.1mm, respectively. The actual survey periods did encompass precipitation differences of this order, with 441.7mm recorded at Wapenamanda on thirty-six raindays during Period I, and only 137.2mm on twenty-six raindays during Period II.

The data were gathered through a combination of observation

4. For a detailed discussion of the methods used and of the general level of reliability and confidence limits of the data, see Appendix 4.

and daily interviews in which all activities were considered except for resting, eating, and sleeping, and a few others carried out on a somewhat casual basis (often after nightfall in and around the house). Of these last the most important at Modópa are the routine preparation of food, making string bags, caring for young children, informal visiting between members of the locality group, and part at least of the harvesting of "business" crops and pulping of coffee. However, some attempt has been made to estimate the labor requirements of several of them (see Table 22).

In calculating the labor inputs for the various tasks the material has been placed wholly within its cultural context, where an activity is defined as commencing and terminating with departure from and return to the house or to a second activity, and where no attempt is made to consider the efficiency with which it is executed or to isolate time spent in traveling, resting, and so on.

The activity patterns of thirty-six individuals (seventeen males and nineteen females) were considered in the course of the survey. The actual size of the sample varied from time to time due, in part, to one arrival (a youth returning from an extended visit to a relative) and one departure (a girl leaving to marry), but also due to a decision on my own part to modify its composition. This was made following Period I and resulted in the exclusion of one household, the sole representative of its patrilineage, to permit the inclusion of a number of individuals not previously recognized to be functionally members of the other nine households because they resided elsewhere. The actual size of the sample ranged from twenty-nine to thirty persons during Period I and thirty-two to thirty-three during Period II. On account of these and other, temporary, fluctuations in the size of the population, the data are expressed in terms of "hours per man-day" or "per man-week" actually resident. This conversion, while obscuring some aspects of the periodicity of activities, does permit realistic estimates to be made of the activity patterns of an "average adult" and of the labor requirements of different tasks over extended periods.

The availability of labor

Although the survey covered a total of 2,615 man-days the day-to-day availability of labor in the locality was found to be influenced by several factors, of which sickness, mourning, and temporary absences were the most important (Fig. 9).

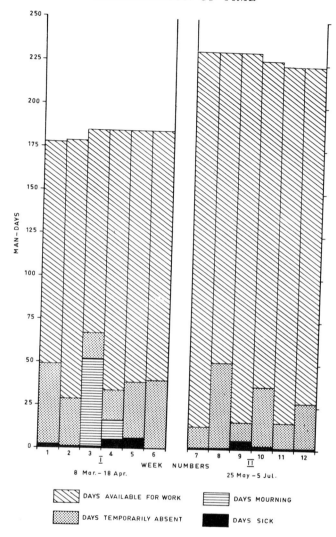

Figure 9. Modópa sample community: potential working days, and days lost through absence, sickness, and mourning

The incidence of sickness appears to be low when compared with coastal and subcoastal populations. Any explanation for this is likely to be found in a lower occurrence of parasitic infections and, in particular, the almost total absence of malaria, a disease which is particularly debilitating at lower altitudes. These, in turn, may be related to the apparent adequacy of Aruní diet (see discussion in Chap. 4). At Modópa only 1 percent of potential activity time was lost through sickness at home (plus a further 0.6 percent through absences caused by sickness—principally hospitalization). Most of the ailments witnessed were acquired in the course of work—cuts, splinters, sprained and broken bones—although several people, one a member of the sample, suffered from leprosy. By contrast, in one subcoastal area, the Popondetta subdistrict, sickness imposed more serious limitations on the level of activity (see Waddell and Krinks, 1968:74, 128–30). In one village it resulted in the loss of an estimated 4 percent of potential activity time (and a further 0.5 percent through absence induced by sickness), and in another village 4.3 percent (plus 3.2 percent in connection with related absences).

While the death of a kinsman precipitates both ritualized mourning and feasting it also commonly results, among close relatives, in the temporary suspension of all work apart from some harvesting to meet daily food requirements. Such suspensions are, understandably, fairly uncommon and over the twelve weeks took up only 2 percent of potential activity time. This was, however, restricted to two weeks following the death of the stepfather of one of the householders, and during this particular period the figure rose to 15 percent.

Short-term absences are defined as involving at least one night, and generally more than twenty-four hours, away from Modópa. They have been isolated from the body of the data for two main reasons. First, the information itself is much less accurate, both because the reasons given for being away were not always clearly defined and because an overnight absence invariably involves a considerable proportion of time spent sleeping or being otherwise inactive. Second, even a single night away from the locality can have a disruptive effect on the agricultural routine, due to the clearly defined division of labor between the sexes and the substantial dependence of the pigs on cultivated foods. In fact, on account of the pigs, it is usual for only one adult member of a household to be absent at a time, and on no occasion were all the members known to be away.

Details of short-term absences from Modópa are presented in Table 20. A total of 328 man-days, or 12 percent of potential activity time, were spent away from the locality for almost exclu-

TABLE 20

Modópa Sample Community: Man-Days Absent from the Locality, by Cause *

Cause of Absence	Period I		Period II		Total		Percentage of All Days
	Days	%	Days	%	Days	%	
Subsistence food production							
Pigs (feed and fetch)	2.25	1.3	1.25	0.8	3.50	1.1	0.1
Other subsistence tasks							
House construction	1.50	0.8	9.50	6.4	11.00	3.4	0.4
Commercial crop production	...	...	...	...	...	...	...
Commercial							
Market commercial crops	0.25	0.1	...	...	0.25	0.1	
Paid work (seek)	1.00	0.6	...	...	1.00	0.3	
Purchasing	0.75	0.4	...	...	0.75	0.2	
Playing "lucky"	5.00	2.8	...	...	5.00	1.5	
Subtotal	7.00	3.9	...	...	7.00	2.1	0.3
Other external sector							
Council work (court)	0.75	0.4	...	...	0.75	0.2	
Church service	4.50	2.5	...	...	4.50	1.4	
Clinic/hospital	7.75	4.3	9.50	6.4	17.25	5.3	
Subtotal	13.00	7.2	9.50	6.4	22.50	6.9	0.9
Social/ceremonial							
Tíe (incl. seek *saádt*)	34.00	19.0	11.75	7.9	45.75	14.0	
Sadárú	7.75	4.3	37.50	2.5	45.25	13.8	
Marriage	1.25	0.7	12.75	8.6	14.00	4.3	
Mourning	58.75	32.8	...	...	58.75	17.9	
Ceremonial (various)	8.00	4.5	...	...	8.00	2.4	
Visiting	45.75	25.5	66.50	44.7	112.25	34.2	
Subtotal	155.50	86.8	128.50	86.4	284.00	86.6	10.9
Total	179.25	100.0	148.75	100.0	328.00	100.0	12.5
Total Days Present	1,247		1,368		2,615		87.5

* In this and all subsequent tables where data are expressed in terms of man-hours and man-days the columns of figures do not necessarily add up, due to rounding.

sively social and ceremonial reasons. The most important single cause, which accounted for over one-third of all the man-days absent, was visiting. The term conceals a variety of motives ranging from the receipt of gifts of food from kin to the negotiation of bridewealth payments and may even involve rendering assistance in garden work. Thus one aged widow, while ostensibly living with her son at Modópa, regularly visited her married daughter with the express purpose of helping in domestic tasks. Likewise mourning, the cause of one-third of all absences during Period I but none during II, primarily involves a public gathering at the bereaved people's residence and attendance at the feast to mark their emergence from retirement; however other considerations may enter in. At the start of Period I a small child belonging to the sister of the "committee" at Modópa died. The latter immediately sent one of his two wives to stay and tend to her gardens and other needs until the feast to mark the termination of her retirement. This feast was held within two weeks of the child's death, yet the "committee's" wife stayed on until well after the end of Period I. While this extended stay was explained partly in terms of the mourning—"until another feast occurred and all the pieces of sugarcane in the house were formally removed and replaced by fresh"—other considerations assumed some importance.[5] The "committee" had recently received several pigs through the *tée* and, rather than negotiate the Lai gorge, decided to hold them at his bereaved sister's house pending their transfer to another exchange partner. There his wife could easily feed them with sweet potatoes from his sister's garden and from a small plot of land to which he had purchased usufructuary rights (for one dollar).

Another major cause of absences, amounting to 28 percent of the total, is centered on the *tée* and *sadárú* ceremonies, themselves functionally related phenomena. Although the *tée* was not to reach Modópa until March 1967, the preceding year saw a gradual intensification of interest, manifested both in journeys to various points in the lower Lai Valley between Paware and Yalis to ascertain its progress and occasionally to receive pigs, and, more commonly, in visits to affines and exchange partners in the Tchak

5. For an extended discussion of Enga funerary prestations see Meggitt (1965a:181–214).

and middle Lai valleys to solicit loans of pigs for presentation at the Sabakamádá ceremony.

The periodic *sadárú* ceremonies are strictly concerned with instructing bachelors in the appropriate safeguards "against pollution, enervation and deterioration" consequent upon contact with women (Meggitt, 1964:212–17). The event involves both four nights of seclusion and instruction in a special house erected in a remote part of the group territory, and various preparations spread over a period of two or three weeks when the house itself is erected, wigs are made, and decorations and clothing are sought from relatives. At the "emergence festival," when the bachelors return fully adorned and chanting from their mountain retreat, members of the host clan distribute food to the large number of visitors present. Finally, for several days after, the bachelors parade around in their dress visiting other *sadárú* festivals and group territories.

The timing of these ceremonies is closely associated with the progress of the *tée* for, to the more influential members of the group, the "emergence festival" provides an unusual opportunity for gathering to hear reports on developments elsewhere and to determine what action they should take themselves. So, between *tée* festivals, several years may elapse without a single *sadárú* ceremony in the Wapenamanda neighborhood, yet a whole series may be held in quick succession as the *tée* approaches. Thus, during the survey alone three *sadárú* ceremonies were visited by different members of the sample community, two of them involving overnight absences. (For a discussion of the *tée* and related activities, see "The social and economic life of the Raiapu," below.)

Together the *tée*, *sadárú*, mourning, and visiting activities account for over 80 percent of the man-days absent, the balance being distributed among a wide range of tasks. The total pattern reflects the fact that it is only in their social and ceremonial life that the people persistently move beyond the confines of their territory, and that even their contacts with the external sector demand only brief and occasional absences.

The work routine: levels of activity and seasonal variations

If the two survey periods are assumed to be representative of the main seasonal variations in activity patterns, it is estimated that the average adult is absent from his home on 6.5 weeks of the year while during the remaining 45.5 he spends an average of 43.3 hours per week on the activities listed in Table 21.

Six broad groups of activities are recognized, three—subsistence food production, other subsistence tasks, and social/ceremonial —identified primarily with the traditional (or subsistence) sector of the economy, and three—commercial crop production, commercial, and other external sector—identified with the postcontact (or monetary) sector. The data clearly demonstrate that, with 72 percent (31.4 man-hours) of the total man-hours spent on the former, the people are largely preoccupied with traditional activities, while among these it is the tasks associated with food cultivation which demand by far the greatest labor inputs.

Subsistence food production accounts for 49 percent of total activity time. This is absorbed primarily in the range of tasks associated with sweet potato cultivation and secondarily in clearing and fencing mixed gardens. In addition to the continuous process of planting and harvesting, the former demands a thorough working of the soil and the introduction of mulch when each mound is re-established, together with periodic weeding. Hence the very substantial figure of 12.6 hours per man-week.

The fences which bound the open field area require constant maintenance, but this involves little more than periodically replacing rotten stakes. Instead fencing, and clearing, are associated primarily with the mixed gardens. The high figure of 4.6 man-hours, divided almost equally between the two tasks, is explained by the fact that new gardens are established annually and each individual garden or group of gardens must be separately fenced to prevent the incursions of pigs from the surrounding unenclosed land. Proportionately yams require substantially more attention than the other crops associated with the mixed and kitchen gardens, on account of the care taken in the preparation of the sites at which individual cuttings are planted.[6] However, apart from time spent in planting and harvesting, little labor is expended in the cultivation of any of the subsidiary crops.

Fences are erected primarily to control the movements of pigs. These same animals are largely dependent on cultivated foods, yet they receive little direct attention in spite of their very large

6. This is evidenced by the fact that yams (D. *alata*) amounted to only 13 percent of all individual crops found in the sample survey of mixed gardens (see Table 14 for details of the survey).

TABLE 21

MODÓPA SAMPLE COMMUNITY: MEAN TIME SPENT
PER MAN-WEEK ON ALL ACTIVITIES
(In Hours)

Activity	Period I	Period II	Total	Percent
Subsistence food production				
Clearing and fencing	0.8	8.0	4.6	10.6
Sweet potato cultivation	9.7	15.2	12.6	29.1
Mixed/kitchen garden				
Yams	1.6	1.5	1.6	3.7
Other crops	1.8	2.0	1.9	4.4
Pigs	0.4	1.0	0.7	1.6
Subtotal	14.4	27.6	21.4	49.4
Other subsistence tasks				
House construction	1.8	1.1	1.4	3.2
Household				
(sweeping, cooking*)	0.4	0.4	0.4	0.9
Preparation of tools,				
equipment, and clothing	0.3	. . .	0.2	0.5
Collecting firewood	1.9	0.8	1.3	3.0
Hunting	. . .	0.1	. . .	. . .
Subtotal	4.4	2.5	3.4	7.8
Commercial crop production				
Clearing	0.2	0.3	0.2	0.5
Pyrethrum (maintain)	0.1	. . .	. . .	. . .
Peanuts/Irish potatoes	0.2	0.2	0.2	0.5
"Business" crops	0.4	. . .	0.2	0.5
Coffee	1.9	0.6	1.2	2.8
Subtotal	2.8	1.2	1.9	4.4
Commercial				
Market commercial crops	2.7	2.4	2.6	6.0
Paid work	0.2	. . .	0.1	0.2
Purchasing	0.5	0.3	0.4	0.9
Playing "lucky"	0.3	0.2	0.3	0.7
Subtotal	3.8	3.0	3.4	7.8
Other external sector				
Council work	5.6	2.2	3.8	8.8
Church service/work	3.3	2.2	2.7	6.2
Clinic	0.2	0.2	0.2	0.5
Subtotal	9.1	4.6	6.7	15.5
Social/ceremonial				
Tée	0.3	0.2	0.2	0.5
Sadárú	0.5	3.1	1.9	4.4
Marriage	0.2	0.4	0.3	0.7
Mourning	2.5	0.1	1.2	2.8
Ceremonial (various)	0.4	1.1	0.8	1.8
Visiting	1.8	2.5	2.2	5.1
Subtotal	5.6	7.5	6.6	15.2
Total	40.0	46.2	43.3	100.0

* In earth ovens, and, therefore, for feasts only.

numbers. During the day they seldom forage far from their owners' houses, and invariably return to be fed and stalled at night. A few sleep in the unenclosed land, and to these food must be carried daily. Alternatively, when pigs are agisted out, the owner may periodically take food to them.

Other subsistence tasks account for 3.4 hours per man-week and, among these, only house construction and the collection of firewood assume any significance. The traditional style of house is, given the materials available, well adapted to the local climate. Meggitt (1957:161) considers the life of the Mae Enga house to be three to four years and the Raiapu appears to conform to this pattern. However, it is a fairly complex structure, demanding, among other things, a large number of specially cut timbers and a carefully prepared site, and the labor required in its construction is probably in excess of 400 man-hours.[7]

The collection of firewood is something of a problem at Modópa for, in the absence of extensive areas of primary or secondary forest, it is a scarce resource. While *Casuarina* is recognized to be the principal source of supply it is an important building timber and so felled only rarely. Instead much firewood is obtained when sites are cleared for new mixed gardens, and any timber which has served its primary purpose, such as old fence posts and the stakes on which the vines of the yam (*D. lablab* and *P. tetragonobulus*) climb, is also used. In both cases firewood frequently has to be carried from some distance.

The production of commercial crops absorbs only 1.9 hours per man-week and of these 1.2 are spent on coffee. In proportion to both acreage and income, labor inputs in coffee are substantially higher than in "business" crops, both because many of the latter are intercultivated with subsidiary crops in the mixed gardens (concealing some of the labor input), and because regular weeding and pruning of the coffee is required, together with the processing of the cherries to parchment prior to sale. The crude methods of pulping which are practiced serve only to increase these differences between the two crops. "Business" crops are, by contrast,

7. Meggitt (1957) provides a detailed description of the mechanics of Mae Enga house-building. My estimate of 400 man-hours is based on the assumption of an eight-hour working day where six adults work for four days and 20 for one day and where the owner spends 50 hours in the preparation of the timber. Meggitt (1965:43) estimates an average of 42.6 adult male days are spent in the construction of a house, or 340.8 hours.

simply gathered in the late afternoon or evening prior to sale. Of the 3.4 hours per man-week spent on commercial activities 2.6 are concerned with marketing commercial crops—a somewhat larger figure than is required for their production. Both coffee and "business" crops are sold at Kumbasakama, about a 45-minute walk away across the Lai gorge. Opportunities for sale normally occur every Thursday for the former and every Monday and alternate Friday for the latter, but since coffee can be stored in the house for extended periods as parchment, only infrequent trips are made. "Business" crops are, however, perishable and, if a reasonable income is to be obtained, must be sold as the crops mature; consequently it is these which account for 2.4 of the 2.6 man-hours spent in marketing.

Other commercial activities are of little importance. There are few opportunities for paid work locally, although the "committee" often acts as a foreman for Waso Ltd, stimulating production among the Aruní, seeking out any crops which are in short supply, and supervising their sale at Kumbasakama. "Lucky" (a card gambling game that is very popular in New Guinea) is a consuming interest for only a few individuals. Finally most purchasing is done on the occasion of marketing commercial crops.

The most time-consuming contacts with the external sector are those from which no monetary return is derived, namely work for the local government council and Administration, and attendance at church services. These, together with visits to the clinics occasionally held in an adjacent group territory, account for the 6.7 hours per man-week spent in other external sector activities.

Although council work is customarily restricted to one day a week, spent in road maintenance, it assumed much greater importance during the survey following the realignment of the Wapenamanda–Tchak Valley road and the decision to lengthen Wapenamanda airstrip. The road had only been realigned across the slope of the main range at Sabakamádá during the previous year, and, since the ground was still unstable, it suffered from frequent closure through earth slips. For lengthy periods it therefore demanded almost daily attention. The airstrip is vital for shipping out produce of the Wapenamanda area, and, with the prospect of more stringent regulations being applied by the Department of Civil Aviation as to its use, yet with little likelihood of funds for its improvement forthcoming from the Administration, it was decided to extend it by "voluntary" labor. This involved individual clans or groups of clans working on a rotational basis in which each spent three and one-half days in a single week at the airstrip.

Church activities assume importance partly because of the devolution of authority in the Lutheran mission. In most group territories in the Wapenamanda area a church and a vernacular school have been established by the Wabag Lutheran Church,[8] each operated by a paid evangelist and teacher. Further to these, small chapels have been established at various points through each territory and at these the evangelist holds the brief services or instructional classes that have become an almost daily feature of the christian's or catechumen's life.

It has already been noted that temporary absences from Modópa are associated predominantly with social and ceremonial activities. These activities are also an important feature of the weekly routine, with 6.6 hours per man-week spent on them. They are characterized primarily by casual visiting, attendance at "emergence festivals" and bridewealth payments, participation in mourning at a bereaved person's house, and also attendance at a variety of feasts such as follow mournings, baptisms, and the opening of new schools.

Together the activities identified involve a mean labor input of 43.3 hours per man-week. However, substantial variations around this mean occur. These are of two types: first, between survey periods and so, presumably, seasonal in character, and second, from week to week. The main features of these variations are identified in Table 21 and Figures 10 and 11.

The substantial increase in the general level of activity from 40.0 hours per man-week in Period I to 46.2 hours in Period II is essentially a response to an almost doubling in the amount of time spent on subsistence food production (from 14.4 to 27.6 hours per man-week). At the same time a decline was registered in all other groups of activities, with the exception of social and ceremonial ones. Of the five individual activities in which sub-

8. An indigenous church established and largely financed by the Lutheran mission and responsible for routine religious and vernacular school affairs in areas where initial evangelical work and the establishment of congregations have already been achieved.

stantial changes were recorded, two, clearing and fencing (0.8 to
8.0 hours) and council work (5.6 to 2.2 hours), can be viewed as
direct responses to seasonal changes; one, sweet potato cultivation
(9.7 to 15.2 hours), as a partial response; and two, the *sadárú*
ceremonies (0.5 to 3.1 hours) and mourning (2.5 to 0.1 hours),

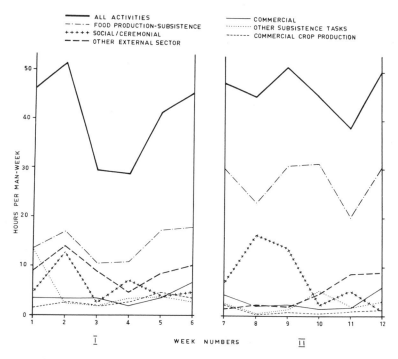

Figure 10. Modópa sample community: weekly pattern of activity

as responses to purely extraneous events. Thus, the onset of the
dry season facilitated bush clearing, necessary for the establishment of new mixed gardens, and also reduced the attention
needed to be given to the realigned road.

The thorough working of the soil, which characterizes the
preparation of sweet potato mounds, is facilitated by dry weather.
However, the reduced amount of time spent in sweet potato
cultivation during Period I must be explained in part by the death
of a senior member of the patrilineage from which most of the
sample was drawn. Over a period of almost two weeks all gardening activities, with the exception of the daily gathering of food,

were suspended, and this accounted for the deep dip in the graph on Figure 10. Without this mourning the general level of activity during Period I might have exceeded forty-five hours per man-week and that of sweet potato cultivation exceeded ten hours.

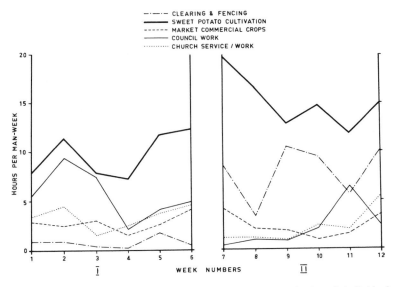

Figure 11. Modópa sample community: weekly pattern of selected individual activities

The occasions of formal mourning and of the *sadárú* ceremonies are directly determined by deaths and the impending *tée*. However, the actual timing of the latter may have been broadly influenced by the availability of yams, since this tuber is an important feature of all formal distributions of food.

While variations in the level of activity occur from week to week, immediate explanations can only be provided for the more substantial ones. The "dampening" effect of the widespread mourning during weeks 3 and 4 has already been remarked upon. Other variations can be related to the rainfall pattern. The amount of time spent on council work (road maintenance) decreased during weeks 4 and 5, in response to drier conditions, and increased substantially during week 11, following a wet spell (Fig. 12). During Period II the three weeks of least activity, 8, 10, and 11, were also the wettest, and a marked fall in the amount of time spent in clearing and fencing was registered.

Other variations can most reasonably be explained in terms of individual inclination and are, anyway, on a very restricted scale. The general conclusion to be reached from the data is that the

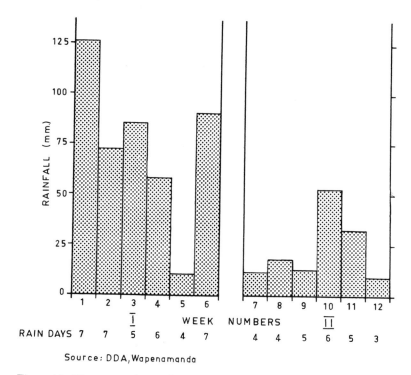

Source: DDA, Wapenamanda

Figure 12. Wapenamanda: weekly precipitation during the survey of activity patterns

Aruní economic system appears to require a fairly constant and regular input of labor, and not the occasional bursts of activity often assumed to be the case for subsistence economies.

Total estimated annual labor requirements and inputs within the agricultural subsystems

To facilitate comparison of the Modópa data with other material and determine differences in the labor requirements of the major agricultural subsystems, the data relating to both time present and absent are amalgamated and some estimates of the total annual labor requirements derived. These estimates incorporate assumptions about time spent on cooking and the manufacture of string bags, activities not covered by the survey. In making these calculations it is assumed that the two seasons, each covered by a six-week survey period, are of equal duration. In view of information contained in Meggitt (1958a), where the period May to September is described as the one of intensive gardening, house-building, and hunting, and the fact that mixed gardens were established during April to October at Modópa during 1966, this assumption appears to be reasonable.

Table 22 details the probable general level of activity for the whole year. With a mean of 47.4 hours per man-week, social and ceremonial activities assume greater significance (11.1 hours), while the time spent on subsistence food production falls slightly (to 18.8 hours). The other groups of activities register no significant changes. In all an adult is assumed to be active about 2,500 hours a year, 1,063.5 of which involve agricultural production and pig husbandry.[9] This input is focused on a cultivated area of approximately 0.23ha[10]—giving an overall rate of 4,610.4 man-hours/ha/annum. However, as Table 23 demonstrates, there are marked variations in inputs from one garden type to another. Most striking is the fact that the mixed-kitchen garden complex records a much higher labor input than the open fields. This former largely reflects the concentration of effort necessary to establish the gardens, where 3,459 man-hours are spent in clearing and fencing alone. In the case of the open fields a much more constant supply of labor is required, but there are no real establishment costs. Similarly there was no major clearing for coffee during 1966 and costs of upkeep are minimal.[11] Finally, pigs require little direct attention in spite of their numbers.

9. In addition perhaps 100 of the "visiting" hours are spent in subsistence agricultural activities.

10. The average of the two figures for mean area under cultivation per able-bodied person (see Table 8). Since the open field area is fairly constant and that cleared for mixed gardens only fluctuates slightly from year to year, the figures are considered to be representative of the annual requirements.

11. The figure is, nevertheless, high. DASF considers 148 man-days/ha/annum to be an appropriate requirement for established coffee. Assuming an eight-hour working day the Modópa figures work out at 281 man-days/ha/annum. The disparity points to considerable diseconomies arising from very small holdings and particularly inefficient processing techniques at Modópa (Shand, personal communication).

TABLE 22

MODÓPA SAMPLE COMMUNITY: ESTIMATED TOTAL TIME SPENT PER MAN-YEAR ON ALL GROUPS OF ACTIVITIES
(In Hours)

Activity	Time Present		Time Absent			Whole Year	
	Mean per Man-Week	Total Hours (45.5 Weeks)	Total Days	Mean per Man-Week*	Total Hours (6.5 Weeks)	Total Hours (52 Weeks)	Mean per Man-Week
Subsistence food production	21.4	973.7	3.5	0.5	3.4	977.1	18.8
Other subsistence tasks	3.4						
String bag making	0.8†	327.6	11.0	1.6	10.7	338.3	6.5
Cooking	3.0‡						
Commercial crop production	1.9	86.4	...	...	...	86.4	1.7
Commercial	3.4	154.7	7.0	1.0	6.8	161.5	3.1
Other external sector	6.7	304.8	22.5	3.4	21.8	326.7	6.3
Social/ceremonial	6.6	300.3	284.0	42.4	275.5	575.8	11.1
Total Mean	47.1	2147.5	328.0	49.0	318.2	2465.8	47.4

* Assuming a seven-hour day.

† Estimate based on data in Salisbury (1962:144–49). At Modópa females own on average 5.2 large string bags (*mádi*) each and males 0.8 small ones (*tuú*). It is assumed that a man's bag requires one-third the time of a woman's to make.

‡ A survey conducted by the author in an Orokaiva village revealed a mean of 5.0 hours per man-week spent in cooking (Waddell and Krinks, 1968:89). The Modópa level is assumed to be three-fifths of this on the grounds that (1) most food is cooked directly in the fire or ashes with little peeling or prior preparation, and (2) fires seldom die because of the bed of hot ash—they merely have to be "revived" immediately prior to use.

TABLE 23

MODÓPA SAMPLE COMMUNITY: MAN-HOUR COSTS
IN AGRICULTURAL PRODUCTION
(Per Adult)

	Total Hours Worked	Mean Cultivated Area (ha)	Man-Hours/ Ha/Annum
Open fields (sweet potato, peanuts, potatoes)	582.4	0.15	4000.0
Mixed-kitchen gardens (incl. all clearing and fencing)	391.3	0.06	6466.1
Cash-crops (coffee only)	54.6	0.02	2248.6
[Pigs	35.2	. . .	. . .]
Total	1063.5	0.23	
Mean			4610.4

Variations within the work routine

1. *By sex.* As in most subsistence economies the principal form of labor specialization is based on sex. Among the Raiapu this specialization assumes a very distinctive pattern with respect to the most time-consuming tasks and therefore has considerable bearing on household composition. As Table 24 indicates, it is primarily in the social and ceremonial activities that there is an equal involvement of the sexes. By contrast the main productive tasks are the primary responsibility of one or the other, with the distinction largely paralleling the agricultural one of open fields and mixed gardens. Thus the whole cycle of sweet potato cultivation—breaking mounds, planting, and harvesting—is the almost exclusive concern of women, while the establishment of mixed gardens—clearing and fencing—and the cultivation of their principal crop, yams, is a male responsibility. Women contributed 92 percent of the time spent on the open fields, while men contributed 85 percent of the time spent in clearing, fencing, and yam cultivation in the mixed gardens but only 20 percent of the time spent in cultivating the other crops. This distinction within the mixed gardens accords with the designation of certain crops (principally

TABLE 24

Modópa Sample Community: Division of Labor by Sex*

	Activity	Total Hours	Percentage Contribution
Activities carried out mainly by men†	Yams (plant)	109.0	100
	Fencing	743.1	98
	Firewood (collect and break)	439.4	97
	House construction	468.5	84
	Council work	1233.4	82
	Clearing	769.1	80
	Sadárú	611.6	67
	Coffee (pulp)	109.0	67
Activities carried out mainly by women†	Sweet potato		
	Plant	433.3	100
	Collect	2375.9	95
	Other crops (collect)	351.5	89
	Sweet potato (break mound)	1278.9	83
	Other crops (plant)	244.4	75
	Church service	883.1	72
Activities carried out by both (men's percentage contribution)	Coffee (collect)	144.1	66
	Yams (collect)	305.5	64
	Coffee (weed/prune)	136.7	54
	Purchasing	124.1	52
	Mourning	397.4	51
	Visiting	718.7	51
	Cooking	127.2	51
	Feasts (various)	252.2	50
	Pigs	233.3	48

	Men	Women
* Total hours active	6577.8	7576.9
Total weeks present	147.9	178.9
Mean activity week	44.5	42.4
(plus cooking		3.0)
(and string bag making		0.8)

† Where one sex carries out more than two-thirds of the work and where the total amount exceeds 100 man-hours (or 0.7% of the total hours active for the whole sample).

yams) as "male" and others as "female." The collection of firewood is largely a by-product of fencing and the establishment of mixed gardens, hence a typically male pursuit.

This distinction in division of labor between the two agricultural subsystems finds added expression both in the associated work routines and in the role of the crops. The staple, sweet potato, is designed to satisfy the day-to-day needs of the cultivators and requires a stable work routine. The mixed garden crops, being only periodically available, merely supplement the diet. Yams, considered the most important of them, are a luxury crop, cooked in earth ovens and eaten with guests or distributed by the men on ceremonial occasions. The gardens require a period of intense activity for their establishment and this is provided by the men. Thereafter, as the crops mature, they are visited only occasionally by the women. A man not only boasts of the size or number of his gardens and finds satisfaction in his ability to invite others to plant with him, but is the subject of some ridicule if he fails to establish any. The gardens are considered male preserves from which menstruating women or men who have had intercourse with women in the preceding twenty-four hours or so are excluded, for fear of damaging the yams.

Although the cultivation of sweet potatoes is unquestionably women's work it is customary for men to attend to the crop themselves on occasion, as when their wives are menstruating[12] or are away from home. However, even in these circumstances a division of responsibility persists where, if a man does gather some sweet potatoes, his wife cannot take any for herself or the pigs. In effect, in cultivating the crop, the male is concerned only with his individual needs, whereas the woman's responsibility is to the whole household and to the livestock.

The overall pattern which emerges is one of distinctive rhythms of work in which the men focus their attention on such irregularly occurring activities as house construction, the establishment of mixed gardens, and intensive work on the road for the council, all designed to satisfy long-term needs and involving deals which extend beyond the household. By contrast the women are concerned with satisfying the day-to-day needs of the household and, beyond that, with participating in the frequent religious services. Consequently, as Table 25 demonstrates, it is in the allocation of time rather than in the general level of activity that the work patterns of the sexes differ. The women spend 57 percent of their time in subsistence food production, with sweet potato cultivation

---

12. In which case the husband must not accept food handled by his wife.

TABLE 25

Modópa Sample Community: Mean Time Spent per Man-Week on All Activities, by Sex
(In Hours)

Activity	Men	Women
Subsistence food production		
Clearing and fencing	9.1	0.9
Sweet potato cultivation	2.3	21.1
Mixed/kitchen gardens		
Yams	2.6	0.7
Other crops	0.8	2.8
Pigs	0.8	0.7
Subtotal	15.6	26.3
Other subsistence tasks		
House construction	2.7	0.4
Household	0.5	3.4*
Preparation of tools, equipment, and clothing	. . .	1.0†
Collecting firewood	2.9	0.1
Hunting	0.1	. . .
Subtotal	6.1	4.9
Commercial crop production		
Clearing	0.1	0.4
Pyrethrum (maintain)	. . .	0.1
Peanuts/Irish potatoes	0.1	0.3
"Business" crops	0.4	0.1
Coffee	1.6	0.8
Subtotal	2.2	1.7
Commercial		
Market commercial crops	2.4	2.8
Paid work	0.2	. . .
Purchasing	0.4	0.3
Playing "lucky"	0.6	. . .
Subtotal	3.5	3.0
Other external sector		
Council work	6.8	1.3
Church service/work	1.7	3.6
Clinic	0.2	0.2
Subtotal	8.6	5.0
Social/ceremonial		
Tée	0.5	0.1
Sadárú	2.8	1.1
Marriage	0.3	0.3
Mourning	1.4	1.1
Ceremonial (various)	0.9	0.7
Visiting	2.5	2.0
Subtotal	8.3	5.2
Total	44.5	46.2

* Including an estimated 3.0 man-hours cooking.
† Including an estimated 0.8 man-hours making string bags.

of singular importance, while the men spend 35 percent of theirs in these same tasks, and their total activity time is more evenly distributed among a diversity of tasks.

2. *By marital status.* A more detailed analysis of the activity patterns of the sexes, as determined by their marital statuses, reveals some implications of the customary distinctions between male and female tasks and illuminates some of the circumstances underlying the complexity of household composition.

While the routine subsistence tasks are considered the almost exclusive concern of women, only married men are assured of being able to adhere to their customarily defined responsibilities. Other adult males must either attach themselves to a family, in which case a female dependent of the household head can assume responsibility for their sweet potato gardens and daily food requirements, or they must become reconciled to their inferior position and execute all the necessary subsistence tasks for themselves. The consequences of either course are serious: in the first, although public approval is maintained, the men must operate largely within the shadow of the household head, assisting him in a variety of ways; in the second, if a man remains unattached for long, curiosity is aroused, and withdrawal from much of public life follows, primarily because he must operate his own sweet potato gardens and so substantially increase his subsistence work load. Table 26 points to some of the tangible aspects of this situation.

The activity patterns of the divorced-widowed-unmarried group of adults are shown to diverge in a number of ways from those of the married. Of all categories the unattached men are the most active. This is in direct response to the amount of time they must spend in sweet potato cultivation—11.4 hours per man-week or 79 percent of all the hours contributed by males. Because of their need to operate both open fields and mixed gardens they are, like women, primarily concerned with subsistence food production. Largely on account of these dictates they spend little time in social and ceremonial activities and were absent from their homes on less than 2 percent of all survey days.

As might be expected, the behavior of the attached men closely approximates that of their married counterparts in all major respects. However, they spend almost 23 percent of their time in council work, perhaps indicative of the degree to which they are subject to the authority of the more influential men with whom they live. The attached women are all over 55 years, and the limitations of age result in their focusing attention increasingly on sweet potato cultivation, which is the least arduous of the main food-producing tasks, and otherwise in attending church services and visiting relatives.

The young unmarried adults evince less interest in the domestic work routine or in commitment to specific tasks. They are both frequently absent (the men on 26 percent of survey days and the women on 18 percent) and are more directly concerned with the social and ceremonial and commercial activities which take them out of the locality. These patterns reflect both the limited responsibilities of younger people and the circumstances in which contacts with potential spouses are made.

Together these variations between groups of differing marital status demonstrate that, while the division of labor is primarily a sexual one, it is directly influenced by the composition of production units, a fact which has some bearing on the wider issues of indebtedness, power, and prestige in the society.

3. *By the size of work groups.* In any consideration of the size and composition of groups associated with Raiapu activity patterns distinction must be made between "work groups" and "assemblies of people." The former are characterized by physical effort directed toward "the purposeful alteration and combination of physical material until it reaches some desired empirical state" (Udy, 1959:2), namely, such acts of production as house construction and agricultural work; and the latter by gatherings to witness and effect transfers of goods and to discourse on matters of common interest, hence primarily the various social and ceremonial activities. Consideration is given here only to the former.

Work groups exceeding two or three persons—members of a single household with perhaps one outsider—are both a rare occurrence and are found only in association with a few specified activities. Most food producing and domestic tasks are characteristically an individual concern. Such are sweet potato cultivation, the operation of kitchen gardens, pig husbandry, household tasks, preparation of tools and equipment, and collection of firewood, all of which are activities of almost daily occurrence and executed principally by women.

As noted above in this chapter (see "Raiapu Concepts of Time

TABLE 26

MODÓPA SAMPLE COMMUNITY: MEAN TIME SPENT PER MAN-WEEK ON ALL ACTIVITIES, BY MARITAL STATUS

| | Married | | Divorced-Widowed-Unmarried | | | Unmarried | |
| | | | Attached* Women (>20 yrs.) | Men (>25 yrs.) Un-attached† | Men (>25 yrs.) Attached* | Men (<25 yrs.) | Women (<20 yrs.) |
	Men	Women					
Number of individuals	7	10	3	2	3	5	6
Total hours active	3003.3	4469.2	1135.2	1108.7	1017.7	1448.1	1972.5
Total weeks present	67.1	104.4	27.1	23.6	22.9	34.3	47.4
Percentage of survey time absent	14.0	8.3	9.8	1.6	4.8	25.6	17.7
Subsistence food production							
Clearing and fencing	7.0	0.8	...	13.3	10.6	9.2	1.8
Sweet potato cultivation	0.9	24.3	26.2	11.4	0.3	0.1	11.4
Mixed/kitchen garden							
Yams	3.2	0.9	0.4	1.6	2.6	2.1	0.6
Other crops	1.5	2.3	3.0	0.2	0.6	0.2	3.7
Pigs	0.6	0.4	0.1	1.0	1.4	0.5	1.6
Subtotal	13.2	28.7	29.7	27.4	15.5	12.1	19.0
Other subsistence tasks							
House construction	2.1	0.2	...	3.6	1.2	3.9	1.2
Household	0.4	0.2	0.1	0.5	0.9	0.2	0.7
Preparation of tools, equipment, and clothing	...	0.4	...	0.2	...	...	...
Collecting firewood	3.3	0.1	...	2.2	3.0	2.5	0.1
Hunting	...	...	...	...	...	0.3	...
Subtotal	5.9	0.9	0.1	6.6	5.1	6.9	2.0
Commercial crop production							
Clearing	...	0.4	0.1	0.4	0.2	0.1	0.3
Pyrethrum (maintain)	...	0.1	0.3	...	...	...	...
Peanuts/Irish potatoes	0.1	0.4	0.1	...	0.2	...	0.3
"Business" crops	0.4	...	...	0.4	0.5	0.2	0.2
Coffee	3.0-	0.5	0.5	0.6	0.6	0.4	1.8
Subtotal	3.5	1.4	1.0	1.4	1.5	0.6	2.5

Commercial							
Market commercial crops	2.9	1.7	0.8	0.6	2.0	2.9	6.2
Paid work	0.5	..	..	..	..	..	..
Purchasing	0.3	0.2	..	0.2	0.7	0.7	0.7
Playing "lucky"	0.8	..	..	..	0.2	0.9	..
Subtotal	4.4	1.9	0.8	0.8	3.0	4.5	6.9
Other external sector							
Council work	6.5	1.4	0.1	6.7	10.1	5.3	1.6
Church service/work	2.0	4.1	5.7	1.1	1.0	1.8	1.2
Clinic	0.3	0.1	..	..	..	0.2	0.4
Subtotal	8.8	5.6	5.8	7.7	11.1	7.3	3.3
Social/ceremonial							
Tée	0.7	..	..	..	..	0.6	0.2
Sadárú	2.2	0.7	0.1	0.9	3.3	4.9	2.6
Marriage	0.2	0.3	0.3	0.2	0.7	0.3	0.2
Mourning	1.9	1.2	0.6	0.8	1.8	0.4	1.1
Ceremonial (various)	0.6	0.4	0.4	0.6	1.0	1.4	1.6
Visiting	3.2	1.6	3.0	0.6	1.4	3.2	2.1
Subtotal	8.8	4.2	4.5	3.1	8.2	10.8	7.9
Total	44.8	42.8	41.9	47.0	44.4	42.2	41.6

* Attached to a family and sharing the work load with a member of the opposite sex.
† No regular assistance received from women.

and Labor"), in house-building and in several tasks associated with the mixed gardens, men actively solicit assistance or at least favor some degree of cooperation. However, such occasions are infrequent. The size of a group is largely determined by the status of the initiator and the range observed was, therefore, considerable. While ten or more adults were seen on occasion to participate in all stages of house construction, from the initial leveling of the site to the completion of the roof, in other cases all but the final thatching was effected by only two or three men.

The clearing and fencing, and to some extent planting, of mixed gardens are often executed by large work groups. Alternatively arrangements may be made between individuals establishing gardens on adjacent sites to coordinate their activities and erect a common fence. As many as twelve adults were seen to clear a site together, the men felling trees and women gathering the debris, and both combining to burn it off. Real economies of effort are achieved in these ways, sufficient incentive being provided by the very high labor inputs necessary for the operation of mixed gardens. Cooperation also results in brief periods of intense activity, permitting full advantage to be taken of dry spells in the weather. Individuals do, nevertheless, establish mixed gardens without assistance, and on no occasion were more than four men observed to be erecting fences together. Both men and women tend to plant their respective crops in groups of three to six persons and, in the case of yams, custom appears to dictate that two people work together, one driving the initial hole and the other modifying it and inserting the cutting.

Consideration of the composition of work groups reveals something of the circumstances of their formation and the underlying motives. House-building groups are generally restricted to residents of the immediate locality, and at Modópa are drawn from both patrilineages represented there. Seemingly, the more influential the initiator the more aid he receives, yet those who render assistance appear to derive little tangible benefit from it and certainly no direct assurance of reciprocal help when it is their turn to rebuild. In the case of work groups associated with the mixed gardens, locality affiliations are less important. Cooperation often follows the fortuitous exploitation of adjacent sites, while assistance is frequently rendered by affines whose group territories are unsuited to the cultivation of yams and many of the associated crops. So, one member of the sample received substantial help from his daughter's prospective husband and father-in-law, who were motivated in part no doubt by a desire to ingratiate themselves but also by the eagerness to be offered usufructuary rights to a section, a common practice with these gardens.

Together the work groups generated by males serve to affirm both their status within the group and their influence beyond it, and they also reflect some of the means by which such status is achieved: namely, through the more extensive cultivation of luxury crops and the provision of opportunities for less well-endowed kinsmen to cultivate such crops for themselves. The groups are not in any way essential for the achievement of subsistence.

The social and economic life of the Raiapu

Social and ceremonial matters absorb a considerable amount of the adult Raiapu's time—an estimated 23 percent of total activity time over the course of a year. While only a few men are active participants in ceremonial affairs, everybody professes interest and is eager to witness displays of group solidarity and formal transfers of wealth.

Three broad categories of assembly are identifiable in terms of their size, composition, and immediate circumstances. The three form a hierarchy wherein the ideology of descent and the system of leadership based on the authority of "big-men" find increasing expression. At the base of the hierarchy is visiting, the casual contacts between individual members of households which extend both within and beyond the group territory. Numbers involved are small, perhaps three or four people, and the events do not normally elicit outside interest. In an intermediate position are the assemblies which focus on life crises and the resolution of conflicts. Here participation is determined by genealogical distance (kinship and affinity) and two distinct groups tend to stand in opposition. The size of the assembly is determined largely by the stature of its initiator, but perhaps twenty to fifty people may be considered the average with casual observers attracted when payments are made. Finally, there are those ceremonies where membership is determined by descent, in this case the subclan or the clan, and where agnates participate both individually and collectively and stand in opposition to a wide range of similarly constituted groups. Such are the *tée* and its related institution, the *sadárú*. Attendance at the festivals may be numbered by the thousand, made up of the host group and both influential and disinterested parties drawn from much of the area through which the exchange cycle operates.[13]

For the Raiapu the *tée* is a consuming interest. It involves several years of preparation in building up holdings of pigs and other valuables, and culminates in a single festival of a few hours' duration. Even Meggitt, who makes but passing reference to the institution in his published material, recognizes it as "an ultimate value" for the Enga (personal communication to DDA, Wabag). Formally, the *tée* comprises a cycle of festivals, organized at the subclan level and following a prescribed sequence that links over 70,000 people along the Lai, Ambum, Sau, Baiyer, and Tchak valleys. Festivals are held at intervals of about four years, and, on the occasion of each, individual members of the host group distribute pigs and pearl-shell to exchange partners (*káita minígi*) from other clans, many of whom are affines. All these exchanges are controlled through a system of debts and obligations (*saádí*), incurred informally prior to the festivals and ostensibly acquitted at them. The degree of equivalence achieved is determined by the relative status of the partners. Thus a debt may simply be settled at a ceremony or it may be paid off with interest as a form of "one upmanship" designed to maintain the relationship and at the same time increase its contractual value.[14] Politically, the *tée* operates at both the individual and group levels: as a primary vehicle for the assertion of individual prestige and influence through the manipulation of the flow of goods, as a means of enhancing the prestige of the host group at the expense of the others, and as an opportunity for establishing alliances with otherwise nonaligned groups. A secondary function of the *tée*, not evident in the festivals themselves, is the economic one of facilitating the distribution of such locally scarce resources as salt, tree-oil, feathers, shells, cassowaries, drums, spears, and (traditionally)

13. At one emergence festival held by the neighboring Yakumáne clan at Kumbasakama on 15 May 1966 an estimated 2,500 people were in attendance, drawn from as far afield as Kompiam, Paware, Wabag, and the Tchak Valley. Elkin (1957:179) also estimates that 2,500 people attended a *tée* festival he witnessed at Kaiperimand near Wabag on 15 July 1950.
14. Freund, personal communication.

stone axes, by means of informal exchanges effected through the network of *káita minígi*.[15]

As has been noted (see "The availability of labor," above), while the *sadárú* ceremonies are in an immediate sense purificatory rituals practiced by the bachelors, their frequency is largely regulated by the *tée* cycle. The "emergence festivals" are the only other public expression of clan solidarity and therefore provide an excellent opportunity for interclan gatherings to discuss the timing of the *tée* festivals.

In life crises, as in the *tée*, issues of group solidarity apply, albeit on a much smaller scale. According to Meggitt (1965a:127) marriage is seen "as a device for transferring the services of a woman from one small-scale agnatic group to another and also as a basis on which political and economic links can be created between agnatic groups of wider span." Childbirth provides an opportunity for reaffirming such links, while death and divorce normally terminate them. Meggitt (p. 136) considers marital rights to operate at two levels: of the individual husband to the woman's sexual, domestic, and economic services, and of the agnatic group to the offspring of that union. Individual prestige is enhanced through the size of the bride-price and through the number of wives and dependent women a man can ultimately obtain.

In all aspects of their social and ceremonial lives the Raiapu forge links and cement relationships through the transfer of goods (and to some extent services), be these women, pigs, garden produce, or traditional valuables. Not only do the activities themselves require a considerable expenditure of time, but a substantial proportion of production is directed toward effecting these transactions. The goods exchanged may have an immediate bearing on the achievement of subsistence but they also result in an increase in production far beyond these minimum requirements—an increase which is utilized for political aggrandizement. Yet, whatever may be the ultimate objective in making prestations, the fact remains that social and ceremonial events reflect to a very substantial degree the levels of economic activity and production in the community.

15. Bulmer (1960b) has made a useful analysis of this exchange system, as it is practiced by the Kyaka. Bus (1951) and Elkin (1953) have also described some of the features of the *tée* among the central Enga.

*Implications of the Activity Patterns
and the Course of Change*

There appears to be little variation between adults in their levels of activity and, presumably, productivity. With the household functioning as the basic unit of production and with an apparently unlimited demand for such goods as pigs (and therefore, indirectly, sweet potatoes) over and above subsistence requirements, it is the availability of labor which primarily determines the size of this productive surplus.

The influential man must have a large work-force available to carry out routine tasks during his frequent absences and to increase the supply of goods available to him from his own holdings. Women are needed to tend the sweet potato gardens and the pigs, men to assist in establishing mixed gardens, collecting firewood, and fencing. While the former must, on account of the constant demand for their labor, become members of his household, as wives, attached widows, and spinsters, the latter need merely cooperate for the duration of the more infrequent tasks with which they are usually associated.

The larger the supply of labor over which an individual can exercise control the greater the surplus of goods he can inject into the exchange system. Thus the most influential member of the sample headed a productive unit composed of three resident wives, six offspring, and one attached spinster, with a cultivated area of 1.39ha and a herd of forty-eight pigs during early 1966. Although per capita figures of resources do not significantly exceed the average for the whole sample, the total production surplus to subsistence requirements and directly available to the head is naturally substantially greater. Such a system operates to the mutual benefit of both parties, for, by becoming attached to a household, the individual widow or bachelor is assured the products of those tasks customarily executed by the opposite sex. The householder, in return for making his own or his wife's labor available to the attached person, exercises control over that part of production which is additional to his or her individual needs.

The Raiapu approach to the organization of their time has been greatly influenced by a number of events associated with European contact: the end of warfare, technological innovations, the demand for cash expressed largely in the commencement of commercial cropping, and direct demands made upon them by the external agencies. Pacification and the change to a steel technology released a considerable amount of labor time, particularly for the men. No accurate data are available on the extent and implications of warfare in the Highlands:

> Exactly what proportion of time was spent on it as against other activities—economic exchange, ritual, ceremony, domestic affairs, gardening, hunting, and so on—is impossible to say. Apart from a few regions where fighting is still continuing, this can only be inferred. But the literature on the Highlands contains some fairly detailed accounts of warfare, including a number recorded from first-hand observations, or close enough to give considerable confidence. In nearly all recorded cases, warfare was an accepted feature of ordinary social living; and the time spent in actual fighting and in direct preparation for it, alone, must have been considerable [Berndt, 1964:183].

Among the Enga, according to Meggitt (1965a:256), war was the most effective means available for expanding territorial boundaries. Everywhere it was "bound up with the struggle for power and prestige" (Berndt, 1964:184), manifested through skill in fighting and the ability to effect alliances. Because cessation resulted in the closure of one of the two main avenues for achieving power, men took an increasing interest in ceremonial activities. This was stimulated by their increased leisure time, by an augmented supply of valuables, by their much greater freedom of movement, and by the elimination of the directly damaging effects of war.

There are many references, in both the published literature (e.g., Bus, 1951:824, and Bulmer, 1960b:12) and Administration reports, to the increasing frequency and scale of the *tée*. DDA observers point out that, whereas traditionally an influential man might have put ten to fifteen pigs into the *tée* and the average person none, now most Enga have at least one pig in it and influential men as many as two hundred. On account of this the ceremony is becoming increasingly difficult to handle. In 1958 and again in 1960 people in the Wapenamanda area sought and obtained Administration support to ensure that all members of the community made *tée* together, thereby preventing the threat of splitting. Such a split did in fact occur in the next cycle when *wakiáma* groups (on the "right" bank of the Lai River) made *tée* during 1964 but the *tubiáma* groups (on the "left" bank) only commenced in October 1965 from Kompiam. This latter branch did not reach Modópa until March 1967.

If Salisbury's (1962:219) assumption that axe work in clearing, fencing, and house-building took three times as long in stone-using times is applied to the data in Table 21, it is estimated that twelve hours per man-week would have been saved through the change-over from a stone to a steel technology.[16] Yet not all the time made available through this change and by the cessation of warfare has been diverted to the *tée* or other ceremonial activities. Sweet potato production must certainly have increased to meet the demand of an enlarged pig population, while a whole new range of activities associated with the external sector have emerged. These activities in themselves account for twelve hours per man-week and variously reflect both the individual and group interests of the other tasks. The position of "committee" is used by one man to assert his power through the settlement of disputes and the supervision of council work, in which large numbers of people are mobilized. Commercial cropping, being still on a small scale, is closely integrated with subsistence agricultural activities and, like them, concerned with both satisfying immediate individual requirements (clothing, tools, etc.) and providing a surplus to inject into the exchange system.

Despite these seemingly considerable changes in activity patterns it is the same considerations of individual subsistence and achieved power founded on agricultural production that dictate the mode of organization of Raiapu time. As Salisbury (1962:138) writes of the Siane, these changes are to be seen simply "as a steady progression from an indigenous base. . . . the structure of society and its activities remain formally the same," whatever their ultimate consequences may be.

16. It should be pointed out that Salisbury's statistic is an extremely crude one, not based on empirical evidence. He writes that the figure "was given to me first by my most reliable informant, who unexpectedly said, when we returned from a day watching and timing gardening operations, 'That would have taken three times as long when we had stone axes.' His remark was the germ for much of the analysis in this book. I checked it extensively by making spot checks, asking individuals whose work I had watched how long they would have taken using stone axes. The consensus was that stone axes took between three and four times as long" (1962:219–20). In the absence of a more rigorous estimate for a New Guinea society Salisbury's assumption must be accepted.

4. Level of Production and Consumption

An analysis of yields of the major crops, general information on the utilization of production, and more specific data on the dietary patterns of several Modópa households serve to illustrate many aspects of the productive system. The most important of these aspects are the place of pigs and the relative importance of agriculture, and the ability of the system to tolerate fluctuations consequent upon partial crop failures or in response to marked changes in the pig population. This same information serves also to illuminate certain incentives for and implications of change within the agricultural system.

Yields of Subsistence Crops

Information on yields was obtained by two means: indirectly, through a survey of all produce collected by three households over two ten-day periods, and directly, by a controlled survey of selected sweet potato plots. The first method reveals the relative importance of the various crops and permits rough estimates to be made of the harvest obtained from the several garden types. The second method gives the potential sweet potato yields obtainable under the environmental conditions prevailing during 1966–67. The difference between the two results indicates the size of the surplus.

Table 27 details the data obtained by the indirect method and demonstrates the almost total dependence on cultivated produce. While children sometimes forage in abandoned gardens for *Zingiber* sp. and *S. palmaefolia* and so on, these provide them with nothing more than snacks while playing. Adults were never known to leave their houses with the sole objective of hunting or foraging

113

TABLE 27

Modópa Sample Community: Level of Production
(By Three Households over Two Ten-Day Periods)

| | Household Mean | | | | | | Per Capita Mean | |
| | Period I (8–17 May 1966) | | Period II (25 Dec. 1966–5 Jan. 1967) | | Both periods | | | |
Item	Kg	%	Kg	%	Kg	%	Per diem (kg)	Per annum (kg)
Cultivated								
Sweet potato	185.5	67.3	180.4	75.1	183.0	70.9	3.79	1383.4
Tubers	...	...	2.2	0.9	1.1	0.4	0.02	8.4
Leaves	29.6	10.7	2.0	0.8	15.8	6.1	0.33	120.4
Setaria palmaefolia	23.6	8.6	1.7	0.7	12.7	4.9	0.26	94.9
Sugarcane	19.6	7.1	1.4	0.6	10.5	4.1	0.22	80.3
Yam (*D. alata*)	3.2	1.2	0.8	0.3	2.0	0.8	0.04	15.1
Saccharum edule	2.6	0.9	3.6	1.5	3.1	1.2	0.06	23.2
Banana								
Pumpkin/gourd	0.1	...	3.9	1.6	2.0	0.8	0.04	15.0
Fruit	1.8	0.6	0.8	0.3	1.3	0.5	0.03	10.0
Leaves	1.5	0.6	0.3	0.1	0.9	0.4	0.02	6.9
Zingiber sp.	1.0	0.4	3.7	1.5	2.4	0.9	0.05	17.8
Corn	0.6	0.2	4.1	1.7	2.4	0.9	0.05	17.9
Plants with edible leaves*								

Psophocarpus tetragonobulus							
Beans	0.2	0.1	1.2	0.5	0.7	0.3	0.01	5.4
Roots	...	...	2.2	0.9	1.1	0.4	0.02	8.2
Yam (*D. bulbifera*)	0.1	...	...	...	...	...	...	...
Irish potato	0.1	...	2.8	1.2	1.4	0.6	0.03	11.0
Dolichos lablab	...	...	1.8	0.8	0.9	0.4	0.02	6.9
Cucumber	...	...	0.3	0.1	0.1	...	...	...
Peanut	...	...	2.5	1.0	1.2	0.5	0.03	9.3
"Business" crops†	3.1	1.1	24.4	10.2	13.7	5.3	0.28	102.2
Coffee	3.1	1.1	...	...	1.6	0.6	0.03	11.7
Hunted/foraged								
Mushrooms/berries	...	...	(0.02)	...	...	...	...	...
Game	...	...	0.1	...	...	...	...	...
Total	275.8	99.9	240.3	99.8	257.9	100.0	5.33	1948.0

* *Psophocarpus tetragonobulus, Amaranthus tricolor, Solanum nigrum*, Brassicaceae, *Rungia klossii, Oenanthe javanica*, (?) *Ricinus communis*.
† Lettuce, tomato, beans, carrots, passionfruit.

in the unenclosed areas. Of the food crops sweet potato dominates, accounting for 71 percent of all produce brought to the house, but the relative importance of this and of the various subsidiary crops changes through the year in association with the mixed garden cycle. During May (Period I) these gardens are near the end of their productive life and *S. palmaefolia*, sugarcane, yams, and *S. edule* are being harvested in large quantities and account for 28 percent of all produce brought to the residences. Yams serve to reduce the demand for sweet potatoes to the extent that, on some evenings, none of the latter may be consumed. During December–January (Period II) the mixed gardens are only just coming into production and few other starchy foods are available, but a wide range of legumes, cucurbits, corn, and various other leafy vegetables are consumed and others produced for sale. Together these items account for 18 percent of total production at this time of year.

Production levels per capita per annum have been derived from these figures and, given the representativeness of the three households,[1] some estimates of yields are derived. If the per capita cultivated area of open field is assumed to be 0.11ha, of cash-crops 0.02ha, and of mixed-kitchen gardens 0.04ha, and if the first is assumed to comprise all the sweet potatoes, Irish potatoes, and peanuts grown, the second all the coffee, and the third all remaining crops, gross yields of 12.84t, 0.58t, and 13.10t/ha/annum are suggested. In other words the close intercultivation and varying maturation periods of crops in the mixed and kitchen gardens result in yields similar to those for the open fields.

Direct information on sweet potato yields was obtained from fifteen mounds, with mean dimensions of 3.11m in diameter and 0.55m in height, and three plots of *yukúsi*, each of 9.29m^2, all scattered through or adjacent to the Modópa terrace sections and chosen because their preparation for planting coincided with the commencement of fieldwork. Close watch was maintained from initial planting to final harvest of the tubers, although termination of fieldwork demanded that this latter take place prematurely in most cases. In the few instances where the final harvest was not brought forward the ground was considered to be "dry" or "not good" and the tubers "not growing well."

1. These have a mean cultivated area of 0.74ha per household, 4.8 members, and a pig:human ratio of 1.7:1.

Significant differences were observed in both the growth pattern and the ultimate yields of tubers from *modó* and *yukúsi*. The initial harvest from the former occurred on average within 24 weeks of planting, while it was estimated the mounds would be broken after 55 weeks. Comparable figures for *yukúsi* were 28 to 60 weeks, respectively, a somewhat longer cycle. In both cases three harvests were normally taken, with a total mean of 20.7kg per mound, or 17.40t/ha of *modó*, and 19.4kg per 9.29m² of *yukúsi*, or 20.87t/ha. These were obtained over periods of 47.7 and 46.0 weeks, respectively. Thus, extended to one year, yields of 18.96t/ha of *modó* and 23.60t/ha of *yukúsi* are suggested.[2]

The data on sweet potatoes point to a substantial difference between yields and the actual level of production. Assuming the per capita cultivated area to be 0.11ha (four-fifths *modó* and the balance *yukúsi*) realizable yields would be about 2,188kg per annum, or 804kg more than the estimated annual production—a daily surplus of 2.2kg. Methods employed at Modópa and circumstances of production preclude similar estimates being made for other crops. Not only is the extent of each very restricted but harvesting is irregular and some crops, such as cucumber, are only in production for two or three weeks of the year. By contrast production and harvesting of sweet potato are maintained with little variation through the year. However, it appears doubtful whether any significant surplus of subsidiary crops is ever produced, although yields probably fluctuate considerably from year to year.

Utilization of Production: The Requirements of the Pig Population

In identifying the large surplus production of sweet potatoes the whole question of crop utilization is introduced. Surpluses of staple foods have been noted elsewhere in New Guinea. Lea (1964:136) reports yam (*D. esculenta*) surpluses of 1.68kg and 0.59kg per capita per diem for two Abelam villages, while in a footnote he mentions similar references:

> The Bureau of Statistics (1963:15) estimates that throughout New Guinea 11 pounds [4.99kg] of food are produced per person

2. In fact one of the three *yukúsi* sections was harvested only twice, the last after thirty-nine weeks. Fifty weeks might be a more realistic estimate of the duration over which such yields would be obtained, giving a yield figure of 21.70t/ha/annum.

per day. This is obviously more than a person could eat. Hogbin (1951:69) estimated that in Busama village, about 15 miles south of Lae, there was an apparent surplus of 12 tons [12t] a month, and that even then "everyone persisted in regarding the gardens as too small." Brookfield (personal communication) reports that yield and acreage measurement in Chimbu suggests that at least 10 pounds [4.54kg] of sweet potatoes are available per head of population per day for human consumption alone.

Table 28 details the utilization of production by the three Modópa households, revealing that 49 percent is consumed by pigs and only 43 percent by humans. Sweet potato tubers are the dominant source of pig food and 64 percent of the crop is given to the animals; 53 percent of the S. palmaefolia crop is also fed directly to the pigs. These figures appear even larger if the refuse and waste associated with the preparation of food for human consumption are taken into account. Leftovers of yams, sweet potatoes, and S. palmaefolia, estimated to be 22 percent, 7 percent, and 80 percent of the original weight, respectively, are all thrown to the pigs. Thus over 90 percent of the S. palmaefolia crop is ultimately consumed by them.

In the light of these facts it seems unsatisfactory to view the difference between actual production and estimated yield simply as a "surplus" serving as an insurance against unexpected losses —it is too substantial. Rather it is suggested the difference is designed to allow for the enormous fluctuations in pig population characteristic of the Highlands pig cycles.[3] A pig is shown to consume 1.4kg of sweet potato tubers a day, while the surplus for the three households was estimated to be 2.2kg per head of population, enough for 1.6 pigs. Further these same households had a pig:human ratio of 1.7:1, somewhat below the Modópa average of 2.3:1. Thus the suggested optimum ratio of 3.3:1 had not been reached at Modópa during 1966. Significantly, however, preparations were commenced for a tée ceremony that finally eventuated

3. A pig cycle is defined as the progression from a very few pigs "immediately after a large pig ceremony to a maximum number immediately before the climax of the next ceremony" (Brookfield and Brown, 1963:58). Among the Enga, tée festivals occur at about four year intervals, but it is not clear what proportion of the total pig population is actually slaughtered in them. Bulmer (1960b:7) considers that the "majority" are. Following Meggitt's observations among the Mae, a pig:human ratio of 1:1 is assumed (1958a:288). Of the total number 75 percent enter the tée, and of these "at least half" are slaughtered (p. 298)—or say 40 percent of the total pig population.

TABLE 28

MODÓPA SAMPLE COMMUNITY: UTILIZATION OF PRODUCTION
(By Three Households over Two Ten-Day Periods)

| | | Quantity | | | |
| | | kg per diem | | | |
	Total kg	(a) Household	(b) Pig	Percent	Percent of production
Consumed by pigs					
Sweet potato					
Tubers	701.5	11.7	1.4	92.2	63.9
Vines	6.7	0.1	. . .	0.9	N.A.*
Setaria palmaefolia	50.6	0.9	0.1	6.6	53.2
Tomato	1.8	. . .	. . .	0.2	9.0
Sugarcane	0.4	. . .	. . .	. . .	0.6
Carrot	0.2	. . .	. . .	. . .	1.1
Irish potato	0.1	. . .	. . .	. . .	2.6
Total	761.3	12.7	1.5	99.9	49.2 percent of total production
Planting material					
Yam (*D. alata*)	18.2	0.3			29.0
Irish potato	1.6	. . .			26.4
Peanut	2.3	. . .			20.9
Total	22.1	0.4			1.4 percent of total production
Sold					
Lettuce	47.2	0.8			96.5
Tomato	15.5	0.3			79.9
Coffee	9.3	0.2			100.0
Sweet potato†	9.1	0.2			0.8
Carrot	7.5	0.1			97.4
Passionfruit	5.5	0.1			86.5
Peanut	5.1	0.1			68.9
Irish potato†	3.0	. . .			33.8
Corn†	2.8	. . .			20.2
Total	105.0	1.8			6.8 percent of total production
Consumed by humans					42.6 percent of total production

* Not available. Most of the vines are used as mulch or planting material.
† All purchased by the researcher except for 1.5kg sweet potatoes.

in March 1967. One of the main criteria in the timing of this festival is that a group's pig population should be at its optimum level since only then can the maximum political and economic benefit be derived from the exchange. The whole operation requires considerable foresight and planning since considerable pressures are imposed on any one group which endeavors to delay the progress of the *tée* too long.

The support of a very large pig population thus appears as an effective means of converting the perishable products of an intensive agricultural system into a more permanent form that can serve a number of purposes: for example, a source of animal protein in a situation where little is otherwise available, a reliable reserve of carbohydrates to be drawn on in the case of serious and unexpected food shortages, and an extremely valuable exchange commodity.[4] It will be demonstrated later (pp. 191–92) that the animals occupy a central place in the Raiapu social and economic system, while convincing evidence will be provided (pp. 179–80) to show that pig husbandry influences the basic principles of farm organization. The limited resources of the unenclosed land mean there is little that is haphazard about their daily feeding: the amount of tubers gathered varies according to immediate requirements, and consequently the distinction drawn between those for the pigs and those for human consumption is not strictly a qualitative one. Finally, variation in the timing of the final harvest and breaking of the mounds is largely determined by the dictates of the pig population, since only inferior tubers are normally remaining at the end (see p. 46).

The ability to plan for and produce such a "surplus" is closely bound up with the cultivation of sweet potato as the staple. Compared with other tuberous-rooted cultigens this crop is extremely adaptable and highly suited to the Highlands. Adaptability implies hardiness, and the sweet potato has the advantage that it continues to produce through extended dry periods. It is also less susceptible to disease than taro (*Colocasia esculenta*), which has suffered greatly in recent years from the depredations of the taro beetle (*Papuana* spp.) and the virus *Phytophthora colocasiae* in various parts of the Pacific. The sweet potato is not only higher yielding and faster maturing than taro or yam but, because of the

4. See Vayda, Leeds, and Smith (1961) for a detailed consideration of the use of pigs in Melanesian subsistence.

universal practice of propagating through vine cuttings, a greater part of the gross harvest is available for consumption. The tuber is also greatly preferred by pigs which, according to a number of sources, will not touch taro in its raw state.[5] Finally neither frosts nor severe droughts present any real hazard to the cultivation of sweet potato in the Wapenamanda area. Consequently, with this as the staple, not only are effective yields higher but the "risk" factor appears much lower than for the other tubers, and so the Raiapu have little need to allow for a large unspecified surplus in agricultural production.

The Adequacy of Aruní Diet

A dietary survey was undertaken primarily to determine the contribution of various foods to the Aruní diet, and in particular to establish the significance of such innovations as recent crop introductions and purchased foods. The survey was conducted in association with the inquiry into the production of foodstuffs, using the same sets of households and observation periods. Each household was visited at least six times a day, whenever possible both before and after meals, to check on food stocks, weigh any refuse or waste, and inquire as to who had consumed the food. Inquiries, and estimates of quantity, were also made of any food eaten away from the house.

The Aruní normally eat twice a day with the main meal in the evening. Preparation of this commences at about 4:00 or 5:00 P.M., following the day's work in the gardens. Although the sweet potato commonly forms the basis of this meal, other foods, depending on the season, are often eaten with it. The sweet potatoes are cooked in the ashes of the fire, as are corn, *S. edule*, and sometimes bananas, while yams and the various greens are either steamed in earth ovens or, increasingly, boiled in pots. Some tubers are set aside in the evening for cooking and eating the following morning, when they are generally consumed alone. Food is not often prepared during the day. If the women are working near

---

5. Watson (1956b:444) quotes Bulmer as saying uncooked taro "does not appeal to pigs." Steadman (personal communication) reports that the Hewa plant taro following the initial clearing of a garden and only erect strong pig-proof fences much later when sweet potatoes are added. In the interim the animals express no interest in the taro. Oliver (1955:27) observes that sweet potatoes "are more tempting to pigs and require sturdier fences than taro gardens do."

their house they may return to prepare a few sweet potatoes, and if they are in the mixed gardens beans or other crops may be cooked in earth ovens. Similarly the men and children may roast some corn, bananas, or *S. edule* over a fire. But hunger is more commonly allayed by frequent snacks of sugarcane, *S. palmaefolia,* cucumber, or *Zingiber* sp.

However, this whole pattern is interrupted on the arrival of important visitors, who are not expected to wait for the customary mealtime. Attention is immediately directed to the provision of food and a trip will most certainly be made to the mixed garden to gather whatever is in season. Yams and pulses or some leafy greens will if possible be included in the evening meal, and preparation of the food may commence in mid-afternoon. Additional food may be harvested early in the morning, for breakfast, if the visitors remain overnight.

It is the hearth- or eating-group which provides the most tangible expression of the basic unit of production, the household. Those who work their gardens in common invariably eat together, wherever they may sleep. So it is the wife of the household head who normally harvests and prepares the food for attached adult males and bachelors and it is to her house that they come to eat. The principal exception to this pattern is provided by polygynous families, where each wife and her offspring eat separately but take some of their food to the husband or perhaps are visited by him to share the meal.

Insofar as the quality of the diet is concerned it is generally considered that Highlands societies experience a high incidence of protein-calorie deficiency among infants and a general deficiency in the protein intake.[6] Both facts reflect the dominant role played by the sweet potato in the subsistence economies, a phenomenon which serves to make the Highlanders a "nutritionally vulnerable population" (Oomen and Malcolm, 1958:116). Oomen et al. (1961:64) amplify this view in stating: "Often over 90 per cent of the calorie intake is derived from this tuber alone. It is responsible for about three-quarters of the total protein intake. Again, the bulk of mineral constituents of the diet come from the sweet potato." This situation is compounded by the rarity, or at least infrequent consumption, of animal protein supplements.

6. Oomen and Malcolm (1958), Oomen et al. (1961), Venkatachalam (1962), Bailey (1963), Bailey and Whiteman (1963), etc.

Such observations are based primarily on work done among the Chimbu and in the Highlands of Irian Barat, where few greens or other tubers with a higher protein content than the sweet potato are shown to be consumed. Among the Aruní, as data on cultivated areas and in-coming produce suggest, the range of subsidiary crops is relatively large. At least one authority (Bailey, 1963:5) has recognized the considerable food value of these, remarking that "the indigenous vegetables are usually much richer than the familiar European ones. They often contain 3–6 per cent protein as against 0.2 per cent, and equivalently higher amounts of some vitamins and minerals." It is against this background that Aruní diet must be evaluated.

Figure 13 shows the percentage intake by weight of sweet potato to be only 63 percent of all foodstuffs, which contrasts with Venkatachalam's (1963:9) figure of 77 percent for his Chimbu sample. Further there are significant intakes of other tubers, yams in particular, and of sugarcane and leafy greens. While many of these minor crops are only available for short periods, one tends to compensate for another and there is no one time of the year when food is characteristically scarce. Although the intake of protein is noticeably higher during December–January (Fig. 14), calorie intakes vary little from one season to the other, and both are considered adequate according to the daily per capita intakes of 25–30g protein and 1,500 calories advocated by Oomen and Malcolm (1958:134). During both periods the contribution from sweet potato remains constant at slightly in excess of 30 percent of total protein and 70 percent of total calorie intakes.

The increased protein intake in the December–January period reflects primarily the consumption of large quantities of quick-maturing crops such as pulses, leafy greens, gourds, and corn from the newly established mixed gardens, bananas from the old gardens, and *Pandanus* nuts, plus the somewhat fortuitous purchase of a quantity of fresh beef following the killing and marketing of a cow in an adjacent group territory. Among these crops only bananas are of limited importance during May, while the others are substituted for largely by yams and *S. edule* from the mixed gardens, together with tinned fish purchased with the proceeds of the sale of coffee.

The contributions of the various categories of foods—traditional, introduced, and purchased—to the daily per capita intake of calories and specific nutrients are detailed in Table 29. The total figures compare favorably with the Chimbu findings of Oomen and Malcolm (1958:40–41) and Hipsley and Kirk (1965:

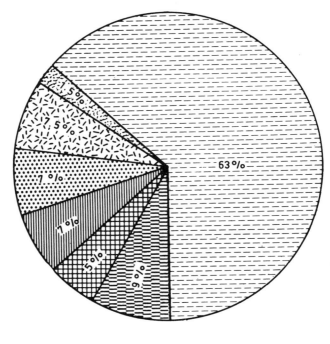

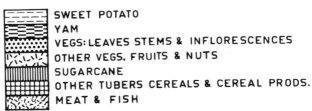

SWEET POTATO
YAM
VEGS: LEAVES STEMS & INFLORESCENCES
OTHER VEGS. FRUITS & NUTS
SUGARCANE
OTHER TUBERS CEREALS & CEREAL PRODS.
MEAT & FISH

Figure 13. Modópa sample community: percentage intake by weight of various foodstuffs

76–83) and reveal the Aruní diet to be adequate in most respects. While the sweet potato is generally the principal source of calcium, iron, thiamin, riboflavin, niacin, and ascorbic acid as well as of calories and proteins, other foods make specific contributions.

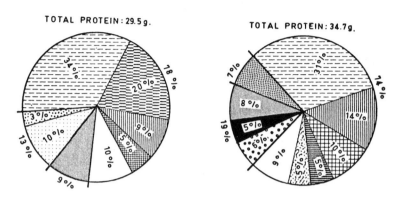

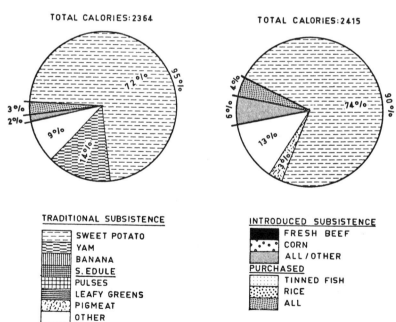

Figure 14. Modópa sample community: composition of diet—daily per capita intake

TABLE 29

Modópa Sample Community: Daily per Capita Intake of Calories and Specific Nutrients*

	Quantity (g)	Calories	Protein (g)	Fat (g)	Calcium (mg)	Iron (mg)	Carotene (I.U.)	Thiamin (mg)	Riboflavin (mg)	Niacin (mg)	Ascorbic Acid (mg)
I 8–17 *May* Total	1911	2364	29.5	7.3	372.8	15.4†	2389	2.1†	1.1†	12.0†	382.6
Percentage contribution:											
Traditional subsistence‡	94	95	78	38	81	89	81	94	92	87	93
Introduced subsistence§	5	2	9	27	11	8	19	6	8	12	7
Purchased‖	1	3	13	35	8	3	...	...	...	1	...
II 27 *Dec.–5 Jan.* Total	1772	2415	34.7	26.8	519.8	15.7	7026†	2.0†	1.1†	13.9†	490.7†
Percentage contribution:											
Traditional subsistence‡	89	90	74	65	91	84	90	90	84	79	94
Introduced subsistence§	9	6	19	18	7	9	10	9	13	20	6
Purchased‖	2	4	7	7	2	7	...	1	3	1	...

* Appendix 5 lists the composition of foodstuffs on which these calculations are based.
† Indicates underestimate. Values for a number of minor items—sweet biscuits, tinned meat and fish, S. *edule*—were not established.
‡ Sweet potato, yam, taro (*Colocasia*), sugarcane, *P. tetragonobulus*, *D. lablab*, *S. palmaefolia*, *S. edule*, banana, gourd, *Zingiber* sp., various leafy greens, cucumber, nut *Pandanus*, pigmeat/fat, opossum.
§ Irish potato, corn, beans, peanut, lettuce, pumpkin, tomato, cabbage, taro (*Xanthosoma*), passionfruit, beef.
‖ Flour, rice, tinned meat, tinned fish, lard, sweet biscuits, coconut.

The leafy greens account for 56 percent of the total carotene intake during May and 85 percent during December–January, while they also contribute largely to the riboflavin and ascorbic acid intakes. Fats are obtained largely from peanuts, fish, meat, and *Pandanus* nut, as is protein.

The relatively high intakes of food, both by weight and by value, require some explanation, either in terms of techniques of data collection and analysis or of aspects of the Aruní economy. The survey was designed to take into account all snacks consumed, including sugarcane, which was apparently disregarded in the other dietary surveys. Many of these items are shown to make an important contribution to the dietary intake. In determining food values, composition tables prepared by others for application in the South Pacific were used wherever possible. These values are listed in Appendix 5, and it seems unlikely that they have resulted in any overestimation. However, some differences in the quantity of food consumed may relate to the estimates of waste and refuse portions at Modópa: these were derived from a series of experimental weighings and applied where the exact portions were not known. Instances of the combined waste and refuse portions as a percentage of total unprepared weight were sweet potato, 7 percent; *S. edule*, 29 percent; corn, 38 percent; sugarcane, 56 percent and *S. palmaefolia*, 80 percent.[7] The common practice of cooking food in the ashes, on the fire or in earth ovens, results in a much reduced wastage, in which the skins are lightly peeled with the fingers following removal. This contrasts with boiling in a pot, for which preparation involves considerable paring with a knife. Thus only 4 percent of the original weight of a banana is removed when cooked in a fire compared with 15 percent in a pot, and the equivalent figures for yams 10 percent and 35 percent, respectively.

It may be presumed that the continuation of traditional methods of food preparation provides a partial explanation for the favorable dietary intake of the Aruní. The role of the subsidiary crops and the various innovations in the food pattern—both crop introductions and purchases from trade stores—would appear to

7. By comparison Rappaport (1967:280) estimates the percentage edible portions of sweet potato to be 80, *S. edule* 40, corn 29, sugarcane 30, *S. palmaefolia* 17, banana 70, and yam 85—all pointing to much higher wastage rates among the Tsembaga.

be more crucial, however. Table 29 reveals that in a number of respects the dietary benefits derived from one or other of the three categories of foodstuffs are out of all proportion to the volume consumed.

Most of the introduced subsistence food crops are grown in the mixed gardens and resemble the traditional ones both in the techniques of cultivation and in their edible portions. Many register high protein and carotene values, with pumpkin tips a particularly good source. Corn and peanuts are important sources of fat and niacin, while fresh beef provides a supplement to the fat and protein intakes. In effect these introduced foods find a ready niche within the ecological system, being both easy to integrate and satisfying recognized "hungers." Although comprising only 5 percent of the total intake by weight, introduced subsistence foods account for 27 percent of the fat and 19 percent of the carotene ingested.

Only 1 percent of all foods consumed, by weight, is purchased, yet it accounts for 35 percent of the fat intake and 13 percent of the protein, for both of which the Aruní register a particularly low intake. In this respect many of the innovations make important contributions to the diet in areas in which it most closely approaches deficiency. However, while most of the starchy foods are consumed with monotonous regularity, others with a high protein value are a much more infrequent component of the diet. Traditionally pigs were only slaughtered on ceremonial occasions and the quantity an individual received was largely determined by his social standing. Similarly *Pandanus* nuts and the indigenous beans are seasonal crops, although peanuts are available throughout the year. The situation has been modified in recent years through the practice of "making business" (marketing) with pig-meat, beef, and other foods, and as a result of the widespread availability of tinned foods in the stores. During December–January a "business dance" was held at Sabakamádá, to celebrate Christmas, and most members of the sample purchased plates of food comprising portions of several of the following items: meat, fish, rice, dumplings, peanuts, and cabbage. This certainly affected the quality of the diet during the second survey; however, these events are occurring with increasing frequency, so that money is becoming the principal factor limiting the consumption of many of the foods.

Conclusion

The data on levels of production and consumption patterns among the Aruní demonstrate the effectiveness of the agricultural system in supporting the large numbers of pigs required for successful participation in the *tée* and in providing the population with a satisfactory diet. The parallel exploitation of open fields and mixed gardens reflects the principal mechanisms whereby these objectives are achieved: the pigs are fed almost entirely on sweet potatoes intensively cultivated in the former, and the people's diet is diversified and improved through the cultivation of a wide range of leafy greens and other minor crops in the latter.

The two most noticeable innovations—new crops and the practice of making "business"—have resulted in an improvement in the general dietary level, in the latter case by making traditional foods, especially pork, more widely available. It is also possible that the introduction of new varieties of sweet potatoes have resulted in increased yields, permitting the support of larger pig populations. Conversely, the abandonment of extensive taro plantings may have been influenced by the increased requirements of pigs. The absence of any serious environmental hazards adds further substance to the view that the crude notion of "surplus" provides an inadequate explanation for the high level of production and associated modes of consumption among the Raiapu, except in so far as the pigs themselves constitute the "surplus."

5. Elements of Order in the System

THUS far the principal features of Raiapu agriculture and society have been described, but no serious attempt has been made to integrate the various facts, nor to establish the relationships between them and the physical environment. Such is the objective of the following three chapters: to establish a crude operational model that demonstrates the functional interdependencies among the cultural, biological, and physical variables within the local ecological system. Again it is the agricultural practices which provide the point of departure for the analysis, the premise being that these act as the primary point of interaction between the society and its environment. Hence it is in terms of such practices that one can best understand the nature of demographic pressures and environmental limitations, and it is in response to these forces that the agricultural practices themselves have evolved. Finally, it is the dictates of these same practices which oblige the population to organize itself in a politically and socially distinctive manner.

It is assumed at the outset that the adaptation is effective, in the sense that the Raiapu are manipulating their environment in an ecologically appropriate manner, and that individual members of the population recognize the basic properties of the system to the extent that they can exploit it to their personal advantage. The analysis vindicates this assumption to the extent that the "regularities" are identified, while some internal flexibility is also demonstrated, which both reflects individual manipulation and indicates persistent evolutionary trends. Thus, this chapter deals with elements of order in the system—Enga perception of ecological constraints, land use techniques in response to both environmental and demographic factors, and an analysis of the economics of location and farmstead organization; Chapter 6 with the cultural devices used to regulate this system; and Chapter 7 with the ways in which the system is currently being modified. From the whole should emerge some idea of the extent to which the Raiapu are arbiters of their own future. The general approach aspires in some ways toward Steward's (1955) view of cultural ecology as an ultimate concern with problems of cultural history and cultural evolution, with, in this case, the mode of analysis foreshadowing a general treatment in Chapter 8 of possible aspects of agricultural evolution in the New Guinea Highlands.

Unlike the preceding description of the Raiapu agricultural system, analysis ranges through most of the central Enga culture area, from Sirunki to the lower Lai and Ninimb valleys. This broadening of the dimensions of the inquiry provides a more effective framework both for handling ethno-ecological information, by encompassing local variations in the form and function of agricultural practices as recognized by the Enga themselves, and for demonstrating empirically the extent to which generalizations can be made about the findings.

Enga Perception of Ecological Constraints

The Enga exhibit a considerable awareness of environmental, and to a lesser extent demographic, constraints operating on their adaptation, and they perceive that many of their agricultural practices are in direct response to these. Further they recognize that the regional variations in these latter, and in the distribution of specific crops, reflect broad ecological differences which serve as partial identification for the various Enga-speaking subcultures. Thus the Mae of the upper Lai Valley and Sirunki area claim sweet potato, taro, and sugarcane as their main crops, cultivated on a short-fallow system where single mounding cycles are interrupted by *pibíná* (*Setaria pallide-fusca*) grass fallows of one to three years' duration. They also admit to a single major garden type in their agricultural system, the mounded *mapú eé* (sweet potato garden). The Raiapu include two further crops in identifying themselves, the yam and banana, and a second garden type, the *amú eé* (yam garden). The mound persists as the principal medium for sweet potato cultivation but the plots are recognized to be under continuous cultivation, whereas the yam gardens operate on a long-fallow cycle. The inhabitants of the lower Lai and Ninimb valleys (Kopóne) distinguish themselves by an abundance of taro and the absence of mounded sweet potato gardens, replaced instead by the intercultivation of all crops in a system of long-fallowing which permits forest regeneration. Finally the Syáka are recognized as sharing some of the attributes of both the Mae and the Raiapu, cultivating sweet potatoes, taro, and sugarcane to the exclusion of yams, and growing the staple in continuously cultivated mound fields. Despite the reiteration of taro as one of the major crops it assumes real importance only among the Kopóne, considered codominant there with the sweet potato.

Within the broad regional pattern the Raiapu recognize themselves to be particularly well endowed, cultivating a range of foods, in particular yams, *S. edule*, and several other greens, which are much desired by the Syáka and Mae. However, all the Enga are almost compulsive innovators, constantly experimenting with new crops and varieties of crops in an effort to improve their resource base; and additional appreciation of the nature of environmental constraints is frequently provided by the varying degree of success that characterize these efforts. For instance, the Irish potato was probably adopted as a major food crop by the Sirunki people in the early 1940's, on account of its ability to withstand frosts. Certainly by 1948 it already seemed plentiful to one Administration observer, and one must assume it was introduced through traditional exchange networks.[1] Among the Aruní one man is currently attempting to grow exotic varieties of banana obtained from Kopóne, another to grow paw-paw. There are similar reports of at least six varieties of banana having been introduced into the Tchak Valley within living memory, where only one was grown before. Finally a number of new varieties of sweet potato, among them *sanim* and *konemá*,[2] have diffused through the whole Enga

1. Freund (personal communication) observed that the Irish potato was cultivated in the Walya area in 1948 and that the people called it *kaspas*, a modification of the Medlpa *katopeng*. This latter is, in turn, derived from the Kate (Finschhafen) word *katofen* which has its roots in the German *kartoffel*. Thus, it is postulated the potato was first introduced by German missionaries into the Finschhafen area, and from there was taken into the Mount Hagen area by indigenous evangelists, whence it was diffused through traditional trade routes.

2. The second can be traced, by name, through much of the Highlands. Bowers (1965b:23) reports it in the upper Kaugel Valley, Powell (personal communication) in the Hagen and Kainantu areas, and Hipsley and Kirk

culture area in the past 30 years. In most cases temperature is considered the major constraint influencing the spread of these crop innovations. Thus the Aruní recognize that temperature conditions are the principal reason why nut *Pandanus* does not bear if it is planted on the terrace sections (1750m MSL) and yam fails if planted above 1850m, while the *Pandanus coneidus* only fruits if cultivated at the bottom of the Lai gorge (1650m MSL). Such an understanding is probably founded on previous experiment.

In so far as the actual techniques of cultivation are concerned, *kidurú* ("ice," frost or hail) and a variety of soil conditions (moisture, depth, and fertility) are recognized as specific environmental constraints. Finally, there is a widespread awareness of a general pressure on resources, most particularly on agricultural land but also, at Sabakamádá, on forest, for everyhere, as Meggitt (1965a: 258) observes, "men point out soberly that . . . land is really the basis of everything important. Men must have gardens to feed themselves, their families and their pigs." However, while this realization is a major determinant of disputes between local groups, no causal relationship is recognized between pressure on resources and stress on agnation. Furthermore the Enga do not perceive their particular agricultural system as reflecting a response to such pressures, except in so far as some individuals explain the proximity of residence to sweet potato garden in terms of a fear of encroachment by adjacent cultivators.

Agricultural practices in response to environmental constraints

Garden types are loosely linked with topographic units, which in turn reflect either microclimatic or soil variations. At Sirunki, "an upland block of relatively subdued topography . . . with a surface lying between 2200 and 2800m M.S.L." (Walker, 1966: 503), mild ground frosts are an annual occurrence—two were reported during 1966—while severe frosts may be expected every few years. Since none of the precontact cultivars is frost-resistant, potential sites for the sweet potato mound field (the single garden type) are evaluated primarily in terms of slight variations in microclimate. Sites, in order of preference, are (1) within the forest or at the interface between forest and grassland, (2)

(1965:38–39) in the Chimbu. The Chimbu believe that this variety, termed *konme*, originates in the Goroka area (Brookfield, personal communication).

the slopes of the depressions within the grassland, and (3) the bottoms of the depressions which comprise either grassland or waterlogged swamp. The first are favored as there "is little ice . . . because the trees cover it." However, the restrictedness of the area under primary forest, its distance from centers of settlement, and the high premium placed on its wild resources prevent most of the Mae at Sirunki from establishing gardens within the forest. Thus a survey of the holdings of a sample of five farmsteads indicated only two out of a total of eighteen gardens to be situated in the forest. Of grassland sites sloping ground is preferred, because crops are damaged only on the occasion of severe frosts. Wherever possible the bottoms of the depressions are avoided because frost damage is recognized to be most frequent there, while to establish a garden often involves digging deep drainage ditches.

Among the Aruní three broad terrain units are identified: the mountain slopes, the terrace sections, and the steep-sided valleys separating them. Specific garden types are closely associated with each, the connection being explained primarily in terms of soil characteristics and only secondarily of microclimatic considerations. The significant soils are *pubutí*, a chocolate-brown, finely structured friable soil; *tugké*, a firm greenish clay containing ocher-colored concretions; and *aoai*, a firm reddish-brown clay without concretions. Of the two garden types the open fields are wholly restricted to areas where *pubutí* is well developed, as an upper horizon overlaying the clays. This soil is thought to be much more fertile than the others (it is said to contain "grease"),[3] is much more stable, and is also easier to work, all of which are important considerations in the preparation of mounds and continuous cultivation of the open fields. *Pubutí* is best developed, to a depth of 0.3m or more, on the terrace sections, and it is here that the open fields are concentrated, to the exclusion of the second major garden type, the mixed gardens.

This second type is restricted to the steep valley slopes, preferably to those parts where some *pubutí* has developed. However, the universal practice of long-fallowing after a single planting means the occurrence of this soil is not considered crucial: rather there is some modification in cropping practices. Where the

3. The Raiapu use the term *ipáge* in the context of composting to indicate that the decomposition process gives "juice" to the soil. An infertile soil is, in contrast, described as *sápu*, or "dry" (Freund, personal communication).

mixed garden is located on *pubutí*, yams and associated crops are planted directly; on "poor" (stony or clayey) ground sweet potatoes are planted following the initial clearing "to break the soil and enable the *Casuarina* to root."

Throughout the middle and upper Lai and its tributary valleys the grassy upper mountain slopes are avoided wherever possible because, according to Meggitt (1958a:302), the "Enga state that such soil [the dark yellow or red clays associated with them] 'has no grease in it,' and that, therefore, yields are much smaller and fallowing time necessarily longer." The Kakoli of the upper Kaugel Valley likewise consider their successional *Miscanthus* grasslands to be of little agricultural value except as a frontier for expansion from the intensively cultivated terrace sections and bottomlands (Bowers, 1968:153, 159). Clarke and Street (1967:7) suggest New Guinean gardeners in general assume that grassland soils can only be effectively exploited through tillage. At Sabakamádá the deforested mountain slope is largely considered "ground nothing," unsuitable even for mixed gardening on account of the altitude. Those obliged to establish open fields there select the shallow depressions, where some *pubutí* has developed and the soils are less prone to drying out. These depressions are also identified as areas where taro, sugarcane, and sweet potato were planted traditionally.

The twin notions of fertility and facility with which the soil can be worked, both reflected in the selection of *pubutí* as the soil with the greatest agricultural value, run through Enga statements about their agricultural practices.[4] Soil fertility is thought to be increased by mulching and by turning pigs into old sweet potato gardens or land being newly tilled. In the latter case "the dung is believed to enhance soil fertility by 'putting grease back into the land'" (Meggitt, 1958a:291); similarly, in the former, "The men say explicitly that composting puts back into the soil 'grease' taken out by earlier crops, and that, without it, they can produce only small and slow-maturing sweet potatoes" (p. 305). Old house sites, with their soils enriched through the quartering of pigs and by food waste, are considered especially fertile and are everywhere selected for planting small plots of luxury crops: *S. palmaefolia, Rungia klossii,* tobacco, gourd, banana, and sugar-

4. This parallels the preference of many Chimbu for *magan wimen*, soils which combine the same characteristics (Brookfield and Brown, 1963:36).

cane at Sirunki; sugarcane, taro (*Colocasia* and *Xanthosoma*), pumpkin, maize, yam, tobacco, carrots, peas, lettuce, and the more exotic varieties of banana at Modópa. Finally, plant growth in the mixed gardens is believed to be improved by pollarding the *Casuarina*, since "too much shade is no good."

The premium placed on ease in working the soil is a reflection of the simple technology. Apart from the hand axe the digging stick was, traditionally, the sole agricultural instrument, and is now supplemented only by the spade. The Sirunki people are loath to let *yagí* (*Imperata cylindrica*) and *sabae* (*Miscanthus floridus*) invade their short-fallows because the lengthy rooting systems of these grasses make the ground "strong" and difficult to clear. Similarly the Aruní do not like to abandon their open fields, in the belief that fallowing makes the "ground too strong."

Together, statements on the function of individual practices suggest a general recognition of the importance of tillage—the need to manipulate the environment in order to obtain yields high enough to support both the pig and human populations. The widespread practice of mounding represents the most tangible expression of a direct technological response to environmental constraints.

Although the Sirunki people are not, strictly speaking, able to say why sweet potatoes are only planted in mounds they do draw a connection between the technique and environmental hazards. Mulched mounds are considered to be "hot" when contrasted with undisturbed soil, and the people are convinced tubers will not develop in unmounded ground. They also state that if vines are planted near the base of a mound either they will be destroyed by frost or the tubers will be so small as fit only for pigs to eat. In this latter context there are two types of distribution in planting vines, *moró* and *wyigí*. In the first vines are planted concentrically around the top of the mound and tubers only develop within the circle, while in the second a more random pattern is assumed which may cover most of the surface area. While both distributions are found at Sirunki, *moró* is more common and is considered to be typical of all the Mae. Wherever *wyigí* occurs at high altitudes the vines are restricted to the uppermost part of the mound.

In the same area two types of *kidurú* ("ice") are recognized, but only one, *pipía* (ground frost), is considered destructive. A light frost simply "burns" the vine and retards growth while a heavier one or successive frosts actually damage the tuber, rendering it inedible. Frosts are associated with clear, starry nights during the dry season. *Tadaki kápa* (hail) may be expected during the wet season but it generally only damages the leaves of the sweet potato vine.

For the Aruní and the Raiapu generally, *wyigí* is the only recognized way of planting sweet potato in mounds, with the vines distributed over most of the surface area. They make no association between mounding and coldness and, perhaps in reflection of this, have two methods of sweet potato cultivation, *modó* (large mounding) and *yukúsi* (small mounding), one broadly linked with level ground and the other with slopes. Further down the Lai Valley from Sabakamádá *yukúsi* gradually displaces *modó* as the accepted medium for cultivating the staple food.

The Aruní consider their climate to be "hot" relative to that of Enga living at higher altitudes, and frost is unknown. Mounding is perceived more in terms of maintaining soil fertility through mulching, but none extend this line of reasoning further to offer it as an explanation for their ability to continuously cultivate the soil. A mound is considered ready to close when the litter has dried out at the surface but is starting to decay beneath—evidence that "the soil is moist and grease is starting to be put in."

Agricultural practices in response to demographic constraints

Meggitt (1965a:218) asserts that the Mae (and, by implication, the Raiapu, see pp. 268-69) "as a whole have access to a limited amount of arable land, as they themselves realise. They have only to look across the valleys to see that no suitable tracts of virgin country remain to be exploited. Consequently land is a scarce good for which individuals and groups compete in various ways." Although population densities are undoubtedly high among the Enga and agricultural land is restricted, only passing mention of these facts is given in explanations of their agricultural practices. It is appreciated that there is little additional land available for open field cultivation at Sabakamádá, compared with an abundance of mixed garden land, but continuous cultivation of the former is not considered to reflect any pressure of population on resources. However, a number of developments at Modópa do suggest some awareness of stress there; for example, the "committee's" decision to leave the "taro ground" as pig grazing and forbid the enclosure of sections for coffee plantings is being increasingly and consciously violated by extensive enclosures for both mixed garden and open field cultivation. Other evidence of land shortage is suggested by the temporary encroachment on to the ceremonial ground for sweet potato cultivation, and by the not infrequently observed practices of planting sweet potatoes in the ridge of a broken mound and establishing small *yukúsi* sections in unutilized ground between *modó*.

Elsewhere among the Enga agricultural practices do not appear to be linked with population pressures. A failure to articulate this may of course reflect an unwillingness to concede a point which accounts for much of the precarious nature of intergroup relations. It may, alternatively, be that agricultural techniques have evolved primarily in response to environmental constraints, which in turn have resulted in much lower per capita requirements of agricultural land than elsewhere in the Highlands, thus eliminating the expected consequences of high population densities among the central Enga. It is the purpose of the following sections, which deal with the operational as distinct from the cognized model of environmental relations, to test this proposition and also the validity of Enga judgments about environmental constraints.

Land Use Techniques in Response to Environmental Constraints

In spite of the widespread interest shown in subsistence agricultural practices in New Guinea, and in the relationships between these practices and absolute densities and types of social organization, they have not been the focus of serious empirical investigation in any strictly ecological or agrometeorological sense. While Brookfield and Brown (1963), the Bureau of Statistics (1965, 1967a, b), and Rappaport (1967) have sought to determine the land requirements of a number of agricultural systems, based variously on crop yields, cultivated acreages, and cultivation cycles, issues of their effectiveness in maintaining equilibrium within the ecosystem have not been given serious consideration. Instead it is assumed that degradation is not occurring, because of the lack of evidence of soil erosion or declining yields, the apparent "conservation value" (Rappaport, 1967:53) of various agricultural practices, and the structural and floristic composition of the regrowth.

Territorial conquest and forced displacement or migration to un-occupied or underpopulated areas are viewed, in the Highlands, as cultural mechanisms designed to regulate the pressure of popu-lation on resources. Brookfield (1962) provides the best summary of the circumstances of "successful" adaptation of intensive sweet potato cultivation to the environmental conditions prevailing in the Highlands. The "greater fertility of the high altitude soils" and the development of special agricultural techniques "in re-sponse . . . to growing population pressure" (p. 252) are thought to be the keys. The techniques include planting *Casuarina* fallow covers to fix nitrogen in the soil, special methods of tillage for erosion control and to "rid the soil of excess moisture," and mulching to raise soil temperature. While many of the assump-tions appear to be legitimate, all are scientifically unsubstantiated and information about the exact nature of the relationships be-tween agricultural practices and environmental constraints and the general effectiveness of the Highlanders' innovations remain scarce.

Clarke and Street (1967), and the larger interdisciplinary re-search project entitled "Human Ecology of the New Guinea Rain-forest" which their and Rappaport's (1967) work foreshadows, have made a first step at placing these assumptions on a firmer basis in conducting yield trials to determine, experimentally, the effect of various cultivation practices on soil fertility. Yet their paper serves only to highlight the paucity of information on this and related topics compared with the detailed investigations conducted in Africa[5] and Latin America,[6] many of which have immediate rele-vance to the New Guinea situation. The development of such a state of affairs reflects, on the one hand, the fact that the few geog-raphers working in New Guinea have been operating within an intellectual milieu dominated by social anthropologists schooled in the British tradition and, on the other, that the CSIRO Division of Land Research has adopted a genetic approach to land in prefer-ence to a search for "ecological zones" and a consequent illumina-tion of climatic-vegetation relationships.[7]

The material presented here represents a break with this tradi-tion in the sense that it is designed to evaluate some of the basic

5. These are largely summarized in Porter (1970).
6. Watters (forthcoming), on the basis of this literature, considers the relevance of ecological factors to shifting cultivation in Venezuela.
7. Watters, personal communication.

assumptions about cultivation practices. It is framed in terms of
the primary distinction that has been identified between open
fields and mixed gardens within the Raiapu agricultural system.
Inherent in this distinction is the proposition that the mixed garden is characterized by an agricultural order which "is integrated
into and, when genuinely adaptive, maintains the general structure of the pre-existing (ecological) system into which it is pro-
jected, rather than creating or sustaining one organised along
novel lines and displaying novel dynamics" (Geertz, 1963:16).
Few or no controls are exercised to rectify the fertility decline associated with clearing and cropping or to prevent weed infestation.
Thus there is often only a single planting, following which the
ground reverts to a natural fallow under which the nitrogen cycle
is re-established, the weeds are eliminated by woody regrowth,
and the soil nutrients are, ideally, restored to their original level.
With the open field, extended periods of cultivation preclude
the restoration of a forest fallow. As a result the associated cultivation practices are characterized by a technical elaboration that
serves to restore equilibrium within the ecosystem and to maintain this through an extended period of cultivation. Techniques
are aimed at controlling soil nutrient and organic matter levels,
primarily through an artificially induced nitrogen cycle; but the
maintenance of soil structure and prevention of weed infestation
are also important objectives.

While the validity of the respective propositions regarding the
distinctive functional properties of the two agricultural subsystems
will be considered, the basis of analysis differs in each case. Thus
the growing body of literature dealing with the effect of shifting
cultivation on the soil permits an evaluation of mixed garden practices exclusively in terms of secondary materials. In contrast little
was known about the effectiveness of open field cultivation in terms
of maintaining equilibrium within the ecosystem. Since, within
the Highlands, the open field assumes its most highly developed
form among the Raiapu, this alone became the focus of direct
ecological inquiry.

The mixed garden

Mixed gardening at Sabakamádá is largely restricted to slopes
of 20–40° along the Lai and its tributary streams. Unenclosed land
is dominated by shrubby regrowth in which frequent associates

are, according to Robbins and Pullen (1965:110), *Antidesma, Agapetes, Acalypha, Callicarpa, Decaspermum, Dodonaea, Ficus* spp., *Eurya, Grevillea, Glochidion, Homalanthus, Leucosyke, Maesa, Macaranga, Osbeckia, Pipturis, Rhododendron, Schefflera, Schuurmansia,* and *Wendlandia.* Sites are cleared by the "slash-and-burn" method and, apart from some tillage at the points at which yams are planted, dibbling is the sole cultivation technique. Selected weeding in favor of arboreal species and the survival of some rooting systems from the previous fallow facilitate its re-establishment following abandonment.

The general consensus (see Nye and Greenland, 1960) is that a shifting cultivation system, if dominated by mature woody as opposed to herbaceous fallows, does not seriously impair soil resources. Further the very long fallows necessary for the re-establishment of high forest are not essential to the maintenance of fertility. On the basis of a study of the secondary vegetation of a tropical montane habitat in Mindanao, Kellman concluded (1967: 209):

> Woody regrowth vegetation with its high litter production, led to a rapid increase in soil carbon and hence soil aeration and infiltration capacity. Some rise in CEC [cation exchange capacity] levels also followed but this did not reach the levels maintained under forest. The rapid nutrient turnover of such woody regrowth may have led to a transient period of high soil fertility during revegetation.

He suggests that the most desirable trees are fast-growing softwoods, which, if small and short-lived, would appear to offer "few advantages to prolonging the fallow beyond 10 years" (p. 210). Nye and Greenland (1960:36, 49) likewise note that litter production under a forest fallow rapidly reaches a high level, while the most rapid accumulation of nutrients in forest vegetation is during the first five years of growth.

Although, in a strictly temporal sense, the fallow periods are of adequate duration at Sabakamádá, the much slower development of woody species at the altitude of the mixed gardens (1650–1830m) results in clearing before the establishment of true secondary forest. On the basis of biomass alone a shrubby fallow is likely to be inadequate for the restoration of fertility, while the small size of the growth forms in association with the loose soils of the valley slopes permits a relatively thorough clearance of garden sites. This in turn serves both to increase the exposure of the soil to surface erosion and, with the removal of at least some rooting systems, to delay the re-establishment of the fallow after abandonment.

Likely effects of the deflection from an arboreal to a shrubby fallow must, however, be considered in relation to prevailing environmental conditions. Notwithstanding the high total precipitation recorded at Wapenamanda, data presented in Table 30 would suggest the very frequent occurrence of small to moderate falls of rain (up to 25.3mm) rather than of very intense downpours of limited duration. On only fourteen occasions during the period 1954 to 1966 were daily falls in the range of 50.8 to 76.0mm recorded, and none of these occurred during the months of June to August when most of the mixed gardens are being established. Consequently, the likelihood of severe soil erosion or leaching is reduced under such a daily rainfall regime.

TABLE 30

WAPENAMANDA: PERCENTAGE OF RAIN DAYS WITH RAINFALLS
WITHIN SPECIFIED LIMITS, 1954–1966

Amount (mm)	Jan	Feb	Mar	Apr	May	Jun	Jul	Aug	Sep	Oct	Nov	Dec
0.3– 6.2	49	46	42	46	55	59	61	54	49	56	49	44
6.3–25.3	42	41	48	44	41	37	34	41	42	37	44	48
25.4–50.7	9	13	9	10	3	4	5	5	9	6	6	8
50.8–76.0	...	...	1	...	1	...	...	...	...	1	1	...
Mean no. of rain days	24	25	26	24	18	15	15	19	22	21	21	24

Humic brown clays, with a *pubutí* (A_1) horizon, are, wherever possible, selected for mixed gardens. These are friable and well structured and have been shown to be relatively fertile particularly with respect to their organic matter content. Rutherford and Haantjens state (1965:93):

> Organic carbon contents of the A_1 horizon are almost uniformly high, whilst in many soils they remain relatively high even in the deeper subsoils, a feature that is particularly pronounced in soils derived from volcanic ash. Accompanying this are generally high nitrogen contents, although the C:N ratios vary greatly (generally between 8 and 17 and up to 25 in some peaty soils). Cation exchange capacities tend to be high to very high.

Other advantages to agriculture may be derived from local climatic conditions. Watters (forthcoming) has summarized the known relationships between macroclimatic factors and fertility decline as applied to Venezuela, concluding that the lower temperatures at higher altitudes result, specifically, in a slower rate of decomposition of organic matter and therefore nitrogen loss. High C/N ratios are considered to be one indication of the slow rate of mineralization of organic matter, and figures for a number of samples taken from the Modópa terrace section are appropriately high, being in the range 11–15 (see discussion of samples on pp. 160–61).

Associated with these natural conditions are a variety of agricultural factors which may compensate for the premature clearing of the regrowth. Most important of these is the apparent trend toward the development of a "controlled" fallow. *Casuarina* are planted in the gardens and the seedlings of these and a number of other fast-growing softwoods, particularly *Acalypha* sp., are protected in the course of selective weeding of the crops, mainly because of their value as building and fencing timbers. The *Casuarina* are not felled during subsequent site clearances unless the timber is specifically required. Consequently, while on the one hand there may be no trees present, on the other the stands may be so dense that individuals are as little as 2–3m apart. Such variations between gardens reflect in part the number of cultivation cycles experienced. Planted and protected in this way, the trees probably function as a valuable source for seeding the abandoned garden —a particularly important consideration in view of the shortness of the fallow and the distance of the cultivated areas from the high forest. Their root systems also have a considerable lateral spread, probably important in limiting the occupation of the garden by herbaceous species and in controlling surface erosion.

It has been suggested that *Casuarina* have a more immediate effect on the control of soil fertility, by fixing atmospheric nitrogen in their root nodules. It is known that twelve of the thirty-five species have bacterial root nodules and it has been demonstrated experimentally (Aldrich-Blake, 1932; Mowry, 1933; Bond, 1957) that four of these, *C. equisetifolia*, *C. glauca*, *C. cunninghamiana*, and *C. lepidophloia*, fix atmospheric nitrogen. *Casuarina* foliage (stems, leaves, and fruit) is also said to be quite high in nitrogen. However, it is not possible on this basis to make any general assumption about the nitrogen fixing status of *C. oligodon* and *Gymnostoma* sp. (*C. papuana*) which occur in the Highlands, although they have been observed to possess root nodules.[8]

The practice of intercultivating twenty or more different crops with varying maturation periods serves both as an erosion control device, through the rapid development of a structured ground cover, and as a relatively abundant source of litter. Pigs rooting through the fallow (unenclosed) areas manure and aerate the soil and, in association with the cultivation practices, undoubtedly influence its fertility.

In the absence of direct evidence on declining soil fertility, judgment about the effectiveness of the natural fallow in the mixed gardens must be suspended. On strictly vegetational grounds there is abundant evidence for a progressive deflection from arboreal to herbaceous associations, directly induced by agricultural practices and reflected in the *Miscanthus*-dominated mountain slopes at Sabakamádá and the numerous *pau* (grasslands) on the terrace sections of the lower Lai Valley. Some *Miscanthus* is found in association with mixed gardens, and further deflection from shrubby regrowth may only be prevented by more consciously "controlled" fallows. Ultimately the recognition of disequilibrium and need for conservation is determined by the importance ascribed to the mixed gardens, and, despite the prestige value of their crops, people and pigs can subsist without them. It is notable that the Aruní think that they have abundant unenclosed land suitable for mixed gardens, while the periodic damage to crops through soil slips has stimulated no technological response in the way of formal erosion control devices. The value of the land on which these gardens are located is not considered simply in agricultural terms. It serves as pig grazing and as an important source of timber, neither of which considerations may be sensitive, in the short run, to any fertility decline.

The transition from forest to grassland

In seeking an explanation for the extensive grasslands of the Highlands, Robbins (1963a, b) has proposed a three-phased vegetational sequence, from forest through dynamic and un-

8. Freund, personal communication.

stabilized sword-grass (*Miscanthus*) regrowth to stabilized dis-climax short-grass communities, which, according to Robbins, reflect both the intensity and the duration of biotic interference. Shifting cultivation is the principal form of interference recog-nized. While some qualifications have been suggested (Brook-field, 1964:32–33), the general proposition has been accepted. Hence it serves as a legitimate basis for evaluating agricultural practices associated with the grasslands, practices which have been considered elsewhere as specifically local and sequential responses to this retrogressive succession (Clarke, 1966).

Two aspects of grasslands agriculture—the fertility status of the soils and, largely as a function of this, "the putative necessity for tilling"—have been treated in a paper by Clarke and Street (1967). They report on a simple but important experiment they conducted among the Maring which was designed to measure the response of sweet potato plants to fertilizer application under a variety of site conditions. Because of their general relevance, the findings will be summarized here.

Apart from confirming the belief that crop yields decline as the length of time of cultivation of a forest-fallowed plot increases, the study demonstrates that tillage raises substantially the yields of grass-fallowed plots, thus implying nitrogen deficiency to be but one of the causes of the relatively low yields obtained from unturned soils. Other explanations were suggested by the physical and chemical properties of these soils: namely, the existence of a "fibrous, relatively compact, greasy, and often wet" surficial or-ganic layer, and of low pH and exchangeable calcium and po-tassium values. They continue (p. 11):

> Both the properties of the surficial organic layer and the low pH are characteristic of soils with a high reducing potential and toxic concentrations of iron and manganese ions (Buckman & Brady, 1960, pp. 251–52, 268–369, 464). As cultivation is the standard remedy for this type of toxicity (Buckman & Brady, 1960, p. 253), it is suggested that an important consequence of turning grass-fallowed soils in humid montane tropical areas is the im-proved aeration and drainage that correct toxic conditions. Com-pared with several other soil samples collected in this vicinity and analyzed at Hawaii the low pH and markedly low calcium content of the unturned grass-fallowed soil point to strong acidi-fication induced by a grassy as opposed to an arboreal vegetation. Drawing on this inference it is suggested that in montane New

Guinea a grassy cover may be an active agent of soil degradation rather than, as is often stated, only an indicator of degradation that has resulted from intensive gardening.

Nye and Greenland (1960:9) assert that the conversion from forest to grassland results in "a permanent lowering of the fertility of the soil" and Kellman's (1967:125–27) study of secondary vegetation in Mindanao would confirm this. He identifies very low soil carbon contents in association with stands of small herbs which are inherited from the cultivation phase and thereafter are maintained or decline even further. This situation he considers to be a direct function of the very low litter falls from the herbs. Specifically, soil carbon contents of about 3 percent are reported, compared with 9 percent or more under softwoods, and litter falls of $200gm/m^2$ per annum compared with 1000gm or more under softwoods and high forest.

Consideration of the vegetation and soils of the terrace sections in the Wapenamanda area provides the necessary framework for evaluating Raiapu open field practices. Robbins and Pullen (1965: 109–11) report a fallow sequence from pioneer weed grasses in the mounds, through *Imperata cylindrica* or *Ischaemum polystachyum*, to *Miscanthus floridus* regrowth, returning without further interference to forest; and they also identify induced short grasslands that are the product of "long-term biotic interference." In fact the intensive cultivation of these terrace sections, coupled with their very thorough clearance, seldom permits the fallow sequence to proceed beyond *I. cylindrica*. As such the fallow can scarcely be considered to aid in the restoration of soil fertility although, at the same time, it is doubtful whether it develops sufficiently to function as an agent of soil degradation.

An analysis of soil samples taken from the Modópa terrace section throws some light on the fertility status of the open field soils. Soil samples were obtained from a profile dug on a 10° slope adjacent to the Modópa ceremonial ground, on a site which had not been cultivated within living memory and which supported *I. cylindrica*. Further samples were drawn from the open field area, both from the topsoil incorporated in the mounds and from the subsoil exposed in mounding. Chemical analyses were conducted by DASF, Konedobu, and the results are presented in Tables 31 and 32.

The undisturbed profile provides clear evidence of leaching,

TABLE 31

CHEMICAL ANALYSIS OF SOILS AT MODÓPA: UNDISTURBED PROFILE

Depth (mm) Identification	Horizon		
	0–255 pubutí	255–635 tugké	635+ aoai
Analysis data			
pH	5.6	5.9	5.8
%N	0.588	0.151	0.101
%C	7.26	0.60	0.38
C/N	12.3	4.0	3.8
% loss on ignition	20.7	8.9	7.3
Total exchange capacity (m.e. %)	26.1	17.3	18.1
% Base saturation	27	47	64
Available P (p.p.m.)	9	10	4
Exchangeable cations (m.e. %)			
Ca	4.9	5.8	7.3
Mg	1.3	1.9	3.7
K	0.45	0.20	0.21
Na	0.3	0.3	0.3
Total metal (m.e. %)	7.0	8.2	11.5
% Total salts	0.015	0.004	0.004
Electrical conductivity (millimho/cm × 10^3 at 25°C)	0.044	0.010	0.010

with the total metal ions and exchangeable calcium and magnesium increasing toward the base. However, generally speaking, it does not exhibit the fertility decline to be expected under a herbaceous cover; the soils are typically acid and free of toxic levels of soluble salts while the carbon level of 7.26 percent in the topsoil is by no means low. The fact that the site has not been cultivated recently has clearly resulted in a build-up in organic matter, paralleled by nitrogen and exchange capacities, in the topsoil under the *Imperata* cover. However, the reduced leaching and improved supply of all major nutrients in the unmulched *pubutí* (1) does point to the potentially deleterious effects of a grassland cover for shifting cultivation. That soil conditions have not deteriorated to the level identified by Clarke and Street (1967) probably reflects, altitudinal factors apart, the relatively high natural fertility and agricultural value of the humic brown clays of the Wapenamanda area. Largely derived from volcanic ash, they have well-developed profiles and, on the terrace sections, deep loamy topsoils (*pubutí*) which are

TABLE 32

CHEMICAL ANALYSIS OF SOILS AT MODÓPA: OPEN FIELD SOILS, MOUNDED AND UNDER CULTIVATION

Identification	1	2	3	4	5	6	aoai 1
Description	Unmulched		pubuti*	Mulched			Exposed
Sequence	0 Weeks	8 Weeks	16 Weeks	24 Weeks	32 Weeks	40 Weeks	Subsoil
Analysis data							
pH	5.4	5.7	5.4	6.0	6.1	6.0	5.0
%N	0.490	0.350	0.319	0.434	0.431	0.439	0.101
%C	5.28	4.98	4.68	5.10	4.92	5.58	0.76
C/N	11.8	14.2	14.7	11.8	11.4	12.7	7.5
% loss on ignition	16.0	19.1	17.0	17.5	16.0	17.4	13.9
Total exchange capacity (m.e. %)	28.0	27.3	24.6	27.6	25.6	28.5	13.5
% base saturation	61	66	70	N.A.	N.A.	N.A.	53
Available P (p.p.m.)	5†	2†	7†	6‡	45‡	26‡	4†
Exchangeable cations (m.e. %)							
Ca	12.8	13.4	12.5	16.0	11.5	14.0	5.4
Mg	3.7	3.5	3.8	4.7	4.2	5.6	1.0
K	0.53	0.73	0.45	0.60	0.47	0.47	0.60
Na	0.10	0.35	0.43	0.29	0.92	0.48	0.20
Total metal ions (m.e. %)	17.1	18.0	17.2	21.6	17.1	20.5	7.2
% total salts	0.018	0.020	0.019	0.018	0.022	0.021	0.006
Electrical conductivity (millimho/cm × 10³ at 25°C)	0.053	0.065	0.063	0.060	0.073	0.069	0.018

* 0.9kg samples were drawn from a depth of 0.3m in ten sweet potato mounds and then reduced by a process of "halving and quartering" to a single 0.9kg sample.
† Determined by Modified Truog method.
‡ Determined by Olsen method.
N.A. Not available.

consistently selected for constructing mounds. It is with respect to this topsoil that the Wapenamanda profiles differ markedly from those described by Clarke and Street. On the basis of this consideration, therefore, the general relevance of their findings is questioned and, insofar as soil conditions are concerned, it is nutrient status rather than toxicity through poor drainage which primarily determines the mode of cultivation at Sabakamádá. However, the full implication of open field practices can only be considered by reference to a wider range of environmental constraints.

The open field

Environmental constraints are not constant through the central Enga culture area and neither are open field practices. At Sabakamádá the ground is considered to be continuously cultivated, though fallowing due to short-term changes in demand, or formerly to warfare, does occur. At Sirunki a single cropping period followed by a short fallow of one to two years' duration is preferred. In all cases, however, the mound is the predominant technique of tillage, and attention is therefore directed to elucidating its ecological characteristics, in order to identify both the nature and extent of particular environmental constraints and the effectiveness of the mound as a mechanism for overcoming them.

A total of 118 mounds were surveyed through the Lai Valley from 1670m MSL near Mambisanda to 2723m MSL at Sirunki. Attention was focused on eight attributes: altitude, slope, soil characteristics, height and diameter, minimum height on the mound surface at which sweet potato vines were located, number of crops present, and age of the cultivator. Altitude was assumed to be the independent variable with the sampling procedure designed to identify any changes which might be related to it. The original intention was to survey approximately 100 mounds within each of four altitudinal groups, 1524–1828, 1829–2133, 2134–2438, and 2439–2743m MSL, but time was insufficient and the 118 were distributed 26, 23, 16, and 53 among the groups, resulting in a marked bias primarily toward the upper and secondarily toward the lower end of the range. The absolute limits were determined, at the lower end, by the displacement of *modó* by *yukúsi* as the dominant form of sweet potato cultivation and, at the upper, by the absolute limit of cultivation. Within each group an even altitudinal distribution was sought but mounds were ultimately selected on a fairly arbitrary basis because attention was restricted to new ones, from each group of which a 5 percent sample was drawn using a random numbers table.

It became apparent on tabulation of the data that no relationship existed between the diversity of mounding techniques, in particular the height of the mound, and age of the cultivator. This latter was therefore discarded as a diagnostic criterion. The remaining information was treated as a classification problem and analyzed by two computer programs designated MULTBET and GOWER. The former is designed to carry out a polythetic agglomerative classification using a centroid strategy (that is, it fuses individuals into groups of progressively increasing size until the entire population is synthesized—groups being defined by the general overall similarity of their attributes), and the latter to investigate the relationships between the groups derived, on the basis of attribute means.[9] The results are presented in Table 33. This shows the progressive division of the population to the cut-off stage in the original hierarchical framework and the identifying characteristics of each group.

The characteristics of the five groups can be summarized in the following manner:

1. Low altitude, moderate slope, small mound with low minimum vine height, a single crop, and *pubutí* with a profile break.

2. High altitude, very steep slope, small mound with low minimum vine height, two crops, and clay soil.

3. Very high altitude, level ground, very large mound with very high minimum vine height, two crops, and *pubutí* with no profile break.

4. High altitude, steep slope, medium mound and minimum vine height, two crops, and *pubutí* with profile break.

5. Medium altitude, moderate slope, large mound, medium minimum vine height, a range of crops and soil types.

In effect the technique of information analysis demonstrates a

9. Details of both programs are available from the Division of Computing Research, CSIRO, Canberra, on whose Control Data 3600 computer the analyses were run. For a detailed discussion of criteria used in the selection of appropriate computer classifications and modes of presentation of results see Rimmer (1968: Appendix).

TABLE 33

CENTRAL ENGA: CLASSIFICATION OF MOUNDS ACCORDING TO SIMILARITY ANALYSIS

| Group Number | Numerical (mean) | | | | | Characteristics — Disordered multistate (percentage distribution) | | | | | | | | | Number in Class |
	Altitude (m)	Slope (°)	Mound Ht. (m)	Dia. (m)	Min. vine ht. (m)	Crops* 1	2	3	4	5	Soil† 1	2	3	4	
1	1864	8.9	0.55	3.14	0.24	79	6	3	12	…	82	15	…	3	33
2	2411	16.0	0.55	3.02	0.24	30	55	10	5	…	30	…	50	20	20
3	2657	2.9	0.85	3.93	0.64	…	91	9	…	…	…	100	…	…	11
4	2575	13.3	0.67	3.63	0.46	3	94	3	…	…	75	19	3	3	32
5	2079	6.9	0.79	4.27	0.43	41	14	14	18	13	45	32	14	9	22

```
|    |    |    |    |    |
160  120  80   40   0
```

Total Information Content

* Number of crops present, where 1 = sweet potato.

† Soil characteristics, where:

1 = *pubutí*: profile break at base of mound.

2 = *pubutí*: no profile break at base of mound.

3 = mixed: *pubutí* plus *aoai* or *tugké*.

4 = *aoai* or *tugké*: no profile break at base of mound.

general increase in mound dimensions and minimum vine height with altitude, but this is considerably modified by slope to the extent that the mounds on steeply sloping ground at the highest altitudes do not differ significantly from those at the lowest. The highest mounds, and more particularly those with the greatest minimum vine heights, occur on level ground at the maximum altitude. The number of crops increases with altitude as does the diversity of soil types. Group 5 is something of a residual one comprising mounds with a diversity of crops and soil types, but it can also be considered transitional in that it is intermediate to the others with respect to altitude, slope, and minimum vine height.

In seeking to provide some explanation for these groupings and for the phenomenon of mounding itself, the fact of the people's absolute dependence on a single crop and therefore of the premium placed on conditions affecting that crop's growth must be taken into consideration. Brookfield (1964:24–25), in discussing the ecology of sweet potato cultivation, identifies three destructive conditions—drought, flooding rains, and frost—with the third as the most serious hazard for the Enga.

According to Fitzpatrick (1965:64) the risk of frost commences at an altitude of about 1524m, increasing thereafter with elevation and topographical variations that promote the concentration of cold air in depressions. Both he and Brookfield (1964:26) state that ground frosts may occur in association with screen temperatures as high as 4.4°C due to radiation loss from the surface, and the appropriate conditions (clear skies) are most likely to develop during the months of June to November.

There are certainly several reports of severe frosts destroying crops. Meggitt (1958a:255) states:

> The worst winter in Enga memory occurred in 1940 or 1941. Gardens as low as 6,500 feet [1981m] were wiped out by weeks of frosts, while above 7,500 feet [2286m] . . . days of sleet (and perhaps snow on the ranges, to judge from men's descriptions) destroyed not only gardens but also food-bearing trees, domestic pigs and wild animals.

Other severe frosts occurred in 1949, 1950, and 1962 according to Brookfield (1964:25). Sirunki might be considered a critical area in this respect. Not only is it situated at the upper limit of cultivation but it is also at the edge of the Wage-Kandep upland, most of which lies above 2438m MSL. This upland is an area where, according to Brookfield (p. 30), the level of persistent cloud formation is relatively high, resulting in more extensive cooling of the ground, frequent frosts, and temperature inversions in hollows and depressions caused by a lack of air drainage from the surface. However, Walker (1966:506, 529) questions some of these assumptions for Sirunki, stating that frosts are rare and, on the basis of limited observations, temperature inversions in the main Lake Ipea depression unusual. In the same paper he circumvents the issue raised elsewhere (i.e., Robbins and Pullen, 1965:112) that some of the grasslands might be natural, resulting from frost-pocket conditions.

Observations carried out by myself at Sirunki tend to support Brookfield's assertions and, in so doing, reveal the particular importance of the practice of mounding in reducing the frost hazard for sweet potato cultivation. At the local level the existence of a nocturnal temperature inversion on clear, calm nights was indicated by the development of horizontal fog banks in the Ipea basin and fringing depressions, and their rapid dissipation at sunrise, generally by a visible process of drainage into the central basin. At the microclimatic level the existence of significant inverted temperature gradients was suggested by the practice of planting sweet potato vines concentrically around the top of the mounds (termed *moró*), common only above about 2400m, and by the widespread recognition that "ice" will kill the vine if it is planted too close to the base of the mound. However, frost-resistant introduced crops, such as cabbage, "Chinese cabbage" (Brassicaceae), corn, and Irish potato, may be planted near the base.

In order to throw some light on the nocturnal pattern of temperature stratification near the ground and the effect of mounding on this pattern, five minimum thermometers were set up in different positions: a screen (1.4m above the ground surface), the top, side, and bottom of a newly planted mound (at 0.84, 0.53, and 0.23m above the residual ground surface), and on cleared but unmounded ground (about 3cm above the surface) already colonized by a few ruderals. The mound was situated at 2662m MSL close to the crest of a low ridge separating a peripheral depression (Nagurésa) from the main Ipea basin. The unmounded site was 6.1m away and slightly downslope of it, while the Stevenson screen was located at Sirunki mission about 1km away and at an altitude of 2653m but in a topographically similar position. The survey was restricted to a few weeks during the dry season when nightly radiation loss was expected to be at its highest.

The results, summarized in Figure 15 and detailed in full in

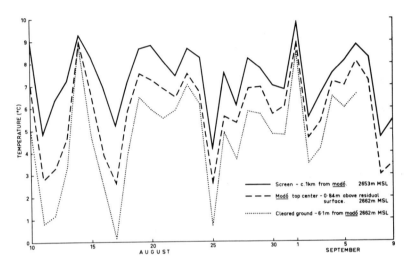

Figure 15. Sirunki: nightly minimum temperature regimes above the ground

Appendix 6, provide unequivocal evidence of a regular inverted temperature gradient near the ground, the dimensions of which do not exceed 1.5°C when the screen minimum temperature rises above 9°C but invariably exceed 3.3°C when it falls below 5.5°C. On the basis of casual observation these variations appear to be explicable primarily in terms of cloudiness and wind speed where, as both increase, the minimum temperature rises and the size of the temperature inversion declines. In all cases the lowest temperatures were recorded on the cleared, unmounded site, these being generally 0.5 to 1.0°C lower than the readings on the mound (modó) itself. The lowest temperatures recorded on the mound were distributed equally among the three positions, the pattern varying approximately with the screen temperature reading. Thus, on the thirteen occasions when the lowest mound temperatures were recorded at the bottom site the screen readings lay between 4.7 and 8.8°C, while on the fourteen occasions when they were recorded at the top site the readings ranged from 7.2 to 10.6°C.

While the distance separating the screen from the other mini-mum thermometers preclude firm conclusions being drawn from these observations, it is apparent that extreme temperature fluc-tuations are characteristic of the climate near the ground and that the degree of the actual inversion increases as the screen temperature falls. The varying observations on the mound suggest that the lowest temperatures are frequently located above the ground surface. However, more important from the agricultural point of view is the phenomenon of consistently lower tempera-tures on the unmounded site. This would suggest that the mound serves not simply to elevate the sweet potato plant above the zone of lowest temperature but also to promote the drainage of dense air away from the vines and downslope, therefore moderating microclimatic inversion patterns but in the process perhaps facil-itating the development of local inversions. The very low tem-peratures at the unmounded site would then be accounted for by the "rough" surface, partially colonized by ruderals, which serves effectively to impede air movement. The effectiveness of the mounds themselves in facilitating air drainage is suggested by their overall distribution—orthogonally, up and down slope—and the practice of clean-weeding both them and the intervening "channels" during the first few months after planting.[10]

The very strong outgoing radiation on clear nights is suggested by the fact that on one occasion, when a minimum temperature of 0.2°C was recorded at the unmounded site, the screen minimum stood at 5.2°C. Whether an inversion of this order can always be expected when screen temperatures fall below 5.5°C will depend very much on local topographic conditions and, as suggested above, Sirunki may be atypical in this respect. Whether there is a concentration of cold air from the surrounding slopes within the Lai Valley is a moot point, and no direct evidence is forthcoming. However, given that extreme radiation loss does occur under clear conditions and that agricultural activity is concentrated on the terrace sections at the foot of the ranges, it is possible that similar gradients develop. If there is assumed to be a slight risk of frost at screen temperatures of 5.5 to 4.4°C and a likelihood at tem-

10. See Geiger (1965:93–102) for a detailed discussion of nocturnal tem-perature in the air layer near the ground.

peratures below 4.4°C, the hazard is a real one at Wabag (2001m MSL). Minimum temperature readings are available for 88 percent of the days during 1957–66 and these reveal an average of 2.1 days per annum below 5.5°C and 0.6 days below 4.4°C. These extremes were restricted to the months of April and June to November, and in only two of the ten years were none recorded.

Although a brief attempt to measure minimum regimes near the ground at Modópa provided no evidence of inversion patterns, it may be that the frost hazard is of significance in determining the altitudinal limits of mounding. The practice effectively ceases at 1675m MSL in the Wapenamanda area, thus approximating roughly with the elevation at which the risk of frost is considered to commence.

While the shape of the mounds is demonstrated to have an important moderating effect on the microclimatic regime of gardens at high altitudes, temperatures both at the surface and within the soil are predictably influenced by other aspects of this agricultural practice. It is known for instance that tillage of the topsoil increases the proportion of air in it, therefore reducing its ability to conduct heat and increasing the amplitude of temperature fluctuations at the surface (Geiger, 1965:152; Slatyer and McIlroy, 1961:2–8). Interestingly the degree to which the mounded soil is worked varies through the area surveyed. In the higher altitudes, as at Sirunki where a short-fallow rotation is practiced, the soil is only very roughly worked. After initial clearing and burning the proposed garden is left for about one year, to be colonized by such ruderals as *Setaria pallide-fusca, Crassocephalum crepidioides, Bidens* sp., *Agrostis avenacea, Arthraxon hispidus,* and *Erigeron sumatrensis,* after which the vegetation is cleared from the ground around the proposed mound sites and thrown to the center. The exposed earth is then roughly broken with a spade or long digging stick and thrown up to form a crude mound. Finally, the earth is broken further and a finer soil "covering" is spread over it. This, in association with the practice of short-fallowing and of resiting mounds on the interstices on the occasion of a second planting, effectively prevents the soil from being worked into the fine tilth characteristic of the continuously cultivated mounds of the Wapenamanda area.

It is possible that this difference in technique may result in the soil being relatively less aerated at Sirunki than at Wapenamanda, so reducing the likelihood in the former of a significant reduction in surface temperatures at an altitude where even slight fluctuations might be critical to plant growth. However, the data on temperature stratification do demonstrate that any possible lowering through mounding is more than compensated for by the manner in which the practice promotes the drainage of cold air downslope.

Observations made at both Sirunki and Modópa at a depth of 0.3m demonstrate that the heat generated by the decomposition of the mulch incorporated in the mounds raises soil temperature slightly. The data, plotted in Figures 16 and 17, demonstrate that

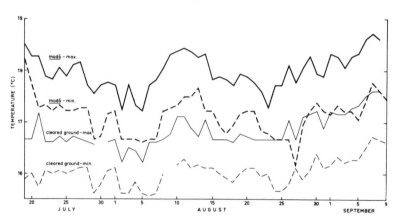

Figure 16. Sirunki: soil temperature regime, 0.3m depth

the range in the mound at Sirunki lies almost entirely above that of the cleared ground, whereas at Modópa a marginal overlapping occurred with the maximum *yukúsi* temperatures slightly higher than the minimum *modó*. The actual survey means in each case were as follows:

Sirunki
modó	max: 18.0	min: 17.1	ra: 0.9°C
cleared ground	max: 16.8	min: 16.0	ra: 0.8°C

Modópa
modó	max: 22.7	min: 21.3	ra: 1.4°C
yukúsi	max: 21.5	min: 19.9	ra: 1.6°C

In both areas maximum temperatures were raised by a similar amount, 1.2°C, but the amplitude in both the mounded and unmounded ground was substantially smaller at Sirunki. Because of the short duration of the observations (approximately 7½ weeks in each case) no direct explanation for this is forthcoming; however, it can probably be viewed as reflecting differing rates of decomposition of the mulch. In both cases the mound observations

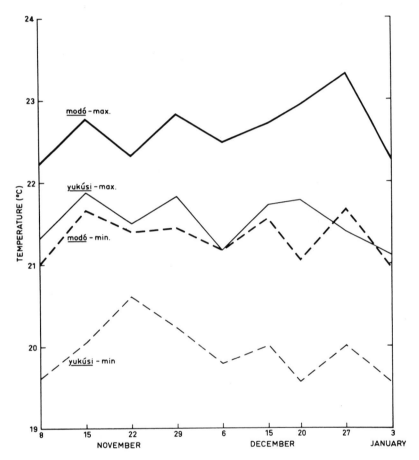

Figure 17. Modópa: soil temperature regime, 0.3m depth

were designed to fall within what might be considered as the most crucial period in the growth of the sweet potato tuber—from initial swelling of the roots to maturation of the first tubers. At Sirunki swelling probably commenced about six months after closure and at Modópa about four months. Given the higher natural soil temperatures at the latter it is possible that most of the litter had already decomposed and little further heat was being generated, thus exposing the soil to greater temperature fluctuations. Certainly no undecomposed mulch surviving in broken mounds was ever observed at Modópa, whereas at Sirunki *Miscanthus floridus* was still readily identifiable in a number of mounds one and a half years after closure.

The greater amplitude in the temperature regime of the unmounded ground at Modópa is explicable in terms of the siting of the thermometer in *yukúsi*, which in this case was a small mound 0.3m high and 0.9m in diameter. Compared with the untilled ground at Sirunki such a soil would be well aerated and therefore subject to more extreme temperature fluctuations.

In the absence of any detailed experimental work on the optimum temperature range of the sweet potato it is not possible to determine the implications of any of these slight increases in soil temperature on plant growth. However, as with tillage, one can only assume the effect of mulching on temperature patterns is insignificant compared with that of general mound topography.

The quantity of mulch per mound appears to be fairly constant, with an estimated 20.6kg in nine mounds averaging 3.5m diameter and 0.64m height at Sirunki, and 20.7kg in ten mounds averaging 3.2m diameter and 0.61m height at Modópa. It may be that mulching plays a subsidiary role at Sirunki in facilitating cropping on a short-fallow system, and it is certainly this aspect of mounding which must be considered most significant at Modópa insofar as it facilitates the continuous cultivation of the soil.

An experiment was conducted at Modópa to evaluate the role of mulching in the maintenance of soil fertility. Shortly after the commencement of fieldwork, ten mounds on the terrace section, all ready for closure, were selected and a 1kg soil sample drawn from the rim of each. Thereafter similar samples were taken from a depth of 0.3m within each mound with, in all, a series of six being gathered over a forty-week period. Each set was reduced by a process of halving and quartering to a single 1kg sample which was dispatched to DASF, Konedobu, for chemical analysis.

It is an established fact that soil organic matter, derived in this case almost entirely from the systematic mulching of mounds, plays a central role in the maintenance or improvement of soil fertility in that it controls to a large degree both the physical and chemical properties of the soil:

> It functions as a reservoir of plant nutrient elements, holds and conserves moisture, helps to preserve soil structure, and provides a favourable environment for various micro-organisms. It is an important constituent of the "exchange complex" of most agricultural soils and is dominant in many. . . . Not only does the soil organic matter hold exchangeable cations—calcium, magnesium, potassium, and sodium, as well as manganese and zinc —against loss by leaching, but its "mineralization" results in the gradual release of such important plant nutrient elements as the non-metals, carbon, nitrogen, phosphorus, and sulphur [Metson, 1961:53].

Consideration of the chemical analyses of the Modópa soils, detailed in Tables 31 and 32, reveals the continuously cultivated and mulched *pubutí* to be in all respects as fertile as in its undisturbed state, while the textural quality is actually improved. This latter is reflected especially in the higher electrical conductivity (evidence of improved aeration) and the higher pH's occurring in the later stages of the mulching inquiry. In this respect too a direct contrast is apparent with the exposed subsoil at the base of the mounds where the much lower figures, particularly for pH, total salts, and electrical conductivity, point to a largely mineral soil with few nutrients available for plant growth.

Nothing conclusive can be said about the fluctuations in the various parameters of the chemical analysis through the sequence of samples from the mulched mounds, because of possible biases related to the sampling method. Thus variations in percent loss on ignition might be explained by one of the series inadvertently drawing on the actual mulch in the mounds. If such possible biases are disregarded, however, the sequence does suggest a gradual decline in nutrient supply to the third sample, evidenced by a reduction in the nitrogen, carbon, and total exchange capacity levels. Thereafter all three, together with pH and salt content, increase markedly, pointing to an improvement in the fertility level of the soil. Such a pattern might be accounted for in terms of the sweet potato plants initially drawing on the existing nutrient supply of the soil (derived largely from the previous mounding cycle), restoration of which only commences between sixteen and twenty-four weeks after closure, as the mulch starts to decompose.

Such a hypothesis is supported by the high C/N ratios in samples two and three which are evidence of the limited assimilation of organic matter at that stage. The actual technique of mulching, in which the litter is covered by soil before a true mulch has developed, probably has the effect of slowing its rate of decomposition, thereby enabling chemical activity and therefore nutrient supply to be maintained for an extended period. On the basis of these data it may certainly be assumed that the practice of mulching the sweet potato mounds results in the establishment of a nitrogen cycle permitting continuous cultivation of the soil.

Not only does mulching make a direct contribution to soil fertility but, in association with the particular techniques of tillage, it is responsible for its loose, friable condition by acting as a granulator of mineral particles (Buckman and Brady, 1960:11). This same process is important in retarding erosion. More problematic, however, is the likely effect of mulching on the soil moisture regime. While organic matter tends to increase the amount of water a soil can hold, granulation and the general practice of complete tillage and mounding increase aeration and improve drainage. The end product of both is of considerable importance in an area subject to both high rainfall and droughts of limited duration.

Flooding rains do not appear to be a hazard among the Enga, as the data in Table 30 show. However, drought is considered a more serious threat, both there and elsewhere in the Highlands. Brookfield (1964:24) links it with frost as the second critical consideration affecting the growth of the sweet potato, critical because the practice of storing the tuber is virtually unknown. Thus Meggitt (1958a:255) remarks, in connection with the Enga, that "in 1941 and 1944 the wet season was late and brief, and people suffered severely from food shortages when the sweet potato crop failed."

Reports of crop disasters due to drought are seemingly in conflict with calculations of moisture balance in the soil. Fitzpatrick (1965:66–68) estimates mean evapotranspiration for Wabag, using mean maximum temperature and vapor pressure data, and concludes that over the years 1954–60 only in four months did precipitation fall below assumed need. Further, "Assuming that up to 4.00 in. [101.6mm] of available water in soil storage could be drawn upon over those intervals when rainfall failed to meet evapotranspiration, it seems unlikely that there would ever have been a case with soil moisture reserves so low as to inhibit growth."

Explanation of the conflict would appear to lie with Fitzpatrick's overestimation of the storage capacity of tilled soils. Brookfield (1964:24) reports that a short drought in the Balim in 1957 caused widespread alarm despite the fact that in no month did rainfall drop below 63.5mm. Droughts of similar proportions are a common occurrence in the Wapenamanda area: in five of the months over the period 1954–66 rainfalls below that figure were recorded (in the range 11.5–51.0mm), while the number of raindays fell below 50 percent in a total of eighteen months.

To determine the effect of tilling, and in particular of mounding, on the soil moisture regime measurements of soil moisture tension close to the surface and under varying conditions were conducted at both Sirunki and Modópa over two periods designed to be indicative of wet and dry season conditions. It was decided to measure the energy state (tension) of soil moisture rather than the total amount present, because this represents the energy necessary to remove water from the soil by plants. Specifically matric tension, expressed as the length (in cm) of a water column necessary to remove the water from the soil by suction, was measured using fiberglass blocks encasing electrodes and a thermistor inserted to a depth of about 8cm in the surface soil. Resistance was then measured on a Wheatstone Bridge, corrected for temperature, and converted to soil moisture tension using calibration charts. The blocks had previously been calibrated on a pressure membrane apparatus at the Division of Soils, CSIRO, Canberra (using thoroughly leached river-bank silt as the medium), for use in Mindanao (see Kellman, 1967, whose methods and suggestions were followed in this inquiry).

The accuracy of the method is not clearly known, although Kellman (1967:77, 80) warns of the "errors introduced" by a restriction of measurement to matric tension and did establish "that at high tensions the blocks became inaccurate." This latter certainly proved to be a problem during the dry season (Period I) at Modópa when a number of measurements had to be discarded. An additional problem arose from the occasional displacement of blocks through gardening activities, and this also necessitated the occasional disregarding of readings. Others were even ingested by pigs. In an attempt to overcome some of the spatial irregularities in tension conditions (also noted by Kellman, pp. 80–81) two blocks were located in each ecological type and the mean derived from the two readings—a technique of questionable merit.

Limitations in interpretation of the data arise from the fact that, without individual calibration of blocks throughout the textural range of soils studied, percent soil moisture content cannot be determined from resistance; further, the relationship between the two is not constant in any one soil. Consequently it is not possible to assume that similar soil moisture tension readings indicate similar percent soil moisture content.[11] Nevertheless the experiment was designed essentially to measure the availability of moisture for plant growth as determined by various agricultural practices and soil types, and tension would therefore appear to be the appropriate parameter. In addition the amplitude of variations over time at a single site does, incidentally, provide a useful basis for comparison of percent soil moisture regimes between sites. Finally, in the absence of any empirical observations from elsewhere in the Highlands, the results are considered to have some intrinsic value.

Blocks were located, at Modópa, in modó (two positions), yukúsi, the fallowed "taro ground" (pubutí, topsoil), and the residual surface between the mounds (tugké, subsoil); and at Sirunki, in modó (two positions), cleared ground (pubutí, topsoil), and the residual surface (aoai, subsoil). Results are presented in Figures 18 and 19.

The rapid increase in soil moisture tension in the cultivated soils at Modópa during the dry season (Period I), and the consequent reduction in percent moisture, provides ample evidence of the risks attendant on complete tillage during relatively dry spells. During July 1966 only 50.1mm of rain fell at Wapenamanda (52.0mm less than the average), while over the whole period 30 June to 10 August rain fell on only twenty days and the maximum on any one was only 17.0mm. At this time of year soil moisture tension fluctuated considerably in response to only very slight variations in total rainfall. Variations in the modó were somewhat greater than in the yukúsi but both experienced very considerable increases in soil moisture tension when compared with the fallow

11. See Williams (1969:51–56) for a detailed discussion of the limitations of this method in the measurement of soil moisture.

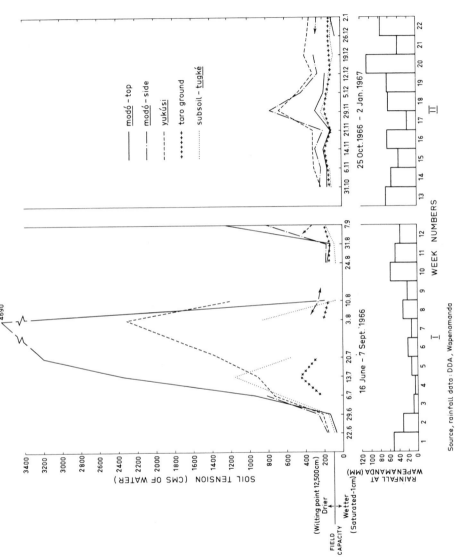

Figure 18. Modóna: soil moisture tension and rainfall regimes

ground. During the wet season (Period II) the cultivated soils recorded slightly higher tensions than the uncultivated but no significant difference was noticed between the two forms of tillage. At Sirunki no noticeable differences were identified between any

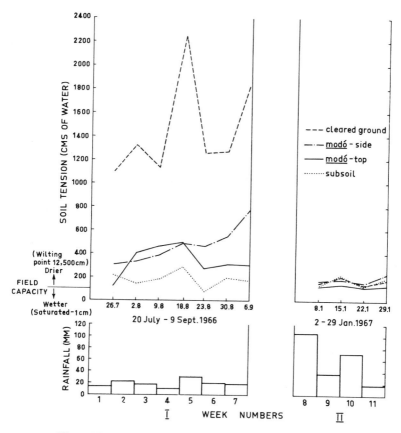

Figure 19. Sirunki: soil moisture tension and rainfall regimes

of the sites during the wet season, but during the dry season soil moisture tension figures were consistently much higher in the cleared ground, while readings in the mound were somewhat higher than in the residual surface. The first may be accounted for in terms of the rapid drying out of the soil on exposure (through clearing and burning).

In general, mounding appears to have a beneficial effect on soil moisture conditions during the wet season when saturation is a possible hazard, but the practice does not appear to be any more effective in improving drainage at Modópa than *yukúsi*, the alternative form of tillage. During the dry season the very high soil moisture tension figures for the mounded soil at Modópa and their rapid response to even slight rainfall variations suggest that the "improved" drainage conditions can have a decidedly deleterious effect on crops when abnormally dry conditions prevail, even for only a few days. That the mulch does not appear to have any regulating effect on the regime in preventing excessive drying out is probably due to it being invariably located at a depth below that at which most evaporation occurs (soil surface to 5cm). Finally the data confirm that evaporation rates are exceptionally high from the deep, finely tilled, agricultural soils.

Conclusion

No single function can be ascribed to the practice of mounding. At Sirunki the objective would appear to be primarily one of reducing the likelihood of frost damage whereas at Modópa the concern is more with the maintenance of soil fertility. With respect to both constraints the technique appears to be effective. Yet this particular form of technical elaboration may provide the explanation for the existence of a third constraint, scarcely identifiable according to meteorological criteria, drought. This, then, is one obvious "cost" associated with the Enga open field system. Interestingly too it is one which might be alleviated by placing the mulch much closer to the mound surface than is presently done, although this in turn might result in damage to the tubers.

If the two agricultural subsystems, mixed garden and open field, are considered together, the need for and benefits deriving from the technical elaboration in the latter readily emerge. Low night temperatures apparently preclude the extensive cultivation of most subsidiary crops above an altitude of about 1850m MSL. This necessitates even greater dependence on a single staple which is itself subject to frost damage—a hazard which is already present at that altitude and increases thereafter. The precariousness of food crop production is compounded by a relative poverty in natural resources and very high population densities. Mounding within open fields not only reduces the risk of crop damage but also permits the intensive use of the best soils and therefore the support of large populations.

In accounting for the need for technical elaboration and the particular form which the response has assumed, the relative facility with which the Highland soils can be intensively cultivated must not be disregarded. Not only are they relatively high in organic matter content but basic differences in soil processes, compared with the lowlands, in all probability result in a much slower rate of humus destruction (Watters, forthcoming) thus permitting more continuous cultivation of the soil without any necessary adjustment in agricultural practices. It is, nevertheless, doubtful whether even the inherently high fertility status of the *pubutí* soils would permit continuous cultivation for thirty years or more without a significant decline in yields, were it not for the practice of mulching.

The practice of establishing *yukúsi* at Modópa prior to *modó* has been assumed to be dictated by technology, because the deep tillage necessary for continuous cultivation is an arduous process when the only instrument available is a digging stick. However, another, strictly ecological, explanation has been suggested for the practice.[12] This is that soil freshly broken from a grass fallow is likely to contain very high percentages of raw organic matter, mostly in the form of roots. Further additions, in the form of mulch, would probably cause both nitrogen and phosphate deficiencies and thus seriously affect sweet potato productivity. These deficiencies result from the micro-organisms using up the readily available sources of these nutrients in the process of decomposing the raw organic matter. *Yukúsi*, then, provides an appropriate medium for cultivating sweet potato while the initial raw organic matter is being broken down to humus. Needless to say the population at Sirunki are in no position to exercise this choice, because of the persistent danger of frosts. However, the fact that the mounds at higher altitudes comprise only coarse and partially tilled soil perhaps serves to reduce the quantity of raw organic matter present, therefore minimizing the danger of serious soil nutrient deficiencies.

Evaluation of the land use practices strictly on the basis of

12. Freund, personal communication.

environmental constraints suggests that an effective equilibrium has been achieved within the open field ecosystem, except for its particular sensitivity to drought. In the mixed gardens at Modópa there appears to be a continuing deflection toward shrubby and grassy regrowth and this must be controlled if soil impoverishment is to be prevented. The apparent trend towards the development of "controlled" fallows, dominated by *Casuarina*, suggests that appropriate measures are being taken. However, the validity of any assessment over time can only be determined on the basis of evidence of demographic constraints, presented in the following section.

Land Use Techniques in Response to Demographic Constraints

To the casual observer the Enga manifest three consuming interests—pigs, land, and women, thus ranked in descending order of importance. The attention lavished on pigs, the characteristic ambivalence of male-female relationships, and the economic importance of both have already been considered. Concern for land assumes a somewhat different form, being expressed in the constant litigation over ownership and, hitherto, in the frequent association of warfare with territorial conquest. Administration officials have noted with concern the proliferation of land disputes and their lack of jurisdiction in these matters. As far back as 1959, thirty-three disputes were reported in the Wapenamanda patrol area (Minyamp, Tchak, and middle and lower Lai valleys), half of them originating in the Tchak. In 1963 there were ninety in the Wabag patrol area (Ambum, Maramuni, and upper Lai valleys) and the situation was considered to be deteriorating. Until the arrival of a native lands commissioner in 1966 disputants were advised to leave all disputed land fallow. However, since such land was invariably arable or, in the higher altitudes, primary forest of considerable agricultural potential, this only aggravated the situation. Concerning warfare, Meggitt (1965a:256–57) notes that encroachment on land was either directly or indirectly the principal cause of interclan feuds in the traditional society, and that "Nowadays the struggle for land is just as vigorous but, because of the Government ban on warfare, people have to rely on fraud and litigation to achieve their ends."

Both phenomena are considered to be a direct expression of population pressure on resources and of current or imminent shortages of land. Academic and Administration observers consider the "arrogance" and "difficult" temperament of the Enga, as identified by plantation employers, to be a further manifestation of these shortages in that theirs is not a wholehearted acceptance of wage employment on the coast.

This assumption of serious population pressures has led, on the practical side, to detailed inquiries into densities, both absolute and effective (McAlpine, 1966), and the quantification of land shortage as expressed in terms of production of the staple food, sweet potato (Bureau of Statistics, 1967a). On the theoretical side it has inspired the thesis that stress on agnation, as manifested in the "coherence and elaboration of the Mae lineage-system," is directly related among highland societies to the shortage of (arable) land (Meggitt, 1965a).

On the basis of its survey the Bureau of Statistics (1967a) does in fact reject the idea of significant demographic constraints operating on the central Enga, an observation which conflicts in some respects with my own findings. Incidental evidence of such constraints is not lacking. At Modópa the ceremonial ground was largely planted over with *yukúsi* and small "business" plots (or kitchen gardens). The restoration of *Pyrethrum* gardens to subsistence food production was in several cases precipitated by a shortage of open field land, and similar explanations are provided for the progressive resumption of the "taro ground." Finally the intensive utilization of the open field area is clearly evoked in the common practice of planting sweet potato vines in the rim of broken mounds and of establishing small sections of *yukúsi* interspersed among the *modó* in places where the remaining *pubutí* is insufficient to mound. Among the Mae, men attempt, under increasing population pressure, "to reclaim small swamps that are normally left as grazing for pigs" according to Meggitt (1958a:304), who also suggests that the almost total absence of virgin land suitable for agriculture is consequent upon the dense populations.

While the indicators are not wanting, what Meggitt and, to some extent, the Bureau of Statistics fail to consider is that previous agricultural practices may provide an important explanation for existing demographic pressures and that the present system may be viewed as a response, and possibly an effective response, to them. Casual observation at Sabakamádá reveals that, although the slopes of the main range are in no sense virgin land, they are considered of little agricultural value and are largely unutilized. They may however be interpreted as a successional grassland that has developed in response to the upward progression of an agricultural frontier no longer operative, but similar to that identified by Bowers (1965b, 1968) in the upper Kaugel Valley (see discussion below, pp. 208–9). Currently agricultural activity assumes the form of intensive exploitation of less than one-third of the group territory, a pattern which is repeated to a greater or lesser degree by all the Raiapu.

Criticism may of course be leveled at a number of specific aspects of Meggitt's thesis, but in more general terms the obvious intensity of Raiapu agricultural activity suggests his basic assumption, that the systems of all Highland groups may be treated as constant, is invalid. Not only may overall land requirements vary from one group to another but the requirements of the component subsystems may differ even more radically, particularly insofar as sweet potato cultivation is concerned. Therefore, with the focus again on the open field/mixed garden distinction, some measures of land requirements are applied at Sabakamádá in order both to identify the degree of demographic constraints and to speculate on the extent to which this agricultural dualism is a product of them.

The greatest concentration of population occurs on the terrace sections, in association with intensive sweet potato cultivation on the terraces themselves and with mixed gardening on the adjacent dissected valley slopes. Hence attention was restricted to these units. Here an estimated 176ha support a total of 237 persons. On the basis of current agricultural practices the carrying capacity of this area was calculated and then compared with the present population to arrive at a "density of occupation index." This latter is described by Brookfield and Brown (1963:119) and provides an indication of the adequacy of land given constant technology and land needs per head. Carrying capacity (W_T) was determined using a simplified version of the method developed by the same authorities (pp. 108–13). This method allows for the two terrain types with their radically different cultivation factors, and is expressed as:

$$W_T = \frac{(a_1C_2 + a_2C_1)L}{L(C_1C_2L)}$$

where:

	Terrace sections 1	Dissected valley slopes 2
Total area, A	72ha	104ha
Cultivable %, P^+	80	65
Cultivable proportion $(AP/100)$, a	57.6ha	67.6ha
Cultivation factor, C^*	1	15
Mean area under cultivation per capita, L	Total:	0.17ha

$^+$ In 1 the balance is accounted for primarily by paths, fences, and houses, plus "taro ground," or is utilized by the local Lutheran congregation; in 2 the balance comprises stream beds or slopes too steep for cultivation.

* Being the number of garden areas required to complete the cycle of cultivation and regeneration, and determined as

(Fallow period + Cultivation period) ÷ Cultivation period

and calculated as:

$$W_T = \frac{[(57.6 \times 15) + (67.6 \times 1)]\,0.17}{0.17\,(1 \times 15 \times 0.17)}$$

$$= \frac{931.6 \times 0.17}{0.17 \times 2.55}$$

$$= \frac{158.4}{0.43}$$

$$= 368$$

This carrying capacity of 368 persons contrasts with a resident population of only 237, resulting in an occupation density index of only 0.6–0.7. Against this observation must be set the fact that a large number of nonresidents exploit the area. Three small terrace sections, all unoccupied and amounting to 7ha, are cultivated primarily by Keamádá residents from the main range slopes. More important, the dissected valley slopes are utilized by people from other parts of Sabakamádá as well as members of other local groups. In all perhaps 25 percent of mixed garden land is cultivated by nonresidents. If the appropriate modifications to the calculations are carried out the effective occupation density index rises to 0.7–0.8.

The calculations assume the several agricultural subsystems to be practiced on both types of land, whereas in fact the continuously cultivated open fields are largely specific to the terrace sections and mixed gardens to the dissected valley slopes. In practice therefore an optimum density may be achieved on one terrain type before another. Ecological evidence shows the open fields to be in equilibrium, but the mixed garden fallows appear to be characterized by a continuing deflection toward a shrubby and, presumably, herbaceous growth, a situation that is in fact being rectified by the establishment of "controlled" *Casuarina* fallows. The much shorter fallow period of the 1966 mixed gardens (averaging eleven years) compared with that of the 1965 gardens (averaging fourteen years) may also indicate increasing pressures within this subsystem, as may the growing evidence of removal of topsoil after heavy rain.[13]

This method of determining demographic pressure is an extremely crude one given the quality of the data incorporated, and one or more of the parameters may be substantially incorrect. However, it does highlight the general efficacy of the major, open field subsystem in reducing land requirements under conditions of high population densities and at high altitudes. Were a simple long-fallow system to be operative at Sabakamádá, with a cultivation factor of 15 and a per capita subsistence requirement of 0.14ha, the *whole* group territory could only support an overall population density of 43/km².[14] Such a figure assumes both 90 percent of the total area to be cultivable and the natural fallow to be of adequate duration for the restoration of soil fertility, two questionable assumptions. Even if these are allowed for, the density compares unfavorably with the present overall figure of 71/km² in which over 70 percent of the territory—the forest and main range slopes—remains largely unutilized for agriculture.

The calculations do not, however, take into account any inequalities in access to land. The observed indications of a shortage of open field land on the terrace sections are in all probability a product of a tenurial situation characterized by a marked "fixity of interests." This particular phenomenon is not then indicative of a strictly demographic constraint but rather of the manner in which the system as a whole is regulated, as outlined in Chapter 6.

Although both McAlpine (1966) and the Bureau of Statistics

13. Freund, personal communication.
14. Determined by Allan's (1949) equation where: per capita requirements of land $= 100 \dfrac{CL}{P}$.

(1967a) have rigorously analyzed the nature and degree of population pressure on resources among the central Enga, their differing assumptions concerning both "land used" and cultivation factors, and known regional variations in agricultural practices, make generalization on the basis of the Sabakamádá findings difficult. McAlpine has, presumably, defined, "land used" to cover all areas showing evidence of agricultural activity, which would exclude at Sabakamádá only the forested ridge-top. According to this criterion the mean population density for the high population concentrations in the Lai and Tchak valleys[15] is 83/km². The Sabakamádá figure lies slightly below this at 77/km². The advantageous position of the Aruní gains further credence through data presented in the Bureau of Statistics survey (p. 5) which shows community 7 (which includes Sabakamádá) to be the best endowed of all, with 3.62 gardenable hectares per capita.[16] By contrast the lowest recorded figure is 1.14ha, near Wabag.

Overall demographic pressures are therefore relatively low at Sabakamádá, and those that exist are induced by particular aspects of the agricultural system. In identifying this association no allowances are made for the efficiency of the various agricultural practices, in terms of maintaining the fertility status of the soil, minimizing labor inputs, and so forth. At Sirunki short-fallowing rather than continuous cultivation is practiced, and Meggitt (1958a:302) reports similarly for the Mae around Wabag. Sweet potato land requirements are therefore obviously increased. Other considerations operative at the higher altitudes include declining yields and an increasing frost hazard. The first may result in higher per capita cultivated areas, as there is no evidence for smaller pig populations or lower consumption levels,[17] and the second in a reduction in the cultivable area. Thus, according to the Bureau of Statistics (1967a), average annual sweet potato yields fall from 24.2t/ha at 1524–1905m MSL to 20.1t/ha above 2286m on slopes of less than 10°. The forested parts of group territories, which may

15. The upper Lai, Wabag, middle Lai, and Tchak census divisions, which approximate the Bureau of Statistics (1967a) Wabag survey area.
16. A corrected figure to include "deep, well drained soils" on slopes greater than 35°.
17. Meggitt is, unfortunately, no guide on this matter. He (1958a:311) estimates the mean cultivated area per household under sweet potatoes to be only 0.2ha and makes no mention of pig requirements; the figure therefore appears absurdly low.

be taken to reflect those areas located above the upper limit of cultivation, amounted to 20 and 23 percent in two cases investigated by Meggitt (1958a:311) near Wabag, compared with only 5 percent at Sabakamádá. Under such circumstances per capita land requirements for sweet potato (including the few supplementary crops grown separately but under roughly similar conditions) are clearly much higher than at Sabakamádá.

If the per capita cultivated area among the Mae is assumed to be 0.14ha (equivalent to the open field plus cash-crop/kitchen garden at Sabakamádá, and therefore not allowing for any possible increase due to lower yields), the cultivation factor to be 4 (based on Bureau of Statistics, 1967a:5, description of practices), and the cultivable percentage to be 70 (allowing for forest, plus settlement and other uses), individual requirements are calculated to be 0.8ha, giving an optimum density of $125/km^2$.

Two related questions arise from this calculation: first, whether the extensive cultivation of supplementary crops (mixed gardening) is not practiced among the Mae because of environmental constraints or because of the increased land requirements of sweet potato in association with higher population densities, and, second, why short-fallowing is practiced at all in preference to continuous cultivation of sweet potatoes?

While yams probably do not grow successfully above about 1850m MSL, S. *palmaefolia*, surgarcane, corn, and the edible gourd are cultivated even at Sirunki, and bananas and P. *tetragonobulus* are common in the Wabag area. The point at which extensive mixed gardening ceases (around Yaibos in the Lai Valley) is not therefore strictly an ecological one. The distribution does, however, roughly coincide with the lower parts of the Bureau of Statistics' communities 7 and 8 around the confluence between the Lai, Tchak, and Minyamp valleys, where per capita gardenable areas approach 3.6ha, compared with 2.4ha or less elsewhere. Mixed gardening may therefore be affected by the relative abundance of agricultural land. On the other hand, were continuous cultivation of sweet potato to be practiced by the Mae additional land would be available for mixed gardening. In terms of minimization of labor costs as well as of land requirements, short-fallowing is undoubtedly less efficient than continuous cultivation. In spite of this the Mae persist in fallowing their gardens, probably at the direct expense of reducing their areas under subsidiary crops.

A purely cultural interpretation of the difference may be dismissed, on the grounds of intensity of Mae-Raiapu contacts and the number of other uniformities. The only possible explanation forthcoming is one based on the agricultural value of their respective lands.

It must be presumed that the fertility status of the soils around Wabag is generally lower and that there is insufficient terrace section land to permit the concentration of population achieved in the Wapenamanda area. Evidence for the second point is provided by Perry et al. (1965: map "Land systems of the Wabag-Tari area") but so far as the first is concerned the Bureau of Statistics (1967a:4) does not show any significant variation in the proportion of "deep, well drained soils" through the Lai and Tchak valleys. However, since these soils are identified on slopes of up to and exceeding 35 degrees it is doubtful whether the category is sufficiently discriminating to have much meaning for sweet potato cultivation. Of the land which would have been included within this category Meggitt (1958a:302) notes, "In many places . . . the grassy slopes are covered with but a thin layer of humus resting on dense yellow or red clay many feet deep." At Sabakamádá a considerable depth of topsoil is required to work *modó*, preferably 0.3m or more, but this does not appear to be the case at higher altitudes, probably because the topsoil is generally shallower. It would seem reasonable to suppose therefore that the soils of the steeper slopes in the Wabag area, which must perforce be cultivated, are not only unstable but relatively infertile and so require frequent fallowing.

If it is presumed that the Mae are exercising some degree of choice in maintaining sweet potato production at a high level, but are foregoing extensive cultivation of subsidiary crops because of the tuber's increased land requirements, it is because the former are much higher yielding, ecologically tolerant, and greatly favored by pigs. Everywhere agricultural practices may be viewed as a generalized response to both demographic and environmental variables. Artificial regulation of the fertility status of open field soils is necessitated by the very high population densities found throughout the central Enga, but continuous cultivation of sweet potatoes at Sabakamádá is possible only because of particularly favorable topographic conditions. Where sufficient land is available and ecological conditions are favorable the open field/mixed garden division appears as an effective adjustment to conditions, and only where population densities are particularly high does the problem of an adequate fallow period re-emerge. And even this is amenable to a solution through the change from a natural to a controlled *Casuarina* fallow.

The Economics of Location

The form and composition of the Raiapu resource complex has provided the framework for the whole of the preceding discussion of their agricultural practices: of the deep, fertile soils of the terrace sections used almost exclusively in the continuous cultivation of sweet potatoes, of the unstable but climatically favorable dissected valley slopes devoted to the shifting cultivation of a diversity of luxury crops, and of the impoverished soils and vegetation of the main range slopes which are, wherever possible, avoided. The general concentration of settlement on the terrace sections is considered to reflect these preferences, while the actual form assumed within the several agglomerations reflects the zonal localization of the major resource. It is only, however, at the level of the individual residence that the various economic, behavioral, and topographic factors are clearly identifiable. Here, at "the point of origin for all the inputs which have to be applied to the land of the farm . . . [and] the point to which all the produce of the farm is brought" (Chisholm, 1962:47–48), the threads of spatial and temporal organization, of production and consumption patterns merge, and it is possible to identify both the underlying rationale of the system and the efficiency of the Raiapu solution.

Schematic representation of a Raiapu farmstead is attempted in Figure 20. To the extent that holdings of individual farmsteads are intermingled the figure is misleading, but it is accurate in terms of both general relationships and relative distances. The open field/mixed garden dichotomy is the most striking feature: the one characterized by permanent cultivation and covering about 16 percent of the total area, the other by impermanent, covering the balance and functioning also as pig grazing and a timber source. The boundary between the two is marked by a major fence-line delimiting the holdings of all those exploiting a single open field area, and by a trackway which regulates the movements of pigs as well as people. The residence itself is located on the open field side of, but adjacent to, this boundary with direct access afforded through the fence to a courtyard fronting on the woman's house. Like the open field the location of the residence is fixed, with rebuilding generally occurring alongside the same site, and the system as a whole is essentially a stable one. So while garden areas may fluctuate marginally from year to year, in response to

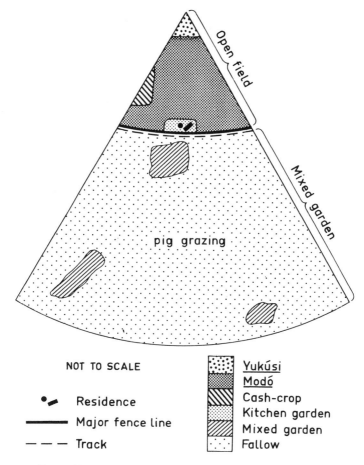

NOT TO SCALE

•⌐ Residence

——— Major fence line

— — — Track

Yukúsi
Modó
Cash-crop
Kitchen garden
Mixed garden
Fallow

Open field

Mixed garden

pig grazing

Figure 20. Schematic representation of a Raiapu farmstead

changing food requirements and the availability of planting materials and as reflected in the area under *yukúsi* in the figure, these require no radical reorganization of the residence and its holdings.

Because of the basic stability of the pattern there is little direct evidence of the processes operative or of the sorts of choices exercised in locating residences. Nevertheless elucidation of the pattern is facilitated at Modópa because the residents themselves consider they have arrived at something approaching an optimal solution in the exploitation of their resource complex, when contrasted with the circumstances prevailing on the densely settled Ráku terrace section or the bleak main range slopes.

The predictive value of the model is based on the assumption that a minimum energy location is sought for the residence in relation to its holdings, and the problem is therefore one of the resolution of parallel forces—the mixed garden and the open field. It is assumed the residence will be located at the point at which the resultant acts, that is, the center of gravity. This point is determined by drawing a line at right angles to the forces and dividing it in inverse proportion to the values obtained for each.

The validity of the model was tested for the Modópa sample community by using data on cultivated areas, labor inputs, and frequency of visits to arrive at an appropriate weighting for each of the two major subsystems.[18] On the basis of these a mixed garden/open field ratio of 1:3 was derived and this was evaluated against information on traveling times (Fig. 21).

It was found that 90 percent of the open field area fell within a seven-minute walk of the residence. Furthermore this distance seemed to reflect an important threshold in that the seven gardens beyond were either in a neglected state, or gardens to which permissive rights had been granted under special circumstances, or, in one case, the recent acquisition of a man with exceptionally restricted open field resources. Notably, in this last case, the garden was worked by the man himself and not his wife, thus contravening the customary division of labour between the sexes. If the same 90 percent threshold is assumed to apply, the mixed garden complex should lie within a 21-minute walk of the residence. In fact, the mixed gardens established during 1965 lay within 30 minutes and those established during 1966 lay within 24.5 minutes, suggesting a reasonable "fit" with actual practices.

18. Yields were disregarded as being constant. Because of the method of data collection, kitchen gardens were included with the mixed gardens but, on account of their restricted size, it is doubtful whether they significantly affected the solution to the problem. Cash-crop holdings were ignored altogether because of the recency of the innovation and absence of any identifiable impact on residential location.

The discrepancy between the model and the real world, as observed at Modópa, may be accounted for in terms of specific characteristics of the two subsystems, behavioral considerations, and topography. The solution of locating at the margin of, rather than beyond, the open field area appears all the more effective as a long-term adaptive measure in circumstances where open fields are established, and therefore fixed in location, whereas mixed

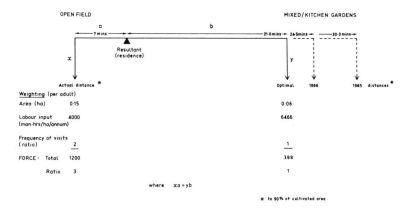

Figure 21. Residential location in relation to agricultural holdings: the resolution of parallel forces

gardens are relocated each year through an extensive unenclosed area. To seek an optimal solution in terms of the latter would require annual resiting of the residence, and the labor costs involved in this would far outweigh the increased economies of location.

From a satisficing as well as an optimal viewpoint residential location adjacent to the open field area also appears as the most effective. The achievement of subsistence and support of the pig population is dependent almost entirely on sweet potato production, while the products of mixed gardens are primarily luxury foods of prestige value. Whereas per capita areas of sweet potato vary little from year to year mixed garden areas vary considerably, because of both individual inclination and, more fortuitously, the availability of planting material. Although the satisficer, disinclined to operate a mixed garden, might in theory better locate within the open field area, this would require either the area's fragmentation to permit the pigs direct access to the houses[19] or the transport of large quantities of tubers to the animals beyond the fence-line and the erection of special pig houses. Location at the periphery appears therefore as a minimum risk location, in the sense of most effective control of pigs, which also approximates closely to a minimum energy location.

Behavioral considerations certainly influence the Raiapu solution to residential location. For example, true optimality in terms of the well-defined sexual division of labor in which women work the open fields and men, primarily, the mixed gardens, would more likely be achieved if the men's houses were further removed from the women's in the direction of the mixed gardens, instead of being adjacent as they are in reality. Fear of encroachment on scarce, improved, open field land is a reason given by some Raiapu for living close to their sweet potato gardens, and this notion is understandable in terms of establishment costs where at least three cropping cycles are necessary before the soil is tilled deep enough to make *modó*.

Finally, in terms of topography, there is a general association at Modópa between residential location and the break of slope separating the terrace section from the dissected valley sides. It might be postulated that, while the most suitable site for settlement is the gently sloping terrace surface, houses are displaced to the periphery because this is a scarce resource which, under conditions of high population pressure, must be devoted entirely to the cultivation of the staple food. The steeper valley slopes are, however, avoided because of the difficulties involved in leveling house sites, problems of access in the wet season, and the general instability of the ground. In fact the association is not universal: although the steeper valley slopes are invariably devoid of settlement, elsewhere, regardless of topography, residences are commonly situated on the fence-lines bounding open field areas. Even at Modópa where the open field abuts on the "taro ground" with no topographic change, houses are situated adjacent to the dividing fence. Elsewhere in the Lai and Tchak valleys terrace sections are frequently more extensive with only portions enclosed for sweet potato cultivation, and here too there is no necessary associa-

19. Thereby running the risk of neglecting sections of the fence-line and facilitating the invasion of gardens by pigs (see, e.g., Brown and Brookfield, 1967:143, quoted on p. 197 below).

tion between residence and change of slope. Where the association does occur it can be considered as largely fortuitous and is not a primary determinant of residential location.

In discussing the problem of location the level of generalization has only been that of the single open field area incorporating perhaps twenty farmsteads, in this case the Modópa terrace section. It is not of course possible for all the individual farmsteads constituting such a group to simultaneously achieve optimal locations, because of unequal competition between them. Similarly, and at a more general level, behavioral constraints, as manifested in the agnatic ideology and in the transmission of rights to land, effectively restrict individual mobility and so place some groups at considerable disadvantage vis-à-vis others. At Sabakamádá this latter is reflected in the circumstances of residents of the main range slopes who, seeking to cultivate mixed gardens, must still establish them on the dissected valley slopes at least a thirty-minute walk away. Similarly those that own large numbers of pigs prefer to agist them with kinsmen resident on the terrace sections because foraging is poor on the slopes; but this in turn often involves carrying large quantities of tubers down to help sustain the animals.

In evaluating the pattern the merits of isolating staple and subsidiary crops in distinct subsystems clearly emerge. The sweet potato far exceeds all others in the total volume produced, fulfills the daily food requirements, and, in the absence of storage techniques, requires continual attention. By contrast the other crops are consumed primarily at small feasts, on ceremonial occasions, or as snacks away from the house, and, except when the gardens are being established, require only infrequent attention. Thus the distinction itself, and the stabilization of one subsystem in association with residences and therefore with the pigs, serves as an effective mechanism for minimizing transport costs.

Needless to say this evaluation in no way accounts for the form of Raiapu farmsteads and location of residences, and current behavior can contribute little to solving the problem because the people themselves claim to be exercising no choices. Instead they view the practice of siting houses adjacent to the open fields as "the fashion of our grandparents." Yet it does point to a close parallelism between the open field/mixed garden dichotomy and dispersed settlement and, on synchronic evidence, leads to propositions about the kinds of processes which have led to the emergence of this pattern within the Highlands. These processes will be considered in the concluding chapter. Meanwhile such speculative thinking is encouraged by the fact that this assessment of residential location does suggest that the Raiapu are making essentially economic decisions, with the topographic and behavioral considerations such as distinguish one Highland society from another being of comparatively minor importance.

6. Regulation of the System

An AGRICULTURAL system cannot be considered meaningfully apart from its social context. Social considerations find direct expression in, for example, the terms of access to land, the sexual division of labor, the composition of a household group, and even the dispersed pattern of settlement. There are causal links between the "network of relationships among men" and the "network of relationships between man and his physical environment" (Frake, 1962:54). Further these links are reflexive in the sense that the social system is a structural mechanism which can be exploited in certain ways or modified in the interests of more efficient utilization of a resource-complex, but the same system can also impose considerable restrictions on both the mode of utilization and actual composition of that complex. In considering aspects of the regulation of the Raiapu agricultural system, attention is focused on what have been demonstrated to be its most significant features: a general pressure of population on resources, a dispersed settlement pattern, an open field/mixed garden dichotomy, and a large, dependent pig population. These features are considered with reference to the clan and its territory, in terms of survival and stability, recruitment of members, and leadership.

Successful analysis of Highlands social structure has proved an extremely difficult task. Such epithets as "loose," "flexible," and "open" have been applied (Langness, 1964:162) to cope with the recurring situations in which:

> . . . we may be hard put to decide, for example, whether descent groups are mainly agnatic with numerous accretions, or cognatic

183

with a patrilineal bias. We find that people are more mobile than any rules of descent and residence should warrant, that genealogies are too short to be helpful, that we don't know what "corporate" means when applied to some groups, that local and descent groups are fragmented and change their alignments [Brown, 1962:57].

Nevertheless, because of the widespread occurrence of groups exhibiting agnatic hierarchies, ethnographers have sought to analyze social structures in these terms and define local groups as founded primarily on descent-group membership (de Lepervanche, 1967: 134). They have been guided in their endeavors by the "African models," particularly of the Tiv and Tallensi as analyzed by Evans-Pritchard and Fortes (Barnes, 1962:5). An awareness that "Highland societies fit awkwardly into African moulds" (Barnes, 1962:5) has deterred some less than others, and Meggitt (1965a:268) has presented the Mae Enga as possessing a "clearly defined agnatic descent system." Furthermore, he proposes that "the coherence and elaboration of the Mae lineage-system are largely a consequence of the limited availability of agricultural land" (p. xv), thereby positioning them at the end of a continuum among Highlands societies. This last proposition has generated a minor, and as yet unresolved, controversy which has tended to inhibit progress toward a more realistic and explanatory definition of Highlands groups.

Meggitt's proposition concerning land availability and stress on agnation has been challenged on a number of grounds. In particular McArthur (1967:284) has shown the percentage of agnates in a Mae clan territory as compared with a Korofeigu local group "might not be so very different if the same system of classifying agnates were followed in both." In considering the Enga and the Chimbu, Brookfield (1970:132–34) notes that not only are Enga population densities lower but, contrary to Meggitt's (1965a:278) assertion, sweet potato yields are comparable. Finally, Meggitt's failure to provide any measure of population pressure on resources by means of a determination of land requirements appears, on the basis of material presented in Chapter 5 (see "Land Use Techniques in Response to Demographic Constraints"), to be a grave omission. The fact remains, however, as Meggitt (1965a) clearly demonstrates, that the Enga do lay considerable stress on the notion, if not on the practice, of agnation—to a much greater extent than do other Highland peoples.

While both Raiapu and Mae appear to accept immigrants readily, they seek from the outset to assimilate them, to make them sever their ties with their true agnates and become unequivocally committed to their host group. Meggitt himself (1965a:46) refers to "the explicit rule that a person may inherit unqualified land rights in one clan only, in return for which he is bound to give undivided allegiance to that group." In effect the transmission of rights to land appears to be not so much restricted as obligating. As elsewhere in the Highlands, descent group (defined in agnatic terms) and local group (defined as co-residents of a named territory) do not coincide, but the Enga are constantly striving to effect a coincidence. If a temporal dimension were introduced to the discussion on agnation some clarification might follow. However, in the present context the problem is rather one of endeavoring to account for Raiapu emphasis upon membership of an agnatically defined group.

The essential weakness inherent in discussions of Highlands social structures has been, according to Langness (1964:164), that "while ethnographer after ethnographer has recognized important discrepancies from the 'African model,' there has been little sustained attempt to see the type of system in terms of its own inherent qualities and tendencies rather than as an aberrant example of a certain type." Both Langness, and more recently de Lepervanche (1967–68), have approached this problem through an investigation of the relations between descent group and local group, in which "the notion of locality as a primary structural principle" (de Lepervanche, 1967:140) has been stressed and the need for achieving solidarity within such a local group considered. In particular the problem is approached in terms of the related issues of land and warfare. Thus de Lepervanche (p. 144), discussing clans with populations of 200–300, writes:

> The relatively small size of these autonomous units seems to be related to ecology and to the need for efficient division of labour in agricultural and other co-ordinated tasks (Salisbury, 1962:208). The type of country and the requirements of shifting cultivation limit the size of the group (Pouwer, 1964:134), yet enough people are needed for defence. Even a small population in the Highlands needs a relatively large amount of garden land for the type of horticulture practiced and because food cannot be stored for long (Hogbin and Wedgwood, 1952:241). Too many people and thus too great a dispersal of gardens and their

cultivators attending them would prohibit convenient assemblies of people for communal tasks and for defence.

In effect allegiance is to the locality, the locality is defined in agnatic terms, and the agnatic idiom is therefore used to achieve and express group unity.

It is particularly important that the social system be considered from the standpoint of locality and local group because the Raiapu are faced with the specific problem of practicing an essentially stable, intensive system of agriculture within an unstable political context. Open field land is improved, requiring a continuing investment of labor over several years until *modó* can be established. At the same time agricultural land is in short supply and is the cause of many disputes. Political instability is based on the fact that the society is an acephalous one, where power is vested in "big-men" who achieve their positions, acquire followings, invite immigrants, and effect alliances between agnatically unrelated groups.

As has been shown (see p. 71) most marriages are with contiguous groups, and it was with these same groups that disputes over land traditionally occurred and were resolved through warfare. Encroachment over territorial boundaries and litigation over land remain a constant threat. In order to counter disputes immigrants were invited, to maintain numbers and help defend clan lands. But in accommodating them solidarity was threatened, because of the constant danger that their loyalties might revert to their natal group, which was often contiguous. In so doing they might continue to assert a claim to land in their host group's territory, leading to its effective alienation and the realignment of boundaries. It is this "infiltration technique," described by Meggitt (1965a:46), which is the real danger associated with the admittance of outsiders. Warfare itself was very destructive, leading either to the alienation of territory or to extensive damage to houses, fences (and therefore gardens), and economically important trees such as *Pandanus*. Nowadays organized warfare has largely ceased but brawling and illicit encroachment across territorial boundaries persist as threats to the clan.[1]

1. Long-smouldering land disputes do occasionally still give rise to premeditated attacks on property and people. Between mid-1969 and mid-1970 at least eight people were killed in three separate fights in the Lai and Ambum valleys, and in one of them thirty-two houses were destroyed by fire and numerous trees felled.

In such a context the agnatic idiom serves to define a person's loyalties. By defining the territory itself in agnatic terms a mechanism is provided for unifying the group that occupies it. While in a number of other Highland societies nonagnates as such are freely accepted, divided loyalties are an anathema to the Raiapu. From the outset individuals are actively discouraged from cultivating land in two clan territories, and in fact this practice is made difficult by the intensity of sweet potato cultivation. Instead a firm commitment is sought from immigrants to one group or the other, this being achieved through the terms of transmission of rights to land.

Apart from the general pressure on resources there are particular reasons directly associated with the agricultural system itself that add further substance to this notional stress on agnation. Dispersed settlement appears, in some respects, as a response to the intensive cultivation of sweet potatoes and large-scale pig husbandry. The disposition of individual residences in relation to their holdings are seen to approximate to minimum energy locations, while the overall pattern of distribution along the boundary of open field areas minimizes the chances of garden invasion by pigs. Finally dispersal of population and pigs probably reduces vegetational disturbance. Rappaport (1967:69) observes that the concentration of large numbers of pigs in association with a single nucleated settlement among the Tsembaga seriously affected the regrowth in nearby garden sites. Six years after cultivation, "trees were only scattered. No canopy had formed, for the pigs had constantly rooted out the seedlings necessary to its development. *Kunai* seemed to be the most important component of the ground cover."

The Tsembaga had, traditionally, a "pulsating" settlement pattern:

> In earlier times the extent to which settlements were scattered was, it seems, directly correlated with the size of the pig herd. During and directly after the pig festival the degree of nucleation was high. As the pig herd grew, however, people would move away, establishing themselves in hamlets. Even these sometimes disintegrated into scattered homesteads as the number of pigs grew even larger [p. 69].

Rappaport proceeds to discuss this phenomenon in terms of relations between co-residents. He suggests that, while conflicts arising out of damage to gardens by pigs may be minimized with dispersal, this latter probably results

. . . in a lowered effectiveness of the social structure. It will be
recalled, for instance, that consensus formation is achieved
through informal conversations, the "talk" eventually "becoming
one." Residential proximity may accelerate this process, residential dispersion inhibit it [p. 155].

More important is the fact that "The process of residential dispersion . . . threatens to reach its logical conclusion: people may
move to residences out of the territory and perhaps be permanently
lost to the local group" (p. 162). For the Raiapu such an outcome,
most likely involving the effective transfer of land as well as loyalty
to a contiguous group, would be disastrous. Where territorial
defence is a vital consideration dispersal is strategically unsound,
except in so far as chances of minor encroachments are reduced.
Contact between co-residents is further reduced by the very low
degree of cooperation between individuals in most agricultural activities.

Local group solidarity is also threatened by a marked individualization of land tenure among the Raiapu. Individuals claim
exclusive rights to most land of agricultural value, this applying as
much to fallowed mixed garden plots as areas currently under
cultivation. Rights are individually transmitted and the possibility
therefore arises of some being acquired by individuals whose
loyalties lie to other local groups.

In the context of settlement and tenure the descent idiom
emerges as an enduring institution binding individuals together
and overriding the changing composition of local groups and individualization of interests, both of which are exploited by "big-
men" in the acquisition of support and influence. By equating
kinship and residence at the level of the clan and by asserting
agnatic ties, and therefore unqualified land rights, with outsiders
only after recruitment, the local group acquires the high degree of
solidarity necessary for survival and the effective operation of its
agricultural system.

Further aspects of political relations between groups, and in
particular the mechanisms by which "big-men" emerge, are revealed through a consideration of the mixed garden/open field
dichotomy. Power is achieved primarily through the manipulation
of resources and, for the Raiapu, land and labour are the basic
resources. However the utility of the products of the two subsystems differs considerably. Sweet potatoes are the staple and every

household must cultivate them in quantity; but by virtue of being universally available they acquire significant exchange value only as fed to pigs and so converted to pigmeat—a very inefficient process that demands a steady investment of labor over an extended period. Mixed garden crops are low yielding, grown in small quantities and over only a restricted geographical area, but they are considered luxury crops and have an immediate exchange value. Further, most of the labor requirements involved in production are absorbed in a few weeks of the year.

"Big-men" are able to exploit this situation to their advantage by means of the customarily defined sexual roles, where women are responsible for the open fields but the mixed gardens are primarily a male concern. Specifically, granting of permissive rights or outright transfers of open field land between co-residents is uncommon. Those with a surplus prefer to let it lie fallow rather than allow others to exploit it, nominally from fear of losing it altogether. The effect of this is to create considerable inequalities in the distribution of open field land and to ensure the presence of a diversity of social types within the local group, ranging from the "rubbish-man" (*kinabúrí*)[2] to the "big-man" (*kamógo*) himself.

Permissive rights are freely given to members of other territorial groups, many of them affines, to cultivate mixed garden sections. Invitations are extended nominally on the grounds of an assumed abundance of mixed garden land, and also because of the obvious facility with which the gesture is terminated—at abandonment of the garden.

Because of the differing work rhythms but complementary sexual responsibilities toward the two agricultural subsystems, it is only those men with female dependents who are able to commit themselves to large mixed gardens and extend invitations to men from other clans to participate. The poor man, poor because he has limited open field resources, has little chance of obtaining a wife or alternatively of marrying a second time following an early divorce. If a man has no wife or is a widower he is faced with two possibilities: either of tending his own sweet potatoes at the risk of public ridicule and with the certainty of having little time available to embark on mixed gardening, or of attaching himself to another household. In the latter case the wife or wives of the

2. The term is a derisory one, applied to bachelors who have largely withdrawn from the competitive system and are no longer eligible for marriage.

head will tend to his pigs and sweet potatoes, but in return he must commit himself to supporting his host. This involves directing all surplus production to him and assisting in various menial tasks, such as gathering firewood.

The "big-man" enlarges the size of his labor force through attracting unattached individuals to his household and is thereby provided with the time to develop extensive mixed gardens and establish an informal network of links with residents of other clan territories, with the object of negotiating alliances, effecting exchanges, and enhancing his reputation generally. In effect he achieves his position through power over co-residents, based firmly on a control over labor as determined by inequalities in access to land and its conventional mode of exploitation, and influence beyond the group, exercised through a personal network embracing other leading men. This pattern accords with that in Sahlins (1963:290) who identifies "internal" and "external" sectors to the "field of influence" of a "big-man": "Within his faction [internal sector] the Melanesian leader has true command ability, outside of it only fame and indirect influence."

Among the Raiapu the first sector comprises a "big-man's" co-residents, effectively encompassing the subclan territory. These are the people likely to assist him in house-building and support him in major exchanges. However the sector may, on the basis of general understanding, extend to the whole clan territory. Meggitt (1967:30) has suggested that this extension is achieved through a system of "oscillating leadership" between the representatives of different segments. Success within the external sector is a function primarily of the amount of time spent in visiting other leading men and in the volume of goods transacted. A firm power base within the internal sector is therefore an essential concomitant.

Most external sector links are established through phratry agnates and through affines and therefore largely involve contiguous groups. Links established by marriage are likely to be the most stable and may even persist after the death of one partner. Furthermore polygyny is desirable because it permits a man to extend his influence through additional sets of affines as well as to increase the size of his labor force.

Connections are difficult to establish beyond the circle of contiguous clans, but such long-range associations may be exceptionally advantageous because of reduced grounds for intergroup conflict (over land) and less likelihood of overlapping interests with fellow agnates. Nonagnatic residents who have unequivocally asserted their allegiance to the host group can make capital out of their status by utilizing the ready-made connections which exist with their true agnates. This facilitates extension of their influence beyond the range of contiguous clans. Meggitt (1965a:40) himself alludes to the fact that agnates are not necessarily better off than nonagnates in pointing out that "quasi-agnates have been nominated and appointed ['luluais,' i.e., Administration officials] in several parishes because they were important and wealthy before Europeans came to Wabaga and were entitled then to speak for the clan on all occasions." At Sabakamádá the emergent *kamógo* and two other influential members of Ayóko subclan are not true agnates but they have been able to profit by their numerous ties with relatives in the Tchak Valley.

It is in the *tée* exchange that the role of the "big-man" is most clearly defined, in terms of the control he exercises over a large share of the product of land and labor in his internal sector and the reputation he acquires through exchanging this with other leading men. A general description of the cycle has already been provided (pp. 108–9). The formal distribution of pigs represents the climax. Months prior to this rows of stakes, each stake about 0.9m high, are laid out on the ceremonial ground and spaced at 1.2m intervals. A pig is roped to each in the ensuing ceremony and one individual determines and effects the distribution of all the pigs in a single row. While both the number and length of rows are likely to increase as the ceremony approaches, more significant is the fact that the length of each row, and therefore the number of pigs distributed, exceeds the capacity of the distributor (*tée akarí*) and his dependents to raise themselves. The maximum number of pigs an adult woman can maintain for any length of time probably does not exceed eight or nine,[3] yet a "big-man" may distribute as many as two hundred pigs, most of them belonging to nonparticipating co-residents and other exchange partners located "up the line." In the latter case a "big-man" must attend their *tée* ceremonies in order to receive the pigs he has been promised so that he can then redistribute them at his own ceremony. This practice requires that a great deal of time be spent in traveling and negotiat-

3. This figure compares favorably with the Tsembaga where, according to Rappaport (1967:158), "a strong adult woman" can only support four.

ing, not to mention the extra food and labor required to support the additional pigs pending the ceremony. The title *kamógo* strictly identifies the individual distributing the largest number of pigs, this achievement being marked by planting a *Cordyline* sp. cutting at the furthest extremity of his line of stakes during the ceremony. In the case of any subsequent disputing of his achievement the plant's position is merely indicated.

While arranged at the subclan level, *tée* exchanges are essentially exchanges between individuals in which the "big-man" regulates the movement of wealth between groups in order to negotiate alliances and other contracts. Because of the great emphasis on exchange as the mechanism whereby power is achieved and intergroup relations are determined, Raiapu social and political life is relatively unstable. Yet it is in this context that an essentially stable and intensive agricultural system is practiced. The two apparently conflicting demands are regulated through the strict association of descent group with locality and the enforced assimilation of immigrants to agnatic status. In this way territorial integrity and group strength are maintained. Stability is enhanced by a marked "fixity of land use" (Brookfield, 1970:135), where the improved value and practice of continuously cultivating open fields discourages owners from risking alienation through granting permissive right of access. "Big-men" are nevertheless able to manipulate the system, by ensuring that inequalities persist in access to agricultural land within the local group and by capitalizing on the conventional division of labor between the sexes. Through their control over a fund of labor and the products of that labor they have both the goods and time with which to participate in extragroup affairs. In this acephalous society the limits to individual power are essentially technological—the productive limits of the system and the capacity of a single man to manipulate them—the clearest expression of the operative considerations being provided by the *tée*, where a man must assemble and distribute as quickly as possible numbers of pigs that are far in excess of his capacity to support, while making the greatest political capital out of the transactions.

7. Prospects for the Future:
The Progressive Modification of the System

REPEATED reference has been made through the preceding chapters to the dynamic character of the Raiapu agricultural system, in which both the mounding and fallow cycles have been stressed, and also the progressive expansion of the open field area through *yukúsi* to *modó* and the deflection of the mixed garden regrowth to shrubby and ultimately herbaceous associations. Reference has been made to the sequence of evaluation, acceptance or rejection, and adjustment characterizing the introduction of new crops or new varieties of existing crops. So the kitchen garden has been cast in an essentially experimental role in which the introductions are first tested and, if liked, either are allocated to one or other of the existing subsystems—e.g., peanuts to the open fields, "business" crops and corn primarily to the mixed gardens—or, like coffee, result in the emergence of an entirely new garden type.

It has been suggested that the Raiapu themselves are "pathological innovators," pragmatists with their eyes set constantly on "the main chance." The changes themselves are not associated uniquely with the contact situation, and certainly not only with the external sector of the economy, although increased mobility has accelerated the rate of change and led to some curious introductions. One of the most striking of these is the agave (Maraylli-daceae), introduced by Hube employees of the Lutheran mission from the Huon Peninsula, and now largely self-propagating below about 1800m MSL, which is highly valued as a source of fiber for making string bags. Another development, the progressive deflection of the mixed garden fallows and increasing use of *Casuarina* as artificial cover, can probably be linked with Flenley's (1967:309)

193

findings. Using radiocarbon dating and palynological techniques he established that c. 100–300 BP "there was an acceleration of forest decline accompanied by a dramatic rise in *Casuarina oligodon* . . . and of *Trema* 2752 cf. *amboinensis* and *Dodonaea viscosa* at Lake Birip." Culturally this important development could have been precipitated as much by an increasing scarcity of timber as by the declining fertility status of the mixed garden soils.

All these processes demonstrate that any suggestion of immutablity of the subsistence system is quite untenable. Further they indicate that a useful framework in which to consider mutations is that of the "ecological niche" wherein the Raiapu are concerned to enrich and increase the productivity of their resource system but not to alter it radically. The nature of their responses to current and to predictable innovations and developments will be considered in terms of this proposition.

While all innovations are considered initially in terms of their potential utility for consumption and exchange, successful adoption is governed by certain important constraints, of land, population, technology, and management. Further, the agricultural system as a whole is influenced by cultural innovations which are not linked in any direct way to the resource system.

Among the Raiapu land is intensively cultivated. Agricultural activity is concentrated on the terrace sections and dissected valley slopes, and the main range slopes are by preference avoided. Because suitable land is scarce, cultivators are unwilling to permit removal of some of it from the subsistence cycle without any parallel reduction in subsistence requirements. Yet this is what commercial cropping, at least initially, requires, so accentuating existing pressures.

The general pressure on resources is aggravated by an expanding population. The Bureau of Statistics (1967a) calculates the average annual rate of increase in the Wapenamanda area (community 7) to be 1.92 percent inclusive of nondependents ("absentees other than children away at school in the same District"). While this figure is below the Wabag survey area average of 2.33 percent, it is considerably higher than their (1967b) Chimbu figure of 1.24 percent. Within the present agricultural context pressures are therefore likely to increase and will be accentuated by improved standards of hygiene and health education. At the same time the local incidence of such pressures is already aggravated by the difficulty of conflict resolution since pacification. Information, derived from Native Death Certificates, was obtained on the cause of death of 304 persons at Immanuel Lutheran Hospital, Mambisanda, over the period 4 January 1963–18 January 1967. The results are presented in Table 34. Immanuel Lutheran

TABLE 34

CAUSES OF DEATH IN MAMBISANDA HOSPITAL PATIENTS
(4 January 1963–18 January 1967)

Cause	Up to 1 yr.		1–14 yrs.		Over 15 yrs.	
	No.	%	No.	%	No.	%
Respiratory infections	51	46.8	18	19.6	15	14.6
Alimentary infections	14	12.8	43	46.7	15	14.6
Childbirth, birth injuries, etc.	19	17.4	. . .	. . .	3	2.9
Malnutrition	4	3.7	5	5.4	1	1.0
External virus infections	4	3.7	7	7.6	10	9.7
Heart diseases	8	7.3	3	3.3	10	9.7
Liver cirrhosis	1	0.9	. . .	. . .	12	11.6
Malaria	. . .	. . .	5	5.4	2	1.9
Tumors/malignancies	. . .	. . .	3	3.3	19	18.4
Other	8	7.3	8	8.7	16	15.5
Total	109	99.9	92	100.0	103	99.9

is the principal hospital serving the Tchak, middle and lower Lai, and Minyamp valleys but there is considerable variation in the degree to which specific health matters are brought to its attention. As yet few children are born there and only a very few injuries and hepatitis cases come to its notice, but a high proportion of respiratory and alimentary infections reach the hospital.[1] The data cannot, therefore, be treated as representative of the population at large, but they do provide some indication of its health status.

Alimentary infections are a major cause of death in all age groups. The most prevalent of these, *Enteritis necroticans*, which is obtained from eating infected pigmeat, accounted for 47 percent of hospital deaths among children. Significantly it is they who are given the internal organs to roast and consume themselves while

1. J. McArthur, senior medical officer, Immanual Lutheran Hospital, personal communication.

the parents cook the rest of the animal in earth ovens for subsequent distribution. Respiratory infections from exposure and the smoke-filled houses are also a common cause, accounting for 47 percent of infants' deaths. Among adults liver cirrhosis, tumors, and malignancies are common. Malnutrition does not appear to be an important immediate cause of death, unlike the Chimbu where it accounted for 27 percent of hospital deaths among 0–5 year olds during 1954–56 (Venkatachalam, 1962:26). However, liver cirrhosis could well be a product of continuing protein deficiency, and susceptibility to alimentary infections would increase for the same reasons (pp. 23–24, 77–78).

Generally speaking, the mortality pattern would suggest that protein intake may be inadequate although it is comparatively high for the Highlands.[2] More important, from the demographic point of view, is the fact that many of the recognized and assumed causes of death could be remedied through appropriate health education and improved housing. This would lead to an accelerated rate of expansion in the population and, therefore, to an intensification of the pressure on resources. Already an increasing Raiapu awareness of health hazards is indicated by their willingness to bring *Enteritis necroticans* and pneumonia cases to the hospital and, among the women, to deliver their babies in the presence of a qualified nurse. Finally there is a considerable self-awareness of being "meat-hungry," and so a desire to increase protein intake and enjoy a more adequate diet.

Farm management problems are introduced by the cultivation of perennial tree crops, such as coffee, side by side with the annual root crops. At the level of the individual farmstead this may simply involve a rationalization of land and labor. However, an upper limit to the area under cultivation is imposed by a technology where, apart from a substitution of steel for stone tools, there has been no radical departure in type and therefore no commensurate increase in productivity. At the group level serious management problems may follow a rapid expansion in commercial cropping where, for instance, it is necessary to regulate the movements of pigs. Brown and Brookfield (1967:143) describe an instance among the Chimbu:

2. But see p. 123. The difference may well be accounted for by the unrepresentativeness of hospital deaths.

. . . the development of a coffee belt in the heart of the enclosed block drew an increasing proportion of the labour and
interests of families away from the fringes. Fences were neglected,
and breached by hungry pigs. To combat the problems that arose,
long avenues of unenclosed land, leading deeply into the enclosed
block, were recreated after 1962. . . . A . . . consequence is
that a much greater length of fence now has to be maintained,
and new breaches led to increasingly frequent change in fence
lines in 1964 and 1965, and to the abandonment of a large garden area in the north, formerly highly valued as sweet potato
land.

A wide range of organizational problems has followed from
contact which, while not directly related, have consequences that
impinge on the agricultural system. Pacification has led to a geographical expansion of the *tée* and the participation of more individuals in each ceremony. Yet there have been no parallel developments in the power structure to facilitate the efficient functioning of the cycle. Individual *kamógo* are able to prevent its
progress, by withholding their pigs, but not to accelerate it. The
tée is therefore becoming increasingly difficult to "manage," delays are extended and frequent, and in the last cycle a split developed between opposing banks of the lower Lai where an interval
of two years elapsed between both branches passing through Sabakamádá. Pig populations are not only substantially larger but tend
to be maintained at a high level for longer, with commensurate
demands on agricultural resources.

The emergence of *kitisenáda* and the concentration of christians
around churches has, to some extent, disrupted the rational arrangement of settlement and land use. Open field areas tend to
become more fragmented and some of the houses are located well
within the fence-lines. At the individual farmstead level the consequences have not been too serious since most converts to christianity have hitherto been poor people, unmarried or monogamous,
with few or no pigs of their own. However, at the group level
stresses analogous to those associated with coffee in the Chimbu
emerge and the general pressure on open field land is accentuated.
Interestingly those of the Lutheran faith have used the authority
of their adopted institution, the Wabag Lutheran Church, to
condemn the *tée* as well as the practice of polygyny.

It is from this perspective that specific innovations can best be
considered. Among commercial crops, *Pyrethrum* cultivation on

the Sabakamádá terrace sections was abandoned within two years of establishment, in part because it utilized the valuable open field land. However, peanuts[3] continue to be grown since the crop is readily rotated with sweet potatoes. During the same two years there has been a rapid expansion in "business" crops (particularly lettuce, tomatoes, peas, and beans), which are readily intercultivated with mixed and kitchen garden crops and also play a limited role in the Raiapu diet. Further they are planted from seed, as are *Solanum nigrum* and *Amaranthus tricolor*, and readily acquire the status of female crops. Between July 1964 and October 1966 Waso Ltd's total monthly purchases of lettuce, tomatoes, peas, and beans increased from 2180kg to 7130kg. Most are grown in the middle Lai and Tchak valleys.

The choice of commercial crops is also influenced by economic considerations, of returns to labor and methods of capital formation. *Pyrethrum* was ultimately rejected because the average 0.04ha holding grossed an annual return of only about four dollars on the Sabakamádá terrace sections. Returns from "business" crops are substantially higher, while additional labor requirements are minimal, and at Modópa these crops now provide the principal single source of cash income. Nevertheless much greater interest is currently being shown in coffee, despite the need for high labor inputs and additional land. The release of land following the abandonment of taro cultivation at Modópa has facilitated the establishment of coffee gardens, while increased returns to labor would follow from economies of scale and improved processing techniques.

The preference for coffee as opposed to other commercial crops is based on differences in the nature of demand within the external sector and on the fact that it more effectively promotes capital formation. "Business" crops are perishable and must be sold as soon as they mature. This is commonly done in small quantities which gross less than one dollar. On the occasions when it is possible to market larger quantities considerable diseconomies follow from the relatively low weight/value ratio of vegetables. Their market value ranges from about 6.4 to 17.2c per kg, and assistance is required to transport such bulky crops, this being normally reciprocated by a

3. Partly consumed and partly hawked in ten-cent bundles at Kumbasakama.

payment from the money received. For example, one Modópa resident received $10.00 for eight string-bag loads of lettuce, yet was obliged to give $6.00 to those who had helped him carry it to the point of sale. Finally, there is no assurance of sale, because the supply of vegetables fluctuates considerably from season to season, with considerable overproduction following the establishment of mixed gardens.

The market value of parchment coffee is 46.2c per kg and, to the Raiapu, there appears to be no limit to demand. Since parchment is easily stored it is often held in the house until the owner has a sackful to sell. This he can transport alone and it may yield as much as $10.00. The mean value of ten coffee sales by Modópa residents was $3.82 compared with only 92c for 147 vegetable sales.

The Raiapu feel considerable need for monetary capital to invest in vehicles, trade stores, and other commercial enterprises, and for use in the settlement of disputes and ceremonial prestations. Given the greater facility for its accumulation from the sale of coffee it is likely that holdings will continue to increase and, in the absence of unenclosed land on the terrace sections, result in the displacement of the kitchen gardens adjacent to the residences.

The rapid development of interest in cattle-raising and "making business" with pigmeat among the Raiapu also reflects the profitability of these enterprises. A steer purchased from DASF for $30.00 and slaughtered after eighteen months will realize about $300.00 when sold in quantities of 1kg or less. Similarly a small pig, weighing perhaps 15–20kg, butchered and cooked with bananas and greens, will gross anywhere between $10.00 and $30.00. The latter innovation dates back only to about 1960, when "making business" was introduced to the Minyamp from Mount Hagen, but it has spread rapidly through the central Enga culture area without any apparent opposition to the idea of selling primarily to kinsmen.[4] Cattle-raising is an even more recent development dating back to about 1964. As yet there are only sixteen stocked projects in the Wapenamanda area, none of them at Sabakamádá, but there is already a two-year waiting list for cattle from individuals who have established the necessary facilities. Paddocks are nor-

4. This contrasts with the Orokaiva where considerable opposition was voiced by older people to the practice of selling meat within the "sympathy-group" (Waddell and Krinks, 1968:119).

mally located on the largely unutilized *Miscanthus* and *Imperata* grasslands and there would appear to be some capacity for expansion on the gentler slopes of the main ranges. Raiapu views of the utility of cattle nevertheless are at variance with those of the DASF. With a "meat-hungry" population the very high return on initial investment from slaughtering after only a few months of fattening results in the Raiapu losing sight of the original objective of breeding cattle.

The development of a monetary economy has stimulated some people to move into the external sector in search of permanent employment. These are the *nai akári* ("new men"), youths who have received some education and are generally disdainful of traditional dress and the pattern of living it represents. As a social type they can be distinguished from indentured laborers who are generally absent for only a few years before returning to reside with their natal groups. Most are employed in the Wabag subdistrict, by Waso Ltd, the missions, and the Administration, but some have found their way to Mount Hagen or are receiving further education outside the district. As yet there are probably only a few hundred such people but they serve as a standard to which many boys aspire, regardless of the capacity of the external sector to accommodate them.

While agricultural developments at the group territory level are conditioned to a very large degree by the pre-existing resource system, more general developments in the social and political spheres are rapidly outgrowing the Raiapu capacity of regulation. These new developments, as have been indicated, can have serious repercussions on the agricultural system. One possibility is that new institutions might be granted certain regulatory powers. For instance during 1966 draft rulings were before both Wabag and Wapenamanda local government councils that were designed to speed the progress of the *tée* and prosecute any individuals found to be responsible for delays. Alternatively, interest in the traditional mechanisms for enhancing individual and group prestige may decline at the expense of increasing investment in vehicles and trade stores. Given the facility with which capital can be accumulated through commercial cropping and the sale of fresh meat, such a trend would be more in harmony with the effective management of the Raiapu resource system. Because of the emergence of new political structures, notably the Wabag Lutheran

Church, the local government councils, and the House of Assembly, and of opportunities outside the realm of agriculture, the system has been altered drastically in both scope and dimension. The capacity of the local ecosystem to absorb all the new innovations without major structural change is clearly in doubt.

8. Conclusion

Regional Contrasts

THE Enga have been identified as one of four Highlands groups manifesting the widest range of technical elaboration in their agricultural systems (Brookfield, 1962). The other three are the Kapauku, Dani, and Chimbu. Each practices, either individually or collectively, "erosion control by permanent banks or walls, swamp reclamation combining main drainage systems and water-level regulation, tillage with mulching and fertilization, and the controlled grazing of livestock" (p. 252). Together the four are viewed as a series of cores with outward gradations to less intensive agricultural techniques, and the intensification process itself is seen as a local one which developed "in response first to growing population pressure and second to the greater fertility of the high-altitude soils." However, Highlands methods in general are considered more intensive than those of lowland New Guinea, which are characterized by simple shifting cultivation, and they therefore serve as a basis for recognizing a distinctive geographical region.

If another aspect of these systems is considered, a somewhat different picture emerges of Highlands agriculture: one in which the open field/mixed garden dichotomy recurs or, in its absence, distinctive crop associations within the enclosed areas where the staple, sweet potato, is segregated from the range of subsidiary crops. These distinctions are identifiable equally in the core as in the peripheral areas and are directly associated with variations in terrain. Thus the Kapauku environment contains two major terrain types: steep mountain slopes flanking flat, poorly drained valley floors (Pospisil, 1963:6–10). Different agricultural methods are

202

CONCLUSION 203

linked with each. On the mountain slopes sweet potatoes are cultivated by means of simple shifting cultivation, where one crop is followed by an eight- to twelve-year fallow. On the valley floor both "intensive shifting cultivation" and "intensive complex cultivation" are practiced, the one characterized by clearing and some ditching, and the other by turning the soil to form a series of rectangular beds each demarcated by a network of drainage ditches. In the first the sweet potato is grown in association with a variety of cultigens ("sugar cane, taro, bananas, several types of greens, cucumbers, gourds, and native beans") and a garden is cultivated "several times in a sequence before it must revert to fallow land." In the second the sweet potato is grown only in association with introduced root crops (manioc and Irish potatoes) and a green (*Amaranthus hybridus*), and plots are cultivated "almost indefinitely." Finally the Kapauku also maintain kitchen gardens adjacent to their houses for cultivating a range of minor traditional and introduced crops.

The Dugum Dani, who inhabit the edge of the Grand Valley (Balim), also have several types of gardens (Heider, 1970:33–42): "the extensive ditched gardens on the low, level floor of the Grand Valley; the gardens at the compounds; and the hill slope gardens." The second are simply small plots of land within, or at the entrance to, the residential compounds, which are devoted to bananas, tobacco, gourds, and a few other vegetables. In effect they are the kitchen gardens of the Kapauku and the Raiapu. More important are the other two. The ditched gardens are the source of most of the food, with sweet potato as the predominant crop, and some taro and yams being grown in association with it. They are intensively cultivated: the soil is tilled and is fertilized with mud removed from the complex network of ditches, and planting cycles are interrupted by grass fallows. The third type, on the hill slopes, are "classic slash-and-burn gardens" where one or two crops are planted prior to long forest fallows. Sweet potatoes are of secondary importance to taro and cucumber, and a range of other crops, such as yams and sugarcane, is also intercultivated.

The Chimbu differ from the other core areas in that, although two types of plots are identified in addition to the kitchen gardens, similar cultivation techniques are applied to both (Brookfield and Brown, 1963:43–54). Sweet potatoes are grown in association with corn but apart from a wide range of subsidiary crops that are intercultivated with one another. Either complete tillage or grid-iron ditching is practiced, in which four or five plantings may be made on a single site prior to fallowing, and one crop association sometimes follows on the other. Fallows are controlled, with *Casuarina* deliberately planted, and on the best ground the cultivation period at least equals the fallow.

This general pattern of internal diversity is repeated throughout the Highlands. The primary distinction among the Kakoli of the upper Kaugel Valley is between "quasi-permanent sweet potato mound fields" which are "characterized by near absence of interplanting," and "mixed vegetable gardens" cleared from forest regrowth and planted only once prior to fallowing (Bowers, 1965b: 17). Similarly the Sina Sina distinguish sweet potato and mixed gardens: the first are predominant and devoted exclusively to the staple while the second include most other food plants (Hughes, 1966). The ground is completely tilled in both cases and short *Casuarina* fallows are typical.

Examples are abundant and further iteration is scarcely necessary. On the basis of them one can, broadly speaking, identify two types of agricultural systems within the areas of close settlement. In one there is a very high degree of intensification, and often effective permanency, in the cultivation of the staple, but this is paralleled by casual, extensive cultivation of the subsidiary crops. In the other there is a general, but lower, degree of intensification through the system as a whole: all gardens are fallowed but the cover is controlled rather than natural. Both types occur in association with a predominantly grassland environment and in both cases large, dependent pig populations are maintained. However, the first appears to be restricted largely to those groups having access to deep, naturally fertile soils—to terrace sections (the Raiapu), river bottomlands (the Kakoli), and broad, level plains (the Kapauku and Dani). Elsewhere the terrain is much more dissected, and topsoils are presumably thinner and more unstable. In such places all agricultural land is fallowed, but the duration of the fallow is effectively reduced.

Individual systems emerge, in these terms, as essentially dynamic phenomena. The frequency of *Casuarina* planting is increasing visibly, partly as a result of pacification but also in all probability due to declining forest resources and reduced fallow periods. Subsystems disappear, as, for instance, taro gardens among the Raiapu and the Kakoli; others, notably cash-crop gardens, emerge and systems adjust to integrate them. In the higher altitudes the forest edge continues to retreat before an advancing, but in some respects "hollow," frontier to be replaced by a successional grassland of a much reduced agricultural value. At Sirunki low night temperatures preclude the cultivation of a wide range of subsidiary crops and the mound field is the only important garden type, but elsewhere the interdependence of the several subsystems within the context of a deflected vegetational succession is readily apparent. Among the Kakoli the quasi-permanent mound fields and mixed vegetable gardens, together with settlement, are concentrated at 2200–2250m MSL in the valley bottom adjacent to the Kaugel River, but about 450m upslope and 1,800m distance is a garden strip bordering on the primary forest. This strip is cultivated according to a "crop-and-abandon method" in which a site is planted from three to five times with intervening short fallows prior to the termination of all agricultural activity. As it advances the forest is gradually replaced by *Miscanthus floridus* grassland, which in turn dominates the zone separating the two areas of agricultural activity and serves to a very limited extent as an agricultural frontier for the more intensive subsystems of the bottomlands.

Within this dynamic framework kitchen gardens provide the medium for evaluating new crops. To a large degree it is the recent innovations which are planted in them, particularly tobacco but also "business" crops among the Raiapu, and manioc and Irish potatoes among the Kapauku. If demand is sufficient and ecological conditions appropriate the innovations are eventually accommodated into one of the major subsystems, or a new one is evolved. Otherwise they continue to be grown on a small scale in the kitchen gardens.

From a regional perspective the particular form that agricultural intensification assumes among the Raiapu is seen to be an essentially local adaptation.[1] However, the general nature of their re-

1. The practice of mounding and associated mulching is not of course unique to the New Guinea Highlands. It has been reported in several parts of Africa and Latin America, admittedly generally in association with poor drainage conditions. Denevan (1966), in seeking to elucidate the aboriginal earthworks and drainage features of the Llanos de Mojos, Bolivia, discusses the phenomena of ridge and mound cultivation, causeways, and habitation mounds as found in other parts of the world.

sponse to the Highland environment is in no sense unique. Most
of the groups segregate the staple from the subsidiary crops within
their gardens, and this is paralleled in three of the four core areas,
as well as in some of the peripheral, by a subdivision into open
field and mixed garden. The one is characterized by intensive tillage and the other by casual planting and natural or controlled
secondary growth fallows. Such a development is a feature of many
agricultural societies. The Tallensi of northern Ghana operate both
"home-farms" and "bush-farms," the former around the house,
under annual cultivation and fertilized with manure, and the latter at some distance and involving simple shifting cultivation
(Hunter, 1967). Somewhat similar was the European run-rig system practiced in the Celtic fringe and parts of north Germany
and Scandinavia until the seventeenth and eighteenth centuries
(Houston, 1953:54–56). This comprised two elements, an infield
of arable land which was manured and continuously cropped, and
an outfield of pasture, parts of which were enclosed from time to
time. In each case the former is commonly viewed as a development of the latter—a process of intensification that is designed
to maximize production on a limited area and compensate for a
degradation of the environment or inherent infertility of the soils.

The Evolution of Highlands Agriculture

A consideration of the synchronic data inevitably leads to specu-
lation on the problem of agricultural evolution in the Highlands.
Diversity within systems and, at the same time, the general parallelisms between them are suggestive of the kinds of processes that
have been, and to some extent still are, operative at the regional
level. But in addition to this they also lead to tentative propositions
as to why intensification has occurred.

Controversy over the origin and development of Highlands agriculture springs from the fact that the current staple, the sweet
potato, is believed to have been introduced to New Guinea only
after the fifteenth century. Two radically different positions have
been assumed: the one, developed primarily by Watson (1965a, b),
postulates an Ipomoean revolution, and the other, largely summarized by Brookfield and White (1968) but also implied by
Clarke (1966), argues for a much slower evolution or succession.
Watson's "revolution" is characterized by the rapid and widespread development of intensive agriculture and an "explosive"

growth of population, prior to which only "intermittent" cultivation existed. He bases his argument on the casual techniques currently associated with the cultivation of a number of subsidiary crops that are presumed to be of greater antiquity in the Highlands—taro (*Colocasia*), *Pueraria lobata*, and sugarcane especially —and, extending ideas first suggested by Bulmer and Bulmer (1964:47) and Brookfield (1964:21–22), postulates an "association between pre-ipomoean and non-ipomoean methods of cultivation" (1965a:298). In support of this argument he invokes a wide range of ethnological data: the recency of *Casuarina* planting, the close association of domestic pigs with a sedentary life and with sweet potato cultivation, the absence of any ritual or magical interest in the sweet potato compared with the earlier crops, and a number of structural, ideological, and material features that are considered to indicate the recency of "nonsedentary bands in the Central Highlands" (p. 303). Heider (1967) has recently come out in support of Watson's interpretation in recognizing a range of "archaic elements" in Dani culture. Specifically he proposes that "there are many aspects of Dani culture which seem more appropriate to a mobile hunting and gathering, rather than an intensive horticultural, way of life" (p. 833).

In their seminar report Brookfield and White (1968) point to the continuities, social as well as agricultural, that exist between Highland and lowland New Guinea. They further indicate that the linguistic and demographic material suggest slow, irregular growth within the Highlands over a long period of time. But the most conclusive support for an "evolutionary interpretation" of agriculture is provided by diachronic evidence from a series of prehistoric dug ditches discovered at an altitude of 1600m MSL in the Wahgi Valley near Mount Hagen. This site has been reported more fully by Golson et al. (1967). A number of artifacts were found within the ditches and a radiocarbon date of $2,300 \pm 120$ years before 1950 was obtained for part of a digging stick removed from the earliest of a series of three ditches. Portions of gourd (*Lagenaria siceraria*) exocarp were also found. The authors note that "the excavated site can be closely compared to the implements and practices of dry land sweet potato cultivation in the area," and conclude that "the site could be reasonably interpreted then as a stratified series of old agricultural systems that had at some stage been abandoned and reverted to swamp" (pp. 369–70).

In summarizing the available evidence, Brookfield and White (1968:50–51) postulate that "the introduction of the sweet potato might cease to be of major relevance to the development of agricultural methods in the New Guinea Highlands." Rather there followed "some empirical modification of already evolved techniques, some shifts in population, and especially an expansion into areas of higher altitude—a process that is still continuing in some parts." Clarke (1966), likewise drawing on synchronic evidence, also ascribes no great significance to the introduction of the sweet potato for his suggested process of agricultural intensification. Instead he sees the development as a direct response to population growth and a consequent deterioration in the environment. Following Boserup (1965), he does not consider this process to be a voluntary one as it is paralleled by a decrease in the output of food per unit of labor and an increasingly monotonous diet: in sum the "quality of human life" deteriorates.

It is apparent that the positions, as represented by Watson on the one hand and Brookfield and White on the other, are not wholly incompatible. The type of revolution that Watson proposes could well have occurred above about 1850m MSL where alternative tuberous crops to the sweet potato mature only very slowly, if at all. Thus in the upper Kaugel Valley, where the lowest zone of settlement is at 2200m MSL on the bottomlands, Bowers' (1968:242–52) proposition that forest recession on the hill slopes has been restricted to the last two hundred years, following the introduction of the sweet potato and the practice of mounding, appears quite acceptable. The proposition itself is based on rough calculations of the present rate of forest recession and it allows for lower estimated populations. She suggests that prior to the innovation of "quasi-permanent mound fields," the Kakoli practiced bush fallowing now typical only of the mixed vegetable gardens, and taro was the major cultivated food.

Bowers' speculative succession appears in general terms to be appropriate to the situation at Sabakamádá and, by extension, to the Raiapu as a whole. Forest resources are scarce and surviving areas on the ridge-tops are no longer cleared for agricultural purposes. However, the main range slopes separating the forest from the intensively cultivated terrace sections are dominated by what are considered to be agriculturally valueless *Miscanthus* and *Imperata* grasslands. Although these are now used only for pig-grazing, informants made repeated reference to the fact that extensive taro gardens were formerly made on the slopes, and that the taro was intercultivated with sweet potatoes and sugarcane. One can speculate that the gardens were operated on a simple shifting cultivation basis and that a gradual shortening in the fallow period resulted in the elimination of secondary growth and its replacement by grassland.

Resolution of the general problem of the origins and development of Highlands agriculture must await further diachronic evidence, particularly in so far as the rate of change is concerned. However, a reappraisal of the synchronic evidence in terms of the systems approach that has been adopted to Raiapu agricultural practices does facilitate the development of some of Clarke's ideas concerning the processes and circumstances of intensification, as well as suggesting ways in which other ethnological phenomena may be causally related to such intensification.

On the basis of regional contrasts and the internal diversity characteristic of individual systems it is postulated that the intensive practices characteristic of the open fields have developed from the more casual mixed gardening with its natural, secondary regrowth, fallow. Thus simple shifting cultivation may, initially, have been practiced by Highlands societies. However, an expanding population and a slow rate of forest regeneration resulted in a progressive deflection of the natural vegetation to a grassland disclimax unsuited to this type of agriculture. Equilibrium within the ecosystem was restored, and at the same time the general level of production increased, by segregating the staple from the subsidiary crops and evolving special techniques for its cultivation. These techniques of intensive cultivation resulted in the substitution of labor for land as a major factor in production by reducing per capita land requirements for sweet potato. This in turn released additional land for the subsidiary crops and enabled the fallow to be lengthened to a period sufficient for the establishment of secondary regrowth. While the open field subsystem adjusted to continued growth in pig and human populations by increasing the area under cultivation and by more permanent use (through mulching and composting), pressures redeveloped in the mixed gardening subsystem and have been intensified since the onset of commercial cropping. Fallow periods tended to decline once more, but this was compensated by an increasing trend towards the planting of *Casuarina* and so the development of a "controlled" fallow, rather than to more general tillage of the soil.

While intensification is in part a response to an expanding human population, an essential concomitant is undoubtedly the large, dependent pig populations. The broad agricultural sequence is perhaps paralleled by another, a trend from nucleated through a relatively unstable stage to a stable, dispersed settlement pattern. It is postulated that dispersal occurs in response to the development of refined agronomic techniques and the increasing concentration of activity within the open fields. Finally the Highlands environment itself can be considered as having facilitated this process of intensification. On the one hand its soils are naturally relatively fertile and, under the lower temperatures, can be assumed to experience a slower fertility decline due to prolonged cropping than those of the surrounding lowlands. On the other the progressive deflection from forest to grassland, consequent upon increasing agricultural activity, is paralleled by diminishing plant and animal resources potentially available to the hunter and food-gatherer and this, in turn, increases the Highlanders' dependence on agricultural production.

The available synchronic and diachronic evidence can, with few exceptions, be interpreted in terms of this speculative sequence. Among the less intensive of the two types of agricultural systems already identified earlier in this chapter, pig and human population densities tend to be comparatively low, settlement is nucleated, and there is a high degree of cooperation involved in establishing new gardens. Thus among the Siane (Salisbury, 1962, 1964), in the Goroka valley (Howlett, 1962), and in the Kainantu-Aiyura area (Schindler, 1952; Powell, personal communication) the soil is only lightly tilled and worked into small mounds similar to the Raiapu *yukúsi*, although shallow ditches may also be dug. Gardens are generally only planted once, and ten to fifteen years may elapse prior to recultivation. The pig to human ratio probably does not exceed 1:2 and the animals derive most of their sustenance from foraging.[2] Population densities are of the order of

2. Korofeigu provides an important exception to this ratio. Here the ratio is estimated to be 3:1, but the animals are used to reciprocate for food received from other tribes on the occasion of recurring shortages consequent upon local droughts. Notably the large numbers of pigs held have resulted in severe over-grazing and sheet erosion (Howlett, 1962:171–72).

30/km² and distribution assumes the form of villages of fifty to over two hundred persons. New garden areas are cleared jointly, "by several men" in the Goroka valley (Howlett, 1962:74) and by "ward groups" who "synchronise" their activities throughout the clan among the Siane (Salisbury, 1962:16). That is, only after some or all of the residents of a village have jointly cleared and fenced garden areas as large as 4ha are they subdivided into individual holdings.

In the three core areas which manifest a clear distinction between open field and mixed garden—Raiapu Enga, Dani, and Kapauku—population densities are much higher, averaging 60–100/km², and large numbers of pigs are supported primarily on the staple food. Karl Heider (personal communication) estimates a pig to human ratio of 3:1 among the Dugum Dani prior to a major pig festival, which compares with my estimated Raiapu optimum of 3.3:1. Furthermore, among the latter, pigs consume almost two-thirds of the sweet potatoes produced. A similar degree of dependence is suggested for the Kapauku, where "grown animals are fed sweet potatoes twice a day" (Pospisil, 1963:11). In some respects the increased focusing of labor and interests in the open fields results in a marked individualization of activity, since the stabilization of fence-lines and minimization of clearing reduces the need for cooperation between households. The remarkably stable, dispersed pattern of settlement and close proximity of residence to garden among the Raiapu and such other Western Highlands District groups as the Medlpa and Kakoli reflects both this individualization and the need to exercise more effective control over the large pig populations.

Kapauku and Dani settlement is, however, nucleated, with villages of about 120 persons characteristic of the former and "compound clusters" of about 50 among the latter. In the Dani case these are relatively unstable groups where "perhaps as few as 30% of the population remains in the same compound for longer than a few months" (Heider, 1967:836). Heider (personal communication) views this instability primarily as a mechanism for "conflict resolution" and, although the circumstances are not known, suggests that it is also indicative of a desire to obtain better grazing for pigs. It has already been observed (see p. 187) that nucleation may be ill-suited to high population pressure on resources, particularly where large numbers of pigs are supported, and a high degree of residential instability among the Kapauku and Dani may be indicative of this. On the other hand one can speculate that nucleation persists in these two core areas because of the need to generate large work groups for at least one open field task—creating and rebuilding the deep drainage ditches (which average 1–2m deep and 2–5m wide). These ditches readily choke with weeds and rushes and the sides collapse, and, in addition to their having to be maintained between plantings, mud and litter are removed from them and spread over the gardens as fertilizer. Mathiessen (1962: 28) reports of twenty or more men participating in such an activity, which differs markedly from the individualistic approach to open field work adopted in other high density areas.

The fourth core area, the Chimbu, does not fit easily into the postulated evolutionary sequence. In spite of population densities averaging 138/km², dispersed settlement, and a marked individualization of agricultural activity, open field location is less fixed than in the other core areas, and no distinctive agricultural techniques are associated with the cultivation of the sweet potato. Instead there is a general but lower degree of intensification throughout the system. Two possible explanations may be provided for the failure of the true open field to emerge: first, differences in terrain, and second, a lower pig population. With the exception of the west Chimbu, there are only very restricted level surfaces with well-developed topsoils. Instead the main zone of settlement is characterized by a series of spurs and valleys and of rubble-flows and landslip areas at the foot of a precipitous limestone escarpment (Brookfield and Brown, 1963: Chap. 4). Slopes are variable and the soils fairly unstable and subject to slipping. Gardens may therefore require frequent fallowing. On the other hand, overall pressures on land may be somewhat less because of fewer livestock and their seemingly reduced dependence on cultivated foods. The pig to human ratio averages about 1.5:1 and the animals consume an estimated "15 to 25 percent of the harvest of a [sweet potato] garden in full production. . . . [However] In old gardens a much higher proportion of the total crop is used in this way" (p. 58).[3]

The Chimbu system may, alternatively, be viewed as a slightly

3. However, Brookfield (personal communication) advises that this estimate is based on a low stage in the pig cycle.

different response to similar constraints since a general but lower level of intensification results in per capita land requirements that compare favorably with those of the Raiapu. The general Highlands process probably commenced at relatively low population densities and, according to the archaeological evidence, intensive cultivation already manifested itself over two thousand years ago. Apart from an expansion of agricultural activity into higher altitudes, the introduction of the sweet potato is likely to have resulted in a greatly increased capacity to support pigs and therefore also in some expansion in the open field area. Although it is not possible to establish whether they were domestic or wild, the animals have certainly been in the Highlands since 5000 BP (Bulmer, 1966). However, numbers were probably small under pre-ipomoean conditions since the most likely staple, taro, is not greatly favored by them except when cooked. In the circumstances the labor required to support pigs would have been higher than at present.

Available palynological and ethnobotanical evidence tend to support the general intensification hypothesis. Flenley (1967:308–9) reports that forest reduction in the middle Lai Valley commenced about 2000 BP, but only between 100 and 300 BP did this accelerate, being accompanied by a marked rise in *Casuarina* and also *Trema amboinensis* and *Dodonaea viscosa*. Notably all three trees are characteristic of either controlled or relatively short fallows in this area. They are not associated in any way with the open fields, and this recent development may therefore be inferred as reflecting increased pressures on the mixed garden subsystem only.

The process of intensification is seen as self-perpetuating in that the gradual conversion of forest to nonforest vegetation necessitates increasing dependence on cultivated as distinct from wild resources. Straatmans (1967), drawing on the available ethnobotanical material, demonstrates the consequences of this anthropogenic succession for the Highlands food-gatherer. Of twenty utilizable genera found in the "virgin forest stage" only one survives to the "short-grass disclimax." To this another five are added, giving a total of six genera or an overall decline of 70 percent through the succession (p. 17).

The object of this speculative exercise in agricultural evolution has been to provide a developmental framework within which to handle the uniformities and differences of Highlands agricultural systems. I have been encouraged to theorize because of the "experimental situation" provided where there are considerable environmental and cultural parallelisms through a large area and population. Because of distinctiveness and relative isolation of the region within Melanesia, there exists the compelling belief that its agricultural systems can be viewed as primarily local adaptations. And it is in terms of this premise that the problem of intensification has been considered.

Agricultural Systems, Ecology, and Evolution

The primary objective of this study has been to describe and interpret the Raiapu Enga agricultural system in such a way as to indicate the sorts of processes that are operative within it. Identification of these processes has, in turn, permitted reasoned assessments to be made about historic as well as future changes. But, more important, an attempt has been made to move beyond a "natural history" approach to cultural ecology, which is concerned simply to identify the specific features of a single system, to a consideration of other systems, and so to comparison and generalization at the regional level. This step has required the simplification of Raiapu agricultural practices to a very low level, specifically to distinguishing mixed gardens from open fields as distinctive subsystems, and to establishing causal relationships in terms of these. The analysis as a whole has been founded on a conception of agriculture as, on the one hand, an integral part of the environment in which it is practiced, and, on the other, the system of livelihood of both a local and a regional population. Further, social and political characteristics of these populations have been assumed to function as mechanisms by which the adaptation is managed. Thus agricultural practices provide the point of entry whence the whole Raiapu ecological system is explored. Anthropologically such a strategy may be considered a sound one for, as Meggers (1954:802) has observed, "The primary point of interaction between a culture and its environment is in terms of subsistence, and the most vital aspect of environment from the point of view of culture is its suitability for food production." Finally, within the New Guinea Highlands this approach to both society and environment is deemed particularly appropriate in view of the almost total dependence of economic systems on cultivated plants and the sophistication that has been achieved in agricultural practices with so simple a tool kit as the digging stick and hand axe.

Information was obtained initially through surveys of the agricultural holdings of a number of households within a local group. A range of data covering general location (terrain), slope, technology (crops, methods of ground preparation, cultivation cycle, etc.), distance from residence, tenurial status, mode of operation and yields, were gathered about each. Using these criteria in association with the Raiapu categorization of garden types, the individual holdings were grouped into a series of subsystems. This information was then considered in relation to data on the overall activity patterns of the adult members of the households and to the ecological evaluation of specific agricultural practices. Finally, more general ethnographic material was incorporated in the analysis, concerning such matters as population size, density, and distribution; social structure; leadership; male-female relationships; ceremonial life; and so forth.

From the whole emerges a view of the Raiapu man-environment system as a pyramidlike structure made up of three distinct but interacting operational levels (see Fig. 22). These are termed natural ecology, generalized adaptation, and individual manipulation. The first comprises the biological resources on which the Raiapu subsist—pigs, sweet potatoes, and the subsidiary crops— and the physical environmental constraints that operate on these —primarily frost and flooding rains. The second encompasses the general manner in which Raiapu local groups, qua populations, exploit these biological resources in order to maximize productivity and minimize risk, while at the same time coping with the pressures on such resources and on available land as determined by the continuing growth in numbers. Significant aspects of the generalized adaptation include the distinctive patterns of distribution and residential organization of population, the system of land tenure and notional stress on agnation, the division of labor between the sexes, and, most important perhaps, the segregation of the staple from the subsidiary crops and the application of distinctive cultivation techniques to each. Agnation here emerges as a mechanism by means of which intensive agriculture is possible within the framework of an inherently unstable political system. In effect, by defining a territory in descent group terms, it serves to bind loyalties to land rather than to individuals, hence giving a degree of continuity over time and space that is not provided by the political leaders of a quasi-anarchic society, and yet which is essential to the practice of open field agriculture.

The third operational level in the man-environment system serves to indicate the fact that individuals manipulate the overall adapta-

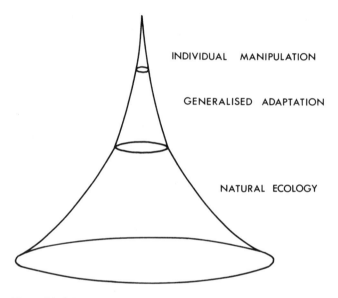

Figure 22. Schematic representation of the structure of the Raiapu man-environment system

tion for personal political gain. Among the Raiapu wealth is founded primarily in agricultural production, and power is achieved largely through the manipulation of the flow of this wealth between individuals and between groups. Hence "big-men" achieve and strengthen their position through careful agricultural planning, in which culturally determined limitations on both the availability of and access to open fields lead to major inequalities in levels of production of the staple food within the local group. These, in turn, result in interhousehold variations in the numbers of pigs supported, and therefore in the opportunities of adult males for marriage. Consequently, the chances of an individual engaging in such economically and politically remunerative activities as the production of luxury crops and the *tée* are also directly affected. Finally, the solution that the powerful offer the impotent, of incorporating them in their households, is a measure that largely benefits the former. The "big-man" thereby increases the size of the labor force at his disposal and the surplus production that he directly controls, in return for protecting the "rubbish-man" from likely public ridicule and isolation.

The distinction between open fields and mixed gardens, however, provides more than the key to an understanding of the Raiapu ecosystem, for it also offers clues as to the evolution of the present intensive system and of Highlands agriculture generally. It serves as a means of crosscultural analysis and, thereby, as a basis for assessing the present understanding of the circumstances and processes of agricultural intensification.

The omnipresence of slash-and-burn cultivation (mixed gardening) as an integument of agricultural systems in the Central Highlands and the association of intensive cultivation (open field agriculture) with the four core population concentrations point to both the prior origin of the former and the interpretation of the latter as a response to increasing pressure on resources and progressive environmental modification. A range of incidental evidence has been presented in support of this proposition, including an experiment designed to establish the relationship between soil fertility and cultivation practices (Clarke and Street, 1967), observations on the contemporary dynamics of Kakoli agriculture (Bowers, 1965b), and palynological evidence for vegetational changes in the Lai Valley (Flenley, 1967). However, while a close relationship between population density and agricultural intensification is indicated, the data that have been presented do not lend themselves to a simple Boserupian-type interpretation of this latter. Boserup's (1965) thesis is, essentially, that the more intensive the agricultural system the lower the productivity of labor. Hence major technical innovations only occur when it becomes necessary to increase output to compensate for the deterioration in yields that occurs in response to increasing population pressure on resources. In sum, intensification is conceived of as essentially an involuntary, or economically disadvantageous, process serving to prevent a fall in output and demanding progressively larger labor inputs.

The Central Highlands evidence suggests that intensification is a more complex process than that. While the data clearly demonstrate that high population densities can only be supported by intensive agriculture, on account of induced vegetational changes and limited land availability, there is little to suggest that extensive systems are inherently more productive than intensive ones. Indeed at Sabakamádá, similar yields per unit area under cultivation are obtained from the two major subsystems, while mixed gardening demands significantly higher labor inputs than open field cultivation. Furthermore *yukúsi* appears to be a more productive form of tillage than *modó*. With such conditions limited intensification should, theoretically, occur independently of population growth because it results in higher levels of productivity and more leisure time. And, in fact, one might hypothesize on the basis of the Wahgi Valley archaeological evidence (Golson et al., 1967) that just such a development did occur at very low population densities in the Central Highlands. What little evidence there is on the productivity of different tropical agricultural systems generally is conflicting, for, contrary to Boserup's assumptions, there are certainly some indications that returns to labor may be significantly higher for intensive systems (see Ho, 1968).

There is, nevertheless, one major distinction between extensive and intensive systems which most authorities recognize, and which would serve to support Boserup's evolutionary sequence if not her exact explanation for it. They have contrasting rhythms of work, with the extensive systems characterized by major fluctuations in levels of agricultural activity through time, and the intensive by sustained inputs throughout the agricultural cycle. For simple social systems, like those of the Central Highlands, the former routine has the merit of providing the majority of the population with abundant opportunity for participating in the various social and ceremonial activities which serve as the mechanisms for exchanging goods and services and acquiring political power. The latter tends to tie the majority of the population more closely to the land, hence providing the appropriate preconditions for the creation of a rural peasantry, where only a controlling minority is endowed with sufficient leisure time to become active in the social and political life of the society. Such a factor could well serve to delay intensification until demographic and environmental constraints demand it, and certainly it does serve to demonstrate the circumstances in which the social and economic differences presently characteristic of the core Highlands populations take root.

The greatest weakness in Boserup's thesis, indicated by this study of Raiapu agriculture, is its failure to account for physical and biological variables in the ecosystem. Boserup abstracts cropping systems from the environment and overlooks the significance of the types of resources exploited. She implies that absolute carrying capacities can be identified for each level of intensification. The Central Highlands information clearly indicates that this is in no sense possible. Under certain circumstances intensive cultivation develops in direct response to environmental variables, and independently of any variations in population size or density. Such is certainly the case among the Mae Enga at Sirunki, where mounding is dictated by the existence of a persistent frost hazard. Furthermore it is suggested that any general explanation for the distribution of mound cultivation among the Enga must be couched in terms of environmental variables.

Of more general significance in the Central Highlands are the ecological dictates of certain major food crops. While the sweet potato can be cultivated with little difficulty up to an altitude of c. 2700m MSL, such pre-ipomoean crops as yam and taro have a much more restricted distribution and more demanding ecological requirements. On account of this basic distinction it is postulated that the populations subsisting on these latter were largely confined to the valley bottoms at altitudes below c. 1700m MSL, and they were obliged to establish elaborate drainage systems in order to cultivate their staples. The prehistoric dug ditches of the Wahgi Valley may, thus, be interpreted as having been developed in response to the dictates of the resources exploited, which in turn served to restrict the populations to these areas. The introduction of the sweet potato served to release them from the constraints imposed by the resources and so assume a lower density distribution. Both factors permitted more extensive agricultural practices to be adopted. Re-intensification only occurred at altitudes where frost became a hazard, and once population densities increased.

In conclusion, the Central Highlands evidence indicates Boserup's population density/agricultural intensification equation requires modification in terms of the biological, and in turn the physical environmental variables. The basic issue as to whether it is an involuntary process remains, for there is little concrete evidence to suggest that productivity declines with intensification.

The only significant factor likely to discourage voluntary intensification is the greater regularity of agricultural inputs required in open field cultivation. Certainly a more complex explanation than that proposed by Boserup is required to account for the significant geographical and historical variations in adaptive strategies within the Highlands. However, further local studies are a necessary prerequisite to such enquiry, for it is only at this level that one can isolate the uniqueness and establish the regularities that are required to lead cultural ecological research toward more general theory.

Appendix 1

Characteristics of the Modópa
Sample Community

1. *Crude population structure*

	No.
Married men	7
Married women	10
Divorced/widowed men	3
Divorced/widowed women	3
Unmarried men, 15+ years	6
Unmarried women, 15+ years	5
Children, 0–14 years	11
Total	45 (21 males and 24 females)

In addition 4 unmarried men are absent in wage employment.

2. *Demographic changes*

	Feb. 1966	Births	Deaths	Arrivals	Departures	Jan. 1967	Net change
No.	45	1	1	1	4	42	−8.9%

3. *Household size*

No. of households	No. of persons Average	Range	Labor units Average	Range
10	4.5	1–11	2.9	1.0–5.9

Labor units were calculated on the following basis:

Age (in years)	5–9	10–14	15–19	20–44	45+
Males	0.1	0.3	0.8	1.0	0.8
Females	0.2	0.4	0.7	0.8	0.6

221

4. *The composition and form of households*

Composition	No. of houses in residence				Total
	1	2	3	4	
Divorcee (male)	...	2	...	...	2
ditto + dependents (both sexes)	...	1	...	...	1
Elementary family	1*	3	...	...	4
ditto + attached adult and dependent	...	1	...	...	1
Polygynous family + attached adult	...	1	...	1	2
Total no. of households	1	8		1	10

* A *kitisenáda*.

Note: Three bachelors, attached to one or other of the households, sleep in their own *patáge áda*. Two of the dependents (widows) sleep in the *kitisenáda* of a household outside the sample.

Appendix 2

Supreme Court Cases Heard at Wabag, May 1964 to October 1966

A TOTAL of 33 cases, involving 46 males, were heard over a period of 18 months. Of the 46 men, 25 were accused of intergroup feuding. The balance, 21, were accused of individual crimes, and, of these, 17 (68 percent) were charged with wilful murder (or attempted murder) of their wives or of co-respondents in a marital dispute. All but one were monogamous and, from their statements, appear to have been men of low social standing, poor and sometimes old, whose wives were constantly threatening to desert them.

The following statements are typical of those made by the accused.

1. *From near Wabag.* "She would not live with me. . . . my wife would not come back. . . . I spent my time from then on following my wife's wanderings."

2. *From near Kompiam.* "Every time I brought my wife back from her first husband I told her she could not go back to him but she would not agree and would return to him." His wife's brother had told him, "You and the first husband can live in one house. . . . You are both of no consequence."

3. *From near Kompiam.* ". . . she did not like me and she was always angry with me. This woman . . . did not like living with me. . . . she would not sleep with me and resisted all my advances. . . . She always called me 'rubbish.' "

4. *From Yaramanda.* "Her mother and father were always persuading her to leave me and go back to their place. I have used up many pigs in getting her to come back to me."

5. *From near Wapenamanda.* "My wife . . . did not like this place and did not stay with me all the time. She was always going

223

back to her people and to my people. . . . I had to cook my own food while my wife spent her time with her mother."

Most apparent from these statements is the insecurity of the accused, who were obliged to suffer the indignity of supporting themselves while making repeated payments to affines to facilitate the return of their wives. The crimes appear to have been unpremeditated and the accused invariably presented themselves to the Administration afterwards.

Appendix 3
Principal Raiapu Cultigens

Name			No. of Named Varieties	Sexual Designation*	Antiquity	Remarks
Botanical	Common	Raiapu				
FOOD PLANTS†						
Amaranthus tricolor	...	yakú‡	?	F	Traditional§	Both a subsistence and a "business" crop; "hawked" at Kumbasakama
Arachis hypogaea	peanut	kalyípu	1	...	Introduced c. 1946 from ANGAU farm in Tchak Valley	
Brassicaceae		kéba	?	F	Traditional	Principally a "business" crop
Brassica oleracea	cabbage	...	1	...	Probably introduced by Administration in 1940's	
Colocasia esculenta	taro	máa	23	F	Traditional	Both a subsistence and a "business" crop
Cucumis sp.	cucumber	tobéla	?	F	Traditional	
Cucumis sativus	cucumber	...	1	...	Introduced in 1950's by Lutheran mission	
Cucurbita pepo	pumpkin	...	1	...	Introduced in 1950's by Lutheran mission	Both a subsistence and a "business" crop. "Tips" (shoots and young leaves) eaten, as well as the fruit
Daucus carota	carrot	...	1	...	Probably introduced by Administration in 1940's	"Business" crop
Dioscorea alata	yam	amú	11	M	Traditional, apart from 1 variety introduced from coast in 1950's by a Lutheran evangelist	
Dioscorea bulbifera	yam	édaganigo	1	F	Traditional	Tubers and bulbils eaten
Dolichos lablab	lablab	tupáila	2	F	Traditional	
Hydrocotyle javanica	...	yai-íbi‡	?	F	Traditional	

Ipomoea batatas	sweet potato	*maṗú*	35	F	Traditional, apart from 10 varieties introduced since 1940's by Administration employees and from ANGAU farm	Principally a "business" crop.
Lactuca sativa	lettuce	...	1	...	Introduced in 1950's by Lutheran mission	
Lagenaria sp.	gourd	*saníma*	?	F	Traditional	Fruit normally eaten immature; seeds only of mature fruit eaten
Lycopersicum esculentum	tomato	...	1	...	Probably introduced by Administration in 1940's	Principally a "business" crop. Overripe fruit fed to pigs
Musa spp.	banana	*saé*	9	M	Traditional, apart from 3 varieties introduced in 1960's from the lower Lai Valley	
Pandanus sp.‖	nut pandanus	*ága*	?	M	Traditional	
Passiflora sp.	passionfruit	*buḷáṣa*	1	...	Introduced in 1940's by Administration	Principally a "business" crop
Phaseolus vulgaris	bean	...	1	...	Probably introduced by Administration in 1940's	Principally a "business" crop
Pisum sativum	pea	...	1	...	Introduced in 1950's by Lutheran mission	Principally a "business" crop
Psophocarpus tetragonobulus	winged bean	*aḷógo*	13	F	Traditional	Seeds, leaves, and tubers eaten
?*Ricinus communis*	castor oil plant	*kaliṗáne‡*	3	F	Traditional	
Rungia klossii‖	...	*kiagaṗu‡*	2	F	Traditional	
Saccharum edule	coastal pitpit	*kuni*	?2	F	Traditional	
Saccharum officinarum	sugarcane	*lyáa*	8	M	Traditional	
Setaria palmaefolia	highland pitpit	*mína*	7	F	Traditional	
Solanum nigrum	...	*takúta‡*	?	F	Traditional	
Solanum tuberosum	Irish potato	*samúu*	?	...	Probably introduced in the 1930's from the Mt. Hagen area	Both a subsistence and a "business" crop
Xanthosoma sagitlifolium	taro kongkong	...	1	...	Introduced (in 1950's?)	
Zea mays	corn	*kaníṗá*	1	...	Introduced c. 1946 from ANGAU farm	
Zingiber sp.	ginger	*aráma*	?3	F	Traditional	

Appendix 3 (cont'd)

Name			No. of Named Varieties	Sexual Designation*	Antiquity	Remarks
Botanical	Common	Raiapu				
OTHER USEFUL CULTIVATED PLANTS						
Acorus calamus‖	sweet flag	répa	?	M	Traditional	Ritual use; fed to pigs and planted by bachelors in the sádará ceremonies
Bambusa sp.	bamboo	?kemá	?	M	Traditional	Used as a water container, sharp-edged tool, and in house construction. Planted around residences
Broussonetia papyrifera	paper mulberry	koralé	?	?	Traditional	Source of fiber, and bark used to make "tapa" wig coverings. Planted in mixed gardens
Casuarina oligodon‖	casuarina	yavúti	?	M	Traditional	Building timber. Planted around residences and as a "controlled" fallow in mixed gardens
Coffea arabica	coffee	...	1	...	Introduced in early 1950's by Lutheran mission	Cash-crop
Cordyline sp.	tanket	akaípu	?	M	Traditional	Leaves used for clothing. Planted as fence and boundary marker
Eleocharis sphacelata	putput	kúlá	?	F	Traditional	Used to make women's aprons. Planted in small pools
Ficus dammaropsis‖	highland breadfruit	yakatí	?	?	Traditional	Leaves and stems eaten with pigmeat. Planted around residences
Marayllidaceae	agave	...	1	...	Introduced (in 1940's?)	Source of fiber for making string-bags, etc.
Nicotiana tabacum	tobacco	muti	5	?	Traditional (?)	Stimulant; planted under the eaves of houses
Pyrethrum cinerariifolium	pyrethrum	...	1	...	Introduced in 1963 by DASF	Cash-crop

* As applied to traditional crops only. M: Male, F: Female.

† In addition single instances of the following were observed: *Capsicum* sp, *Carica papaya*, *Manihot dulcis*, and *Pandanus coneidus*.

‡ All subsumed within the category *dóa* (leafy greens).

§ Defined as those plants whose origin is not linked with European contact.

‖ Semicultigens.

Appendix 4

Work Organization: Methods of Inquiry and Validity of the Data

A HIGH degree of accuracy was sought in the inquiry into activity patterns at Modópa. In order to overcome the doubtful reliability of informants' estimates of time spent on individual tasks, a rigorous method of observation and interview was devised which required the undivided attention of a specially trained assistant. In so far as was possible the movements of selected adults to and from their houses were observed throughout the day for the duration of the inquiry. These movements were recorded in a diary and the time noted. General observation was supplemented by a thrice-daily visit to the houses, at 9 A.M., 12 noon, and 3 P.M., when their presence or absence was recorded. This information served as a datum for checking any unobserved movements. Finally their houses were visited again each evening and the informants questioned, with the aid of the diary, on all activities they had carried out during the day. On this basis accurate determination of the time devoted to different tasks was generally possible. In the course of questioning, the location of each activity was established as well as the names and numbers of individuals participating. As a result information was also obtained on the amount and proportion of time spent traveling and on the size and composition of work groups for the various activities.

Such detailed inquiry was demanding of both the observer and the observed. It resulted in limiting the survey to two six-week periods representative of seasonal variations in activity, and it imposed considerable limitations on the size and composition of the sample. About thirty individuals were the maximum that could be considered without any substantial reduction in accuracy of the survey, and it was necessary that they all reside within five to ten minutes' walking distance of my house. A random sampling procedure was therefore out of the question. Such a procedure would not, anyway, have been particularly suitable for obtaining information on the form and extent of cooperation between individuals.

For methodological as well as logistic reasons the sample was drawn from a single locality group: the residents of the Modópa terrace section. In the first period ten households were surveyed, nine of which were members of a single patrilineage, and inquiry was restricted to these same nine for the second period. The population therefore comprised a clearly defined social group that was, at the same time, sufficiently diverse in composition to provide some indication of individual and household variations in activity patterns. The main characteristics of the sample are indicated in Appendix 1. For the purposes of the survey the activity patterns of children were disregarded since it was felt that their contribution to household tasks, where significant, was amenable to qualitative treatment.

The sample can reasonably be considered representative enough to characterize those Raiapu who inhabit the terrace sections and lower slopes of the main ranges, and this would account for two-thirds of an estimated total population of thirty thousand. Whether the intrasample comparisons have any general validity is of course another matter. In order to provide some measure of the significance of the difference between mean weekly figures a "t" test was applied to Tables 21 and 25 and a chi-square test to Table 26. In the case of the "t" test the equation

$$ t = \frac{\overline{X}_1 - \overline{X}_2}{s'} \sqrt{\frac{N_1 N_2}{N_1 + N_2}} $$

was used, where $s' =$ the standard deviation of the population. In Table 21 t was computed to be 4.13 (df $= 10$), and the difference between the means for the two survey periods is therefore significant at the 1 percent level. In Table 25 t was computed to be 2.24 (df $= 34$), the difference between the means for the two sexes being significant at the 5 percent level. In the case of the chi-square test the equation

$$ \chi^2 = \sum \frac{(O - E)^2}{E} $$

was used, where $O =$ the observed, and $E =$ the expected mean. No significant differences were established between the general levels of activity of individuals of differing marital status.

The various tabulations indicate that it is primarily at the level of individual activities that significant differences may be expected between groups, this applying particularly in the case of Table 26. However, to test for this it would be necessary to do an analysis of variance and, in view of the volume of data, have it programed on a computer. This was not done. On the basis of the tests applied it is evident that a high level of statistical significance can be ascribed to some of the data, and it may be expected in other cases. The material as a whole, however, should be viewed rather as a methodological advance, in the sense that a high degree of accuracy can be assumed of the data obtained. What is required now is the extension of the survey to other populations to provide some firm test of the validity of the intrasample differences.

Appendix 5

The Composition of Foodstuffs per 100 gm

(raw weights, edible portion)

Item	Calories	Protein (g)	Fat (g)	Calcium (mg)	Iron (mg)	Carotene (I.U.)	Thiamin (mg)	Riboflavin (mg)	Niacin (mg)	Ascorbic Acid (mg)	Source
Banana	94	1.1	...	8	tr.	400	0.05	0.08	0.60	19.9	1
Beans (eaten green, in pod)	34	2.0	...	50	1.4	200	0.08	0.12	0.50	20.0	6
Beef (mod. fat, whole carcass)	262	16.0	22.0	10	2.5	...	0.07	0.15	4.50	...	6
Biscuits (sweet mixed)	556	5.5	31.0	83	1.2	N.A.	N.A.	N.A.	N.A.	N.A.	3
Coconut meat (green)	230	1.9	10.0	21	2.0	...	0.11	0.01	0.20	3.0	1
Corn (on cob)	102	3.7	1.0	9	0.5	390	0.15	0.12	1.70	12.0	1
Cucumber	11	0.6	...	23	0.3	...	0.04	0.04	0.20	10.0	1
D. lablab	340	22.0	2.0	80	3.5	...	0.60	0.20	2.30	...	4
Ginger (root)	65	2.0	1.0	20	2.5	...	0.16	0.43	0.60	6.0	1
Gourd	28	0.7	...	20	0.6	...	0.04	0.03	0.60	15.0	6
Green leaves (av. of Amaranthus sp. and Rungia sp.)	30	2.7	0.3	369	3.0	9000	0.10	0.20	0.60	60.0	1
Irish potato	75	2.0	...	10	0.7	...	0.10	0.03	1.50	15.0	6
Lard	891	...	99.0	...	...	...	...	...	...	...	6
Leaves, low carotene (e.g. cabbage)	23	1.5	0.2	40	0.5	30	0.05	0.05	0.30	40.0	6
Leaves, medium carotene (e.g. pumpkin)	28	2.0	0.3	80	2.5	1000	0.08	0.20	0.50	50.0	6
Lettuce	19	1.4	...	35	1.0	300	0.10	0.10	0.40	15.0	6
Luncheon meat	335	11.4	29.0	18	1.1	...	N.A.	0.40	N.A.	...	3
Pandanus julianetti	588	10.7	59.0	...	...	...	0.22	...	1.31	...	5
Passionfruit	70	1.5	2.0	9	...	...	...	0.12	1.90	25.0	4
Peanut	335	25.6	43.0	73	1.8	...	1.09	0.13	15.60	...	2

Peas (fresh, shelled)	104	7.0	...	40	2.0	150	0.30	0.15	1.50	25.0	6
Pilchards (canned)	221	18.9	15.0	190	2.6	...	...	...	N.A.	...	3
Pork (fat)	448	10.0	45.0	5	1.4	...	0.43	0.11	2.30	...	1
P. Tetragonolobus (seeds)	97	8.1	4.0	30	1.1	160	0.01	0.18	1.60	37.0	1
P. Tetragonolobus (root tubers)	assume same as starchy root (sweet potato)										1
Pumpkin	44	1.5	...	20	0.7	1500	0.04	0.08	0.06	10.0	1
Rice (highly milled, polished)	352	7.0	0.5	5	1.0	...	0.06	0.03	1.00	...	6
S. edule	38	4.1	...	10	N.A.	N.A.	...	N.A.	N.A.	21.0	7
S. palmaefolia	23	0.4	0.2	21	0.9	830	0.18	0.19	1.40	33.0	1
Sugarcane	58	0.4	...	10	...	...	...	...	...	...	1
Sweet potato	150	0.9	...	15	0.8	...	0.13	0.05	0.70	31.3	1
Taro (Colocasia and Xanthosoma)	145	1.4	...	39	1.0	30	0.10	0.03	0.40	6.2	1
Tomato (with skin)	20	1.0	...	5	0.4	250	0.06	0.04	0.70	25.0	6
Wheat flour (75 percent extraction)	350	10.0	1.0	16	1.5	...	0.08	0.05	0.80	...	6
Yam	107	1.9	...	10	0.9	tr.	0.10	0.05	0.40	5.6	1

Notes: (1) Opposum treated as beef. (2) Chewing gum (0.001g per capita per diem) disregarded as no values found. (3) N.A. = not available.

Sources: 1. Hipsley and Kirk (1965); 2. Massal and Barrau (1956); 3. McCance and Widdowson (1960); 4. Peters (1957); 5. Peters (1958); 6. Platt (1963); 7. Department of External Territories (1947).

Appendix 6

Sirunki: Nightly Minimum Temperature (°C) July–September 1966

			Site*			
				Modó		
Date		Screen	top (84 cm)	side (53 cm)	bottom (8 cm)	Cleared ground
July	17	6.8	. . .	. . .	. . .	. . .
	18	9.9	. . .	. . .	. . .	. . .
	19	10.0	9.6	9.4	9.7	. . .
	20	10.6	9.8	9.9	10.0	. . .
	21	7.8	6.5	6.2	6.6	. . .
	22	8.9	8.3	8.4	8.6	. . .
	23	6.8	5.8	5.3	5.6	. . .
	24	8.4	6.4	6.2	6.3	. . .
	25	5.3	3.8	3.5	3.8	. . .
	26	7.8	6.8	6.7	6.4	. . .
	27	8.0	6.8	6.3	. . .	. . .
	28	5.6	5.1	. . .	. . .	. . .
	29	7.2	6.6	6.7	6.8	. . .
	30	9.3	9.2	9.3	9.4	. . .
	31	9.4	9.3	9.4	9.6	. . .
August	1	8.8	7.7	7.5	7.8	. . .
	2	6.1	3.7	3.3	3.2	. . .
	3	9.2	8.3	8.5	8.6	. . .
	4	9.3	8.7	8.8	8.9	. . .
	5	6.9	5.3	4.8	4.8	. . .
	6	7.2	5.9	5.4	5.3	. . .
	7	6.2	4.6	4.4	4.4	. . .
	8	8.9	6.6	6.6	6.6	. . .
	9	8.3	6.5	6.4	6.3	. . .
	10	8.8	7.0	6.6	6.7	5.1
	11	4.8	2.8	2.2	2.3	0.8
	12	6.3	3.3	3.3	3.1	1.2
	13	7.2	4.7	4.7	4.7	3.3
	14	9.3	8.9	9.3	9.2	8.9

Appendix 6 (cont'd)

		Site*			
		Modó			
Date	Screen	top (84 cm)	side (53 cm)	bottom (8 cm)	Cleared ground
August 15	8.3	6.6	5.9	5.7	4.7
16	6.9	3.9	3.7	3.6	2.4
17	5.2	2.6	1.9	2.0	0.2
18	7.2	5.9	5.5	5.5	3.9
19	8.7	7.6	. . .	7.7	6.5
20	8.8	7.3	7.2	7.1	5.9
21	8.1	6.9	6.6	6.6	5.6
22	7.4	6.5	6.6	6.6	5.9
23	8.7	7.6	7.6	7.7	7.1
24	8.3	6.7	7.0	6.9	6.2
25	4.2	2.6	2.1	2.1	0.7
26	7.6	5.6	5.7	5.7	4.9
27	6.1	5.3	5.4	5.3	3.7
28	8.2	6.9	6.4	6.6	5.8
29	7.8	6.9	6.6	6.6	5.7
30	7.0	5.7	5.8	5.7	4.8
31	6.8	6.1	. . .	5.9	4.8
September 1	9.8	8.9	9.0	9.2	8.5
2	5.6	4.7	. . .	4.5	3.5
3	6.6	5.4	5.2	5.0	4.2
4	7.6	7.2	7.2	7.2	6.5
5	8.1	7.0	7.1	6.9	6.0
6	8.8	8.1	7.8	7.6	6.6
7	8.3	7.2	7.8	7.7	. . .
8	4.7	3.0	3.1	2.7	1.3
9	5.4	3.5	3.2	2.9	1.4
10	7.4	. . .	. . .	. . .	. . .
11	8.5	. . .	. . .	. . .	. . .

* Screen located at Sirunki Mission (2653m MSL) c. 1km distance from other sites (2662m MSL). The cleared ground site was 6.1m diagonally down-slope from the mound (*modó*).

Glossary

akáryáda	man's house
aoai	reddish-brown clay soil
édáda	woman's house
kitisenáda	"christian's house"; a christian family's dwelling with no accommodation for pigs
modó	large, mulched mound carrying a number of sweet potato plants
nai áda	"new house"; built in the style of Administration rest houses and generally a family dwelling
patáge áda	bachelor's house
pubutí	chocolate-brown, finely structured topsoil
saádí	obligation or debt; used principally with reference to commodities that are distributed through the *tée*
sadárú	ritual seclusion of bachelors
tée	ceremonial exchange cycle involving, primarily, the distribution of pigs
tugké	greenish clay soil with ocher-colored concretions
yukúsi	small, unmulched mound carrying a single sweet potato plant

Bibliography

Aldrich-Blake, R. N.
   1932   *On the Fixation of Atmospheric Nitrogen by Bacteria Living
          Symbiotically in Root Nodules of* Casuarina equisetifolia.
          Oxford Forestry Memoirs, No. 14, Oxford.
Allan, W.
   1949   *Studies in African Land Usage in Northern Rhodesia.*
          Rhodes-Livingstone Papers, No. 15, Lusaka.
Bailey, K. V.
   1963   "Nutrition in New Guinea." *Food and Nutrition Notes and
          Reviews,* 20:89–112, Canberra.
———, and J. Whiteman
   1963   "Dietary Studies in the Chimbu (New Guinea Highlands)."
          Journal of Tropical Geography and Medicine, 15:377–88.
Barnes, J. A.
   1962   "African Models in the New Guinea Highlands." *Man,* 62:
          5–9.
Barrau, Jacques
   1958   *Subsistence Agriculture in Melanesia.* Bernice P. Bishop
          Museum Bulletin No. 219, Honolulu.
Berndt, Ronald M.
   1964   "Warfare in the New Guinea Highlands." *American Anthro-
          pologist,* 66 (No. 4, Pt. 2): 183–203.
Bond, G.
   1957   "The Development and Significance of Root Nodules of
          Casuarina." *Annals of Botany,* 21:373–80.
Boserup, Ester
   1965   *The Conditions of Agricultural Growth: The Economics of
          Agrarian Change Under Population Pressure.* London: Allen
          and Unwin. Also published by Aldine, 1965.

Bowers, Nancy

1965a "Permanent Bachelorhood in the Upper Kaugel Valley of Highland New Guinea." *Oceania,* 36:27–37.

1965b "Agricultural Practices and Successional Vegetation in the Upper Kaugel Valley, Western Highlands, Australian New Guinea." Paper delivered at the Northwestern Anthropological Conference. Mimeographed.

1968 "The Ascending Grasslands: An Anthropological Study of Ecological Succession in a High Mountain Valley of New Guinea." Ph.D. thesis, Columbia University.

Brookfield, H. C.

1962 "Local Study and Comparative Method: An Example from Central New Guinea." *Annals of the Association of American Geographers,* 52:242–54.

1964 "The Ecology of Highland Settlement: Some Suggestions." *American Anthropologist,* 66 (No. 4, Pt. 2): 20–38.

1968 "New Directions in the Study of Agricultural Systems in Tropical Areas." In *Evolution and Environment,* edited by Ellen T. Drake. New Haven, Conn.: Yale University Press. Pp. 413–39.

1970 "Population, Society and the Allocation of Resources." In *Geography and a Crowding World,* edited by R. M. Prothero, L. Kosinski, and W. Zelinsky. New York: Oxford University Press. Pp. 129–53.

———, and Paula Brown

1963 *Struggle for Land.* Melbourne: Oxford University Press.

Brookfield, H. C., and Peter J. White

1968 "Revolution or Evolution in the Prehistory of the New Guinea Highlands." *Ethnology,* 7:43–52.

Brown, Paula

1962 "Non-agnates among the Patrilineal Chimbu." *Journal of the Polynesian Society,* 71:57–69.

———, and H. C. Brookfield

1967 "Chimbu Residence and Settlement: A Study of Cycles, Trends, and Idiosyncracies." *Pacific Viewpoint,* 8:119–51.

Buckman, H. O., and N. C. Brady

1960 *The Nature and Properties of Soils.* New York: Macmillan.

Bulmer, Ralph

1960a "Leadership and Social Structure among the Kyaka People of the Western Highlands District of New Guinea." Ph.D. thesis, Australian National University.

1960b "Political Aspects of the Moka Ceremonial Exchange System among the Kyaka People of the Western Highlands of New Guinea." *Oceania*, 31:1–13.

Bulmer, Susan
    1966   "Pig Bone from Two Archaeological Sites in the New Guinea Highlands." *Journal of the Polynesian Society*, 75: 504–5.
    ———, and Ralph Bulmer
    1964   "The Prehistory of the Australian New Guinea Highlands." *American Anthropologist*, 66 (No. 4, Pt. 2): 39–76.

Bureau of Statistics, TPNG
    1963   *Survey of Indigenous Agriculture and Ancillary Surveys.* Konedobu: Government Printer.
    1965   "Report on Intensive Agricultural Surveys in the Maprik Sub-district, 1961–64." Konedobu. Mimeographed.
    1967a   "Report on Intensive Agricultural Surveys in the Wabag Sub-district, 1962–66." Konedobu. Mimeographed.
    1967b   "Report on Intensive Agricultural Surveys in the Chimbu Survey Area, 1962–64." Konedobu. Mimeographed.

Bus, G. A. M.
    1951   "The *Te* Festival or Gift Exchange in Enga (Central Highlands of New Guinea)." *Anthropos*, 46:813–24.

Chisholm, Michael
    1962   *Rural Settlement and Land Use.* London: Hutchinson University Library. Also published by John Wiley and Sons, 1967.

Clark, P. J., and F. C. Evans
    1954   "Distance to Nearest Neighbor as a Measure of Spatial Relationships in Populations." *Ecology*, 35:445–53.

Clarke, William C.
    1966   "From Extensive to Intensive Shifting Cultivation: A Succession from New Guinea." *Ethnology*, 5:347–59.
    1968   "The Bomagai-Angoiang of New Guinea: The World's Most Efficient Farmers?" Paper delivered at the 64th annual meeting of the Association of American Geographers. Mimeographed.
    ———, and John M. Street
    1967   "Soil Fertility and Cultivation Practices in New Guinea." *Journal of Tropical Geography*, 24:7–11.

Conklin, H. C.
    1957   *Hanunóo Agriculture: A Report on an Integral System of Shifting Cultivation in the Philippines.* FAO Forestry Development Paper No. 12, Rome.

de Lepervanche, Marie
1967–
    68 "Descent, Residence, and Leadership in the New Guinea Highlands." *Oceania*, 38:134–58 and 163–89.

Denevan, William D.
1966 *The Aboriginal Cultural Geography of the Llanos de Mojos of Bolivia*. Ibero-Americana No. 48. Berkeley and Los Angeles: University of California Press.

Department of External Territories, Commonwealth of Australia
1947 *Report of the New Guinea Nutrition Survey Expedition*. Canberra: Government Printer.

Elkin, A. P.
1953 "Delayed Exchange in Wabag Sub-district, Central Highlands of New Guinea, with Notes on the Social Organization." *Oceania*, 23:161–201.

Epstein, A. L., and T. S. Epstein
1962 "A Note on Population in Two Tolai Settlements." *Journal of the Polynesian Society*, 71:70–82.

Fairbairn, I. J.
1967 "Waso: An Extension of the Namasu Principle." In *New Guinea People in Business and Industry: Papers from the First Waigani Seminar*. New Guinea Research Bulletin No. 20, Canberra. Pp. 89–97.

Fisk, E. K.
1962 "Planning in a Primitive Economy: Special Problems of Papua–New Guinea." *Economic Record*, 38:462–78.

Fitzpatrick, E. A.
1965 "Climate of the Wabag-Tari Area." In *General Report on Lands of the Wabag-Tari Area, Territory of Papua and New Guinea, 1960–61*. Land Research Series, No. 15, CSIRO, Melbourne. Pp. 56–69.

Flenley, J. R.
1967 "The Present and Former Vegetation of the Wabag Region of New Guinea." Ph.D. thesis, Australian National University. Multilithed.

Frake, Charles O.
1962 "Cultural Ecology and Ethnography." *American Anthropologist*, 64:53–59.

Geertz, Clifford
1963 *Agricultural Involution: The Processes of Ecological Change in Indonesia*. Berkeley and Los Angeles: University of California Press.

Geiger, Rudolf
1965 *The Climate near the Ground.* Cambridge, Mass.: Harvard University Press.

Getis, A.
1964 "Temporal Land-Use Pattern Analysis with the Use of Nearest Neighbor and Quadrat Methods." *Annals of the Association of American Geographers,* 54:391–99.

Golson, J., R. J. Lampert, J. Wheeler, and W. A. Ambrose
1967 "A Note on Carbon Dates for Horticulture in the New Guinea Highlands." *Journal of the Polynesian Society,* 73:369–71.

Haggett, Peter
1965 *Locational Analysis in Human Geography.* London: Edward Arnold.

Harris, David R.
1969 "Agricultural Systems, Ecosystems, and the Origins of Agriculture." In *The Domestication and Exploitation of Plants and Animals,* edited by Peter J. Ucko and G. W. Dimbleby. Chicago: Aldine. Pp. 3–15.

Heider, Karl G.
1967 "Speculative Functionalism: Archaic Elements in New Guinea Dani Culture." *Anthropos,* 62:833–40.
1970 *The Dugum Dani.* Chicago: Aldine.

Hipsley, E. H., and Nancy Kirk
1965 *Studies of Dietary Intake and Expenditure of Energy by New Guineans.* South Pacific Commission Technical Paper No. 147, Nouméa.

Ho, Robert
1968 "A Major Clearing in the Jungle: On J. E. Spencer's 'Shifting Cultivation in Southeastern Asia.'" *Pacific Viewpoint,* 9:173–89.

Hogbin, H. Ian
1951 *Transformation Scene: The Changing Culture of a New Guinea Village.* London: Routledge and Kegan Paul.
——, and C. Wedgwood
1952 "Local Grouping in Melanesia." *Oceania,* 23:241–76.

Houston, J. M.
1953 *A Social Geography of Europe.* London: Duckworth.

Howlett, Diana R.
1962 "A Decade of Change in the Goroka Valley, New Guinea: Land Use and Development in the 1950s." Ph.D. thesis, Australian National University. Multilithed.

Hughes, Ian
1966   "Availability of Land, and Other Factors Determining the
       Incidence and Scale of Cash Cropping in the Kere Tribe,
       Sina Sina, Chimbu District, New Guinea." B.A. (Honours)
       thesis, University of Sydney.

Hunter, J. M.
1967   "The Social Roots of Dispersed Settlement in Northern
       Ghana." *Annals of the Association of American Geogra-
       phers,* 57:338–49.

Kellman, M. C.
1967   "Ecological Studies on the Secondary Vegetation of a Tropi-
       cal Montane Habitat in Mindanao." Ph.D. thesis, Australian
       National University.

King, L. J.
1962   "A Quantitative Expression of the Pattern of Urban Settle-
       ments in Selected Areas of the United States." *Tijdschrift
       voor Economische en Sociale Geografie,* 53:1–7.

Langness, L. L.
1964   "Some Problems in the Conceptualization of Highlands
       Social Structures." *American Anthropologist,* 66 (No. 4,
       Pt. 2): 162–82.

Lawrence, P., and M. J. Meggitt, eds.
1965   *Gods, Ghosts, and Men in Melanesia.* Melbourne: Oxford
       University Press.

Lea, D. A. M.
1964   "Abelam Land and Sustenance: Swidden Horticulture in
       an Area of High Population Density, Maprik, New
       Guinea." Ph.D. thesis, Australian National University. Multi-
       lithed.

Lepervanche, Marie de. *See* de Lepervanche

McArthur, Margaret
1967   "Analysis of the Genealogy of a Mae-Enga Clan." *Oceania,*
       37:281–85.

McAlpine, J. R.
1966   *Land Use in the Wabag Sub-district, Territory of Papua
       and New Guinea.* Division of Land Research Technical
       Memorandum 66/8, CSIRO, Canberra.

McCance, R. A., and E. M. Widdowson
1960   *The Composition of Foods.* Medical Research Council Spe-
       cial Report Series, No. 297, London.

Massal, Emile, and Jacques Barrau

1956   *Food Plants of the South Sea Islands.* South Pacific Commission Technical Paper No. 94, Nouméa.
Matthiessen, Peter
   1962   *Under the Mountain Wall.* New York: Viking Press.
Meggers, B. J.
   1954   "Environmental Limitation on the Development of Culture." *American Anthropologist,* 56:801–24.
Meggitt, M. J.
   1957   "Housebuilding Among the Mae Enga, Western Highlands, Territory of New Guinea." *Oceania,* 27:161–76.
   1958a "The Enga of the New Guinea Highlands: Some Preliminary Observations." *Oceania,* 28:253–330.
   1958b "Mae Enga Time-Reckoning and Calendar, New Guinea." *Man,* 58:74–77.
   1964   "Male-Female Relationships in the Highlands of Australian New Guinea." *American Anthropologist,* 66 (No. 4, Pt. 2): 204–24.
   1965a *The Lineage System of the Mae-Enga of New Guinea.* Edinburgh: Oliver and Boyd.
   1965b "The Mae-Enga of the Western Highlands." In *Gods, Ghosts, and Men in Melanesia,* edited by P. Lawrence and M. J. Meggitt. Melbourne: Oxford University Press. Pp. 105–31.
   1967   "The Pattern of Leadership among the Mae-Enga of New Guinea." *Anthropological Forum,* 2:20–35.
Metson, A. J.
   1961   *Methods of Chemical Analysis for Soil Survey Samples.* Soil Bureau Bulletin No. 12, New Zealand Department of Scientific and Industrial Research, Wellington.
Mowry, H.
   1933   "Symbiotic Nitrogen Fixation in the Genus *Casuarina.*" *Soil Science,* 36:409–21.
Newman, Philip L.
   1965   *Knowing the Gururumba.* New York: Holt, Rinehart and Winston.
Nye, P. H., and D. J. Greenland
   1960   *The Soil under Shifting Cultivation.* Commonwealth Bureau of Soils Technical Communication No. 51, Harpenden.
Oliver, Douglas L.
   1955   *A Solomon Island Society.* Cambridge, Mass.: Harvard University Press.
Oomen, H. A. P. C., and S. H. Malcolm

1958   *Nutrition and the Papuan Child*. South Pacific Commission Technical Paper No. 118, Nouméa.

———, W. Spoon, J. E. Heesterman, J. Ruinard, R. Luyken, and P. Slump

1961   "The Sweet Potato as the Staff of Life of the Highland Papuan." *Journal of Tropical Geography and Medicine*, 13: 55–66.

Oosterwal, G.

1961   *People of the Tor*. Assen: Van Gorcum.

Perry, R. A., M. J. Bik, H. A. Haantjens, J. R. McAlpine, R. Pullen, R. G. Robbins, and G. K. Rutherford

1965   "Land Systems of the Wabag-Tari Area." In *General Report on Lands of the Wabag-Tari Area, Territory of Papua and New Guinea, 1960–61*. Land Research Series, No. 15, CSIRO, Melbourne. Pp. 14–55.

Peters, F. E.

1957   *Chemical Composition of South Pacific Foods: An Annotated Bibliography*. South Pacific Commission Technical Paper No. 100, Nouméa.

1958   *The Chemical Composition of South Pacific Foods*. South Pacific Commission Technical Paper No. 115, Nouméa.

Platt, B. S.

1962   *Tables of Representative Values of Foods Commonly used in Tropical Countries*. Medical Research Council Special Report Series, No. 302, London.

Porter, P. W.

1970   "The Concept of Environmental Potential as Exemplified by Tropical African Research." In *Geography and a Crowding World*, edited by R. M. Prothero, L. Kosinski, and W. Zelinsky. New York: Oxford University Press. Pp. 187–217.

Pospisil, Leopold

1963   *The Kapauku Papuans of West New Guinea*. New York: Holt, Rinehart and Winston.

Pouwer, Jan

1964   "A Social System in the Star Mountains: Toward a Reorientation of the Study of Social Systems." *American Anthropologist*, 66 (No. 4, Pt. 2): 133–61.

Rappaport, Roy A.

1967   *Pigs for the Ancestors: Ritual in the Ecology of a New Guinea People*. New Haven: Yale University Press.

Rimmer, P. J.

1968   "A Framework for Analysing Melbourne's Industrial Structure." Paper delivered at the sixth meeting of the Institute of Australian Geographers. Mimeographed.

Robbins, R. G.
1963a "Correlations of Plant Patterns and Population Migration into the Australian New Guinea Highlands." In *Plants and the Migrations of Pacific Peoples: A Symposium,* edited by Jacques Barrau. Honolulu: Bishop Museum Press. Pp. 45–59.

1963b "The Anthropogenic Grasslands of New Guinea." In *Proceedings of the UNESCO Symposium on Humid Tropics Vegetation, Goroka 1960.* Canberra: Government Printer. Pp. 313–29.

———, and R. Pullen
1965 "Vegetation of the Wabag-Tari Area." In *General Report on Lands of the Wabag-Tari Area, Territory of Papua and New Guinea, 1960–61.* Land Research Series, No. 15, CSIRO, Melbourne. Pp. 100–15.

Rutherford, G. K., and H. A. Haantjens
1965 "Soils of the Wabag-Tari Area." In *General Report on Lands of the Wabag-Tari Area, Territory of Papua and New Guinea, 1960–61.* Land Research Series, No. 15, CSIRO, Melbourne. Pp. 85–119.

———, and R. A. Perry
1965 "Land Use Capability of the Wabag-Tari Area." In *General Report on Lands of the Wabag-Tari Area, Territory of Papua and New Guinea, 1960–61.* Land Research Series, No. 15, CSIRO. Pp. 132–36.

Sahlins, Marshall D.
1963 "Poor Man, Rich Man, Big-Man, Chief: Political Types in Melanesia and Polynesia." *Comparative Studies in Society and History,* 5:285–300.

Salisbury, R. F.
1962 *From Stone to Steel: Economic Consequences of a Technological Change in New Guinea.* Melbourne: Melbourne University Press.

1964 "Changes in Land Use and Tenure among the Siane of the New Guinea Highlands." *Pacific Viewpoint,* 5:1–10.

Schindler, A. J.
1952 "Land Use by Natives of Aiyura Village, Central Highlands, New Guinea." *South Pacific,* 6:302–7.

Slatyer, R. O., and I. C. McIlroy
1961 *Practical Microclimatology, with Special Reference to the*

Water Factor in Soil-Plant-Atmosphere Relationships. Melbourne: CSIRO.

Spencer, J. E.
1966 *Shifting Cultivation in Southeastern Asia.* University of California Publications in Geography, Vol. 19, Berkeley and Los Angeles.
————, and G. A. Hale
1961 "The Origin, Nature and Distribution of Agricultural Terracing." *Pacific Viewpoint,* 2:1–40.

Steward, Julian H.
1955 *Theory of Culture Change: The Methodology of Multilinear Evolution.* Urbana: University of Illinois Press.

Straatmans, W.
1967 "Ethnobotany of New Guinea in its Ecological Perspective." *Journal d'Agriculture Tropicale et de Botanique Appliquée,* 14:1–20.

Udy, S. H.
1959 *Organisation of Work: A Comparative Analysis of Production among Non-Industrial Peoples.* New Haven: Human Relations Area Files Press.

Vayda, Andrew P., Anthony Leeds, and David B. Smith
1961 "The Place of Pigs in Melanesian Subsistence." In *Proceedings of the 1961 Annual Spring Meeting of the American Ethnological Society.* Seattle: University of Washington Press. Pp. 69–77.

Venkatchalam, P. S.
1962 *A Study of the Diet, Nutrition, and Health of the People of the Chimbu Area.* Department of Public Health Monograph No. 4, Port Moresby.

Waddell, E. W., and P. A. Krinks
1968 *The Organisation of Production and Distribution among the Orokaiva.* New Guinea Research Bulletin No. 24, Canberra.

Walker, D.
1966 "Vegetation of the Lake Ipea Region, New Guinea Highlands. I. Forest, Grassland and 'Garden.'" *Journal of Ecology,* 54:503–33.

Watson, James B.
1964 "Introduction: Anthropology in the New Guinea Highlands." *American Anthropologist,* 66 (No. 4, Pt. 2): 1–19.
1965a "From Hunting to Horticulture in the New Guinea Highlands." *Ethnology,* 4:295–309.

1965b "The Significance of a Recent Ecological Change in the Central Highlands of New Guinea." *Journal of the Polynesian Society,* 74:438–50.
1967 "Horticultural Traditions of the Eastern New Guinea Highlands." *Oceania,* 38:81–98.
Watters, R. F.
1960 "The Nature of Shifting Cultivation: A Review of Recent Research." *Pacific Viewpoint,* 1:59–99.
197– *Shifting Cultivation in Latin America.* FAO Forestry Development Paper, Rome. Forthcoming.
Westermann, E. D.
n.d. "The Mountain People: Social Institutions of the Laiapu Enga." Wapenamanda: New Guinea Lutheran Mission (Missouri Synod). Mimeographed.
Williams, M. A. J.
1969 "Rates of Slopewash and Soil Creep in Parts of Northern and Southeastern Australia: A Comparative Study." Ph.D. thesis, Australian National University. Multilithed.

Index

Absences: long-term, 75; short-term, 84, 86. *See also* Intergroup relations

Affines, 72, 74, 107, 190; affinal ties and travel, 70

Agnation, 65, 187, 191; stress on, 10, 169, 184; acquisition of status, 19, 185, 192

Agriculture: evolution of, 4, 8, 10; system, 11, 41, 60, 63–64, 129, 140, 168, 174–78 *passim*, 181, 183, 187, 202, 204–5; intensity of, 169–70, 174, 204, 209, 210, 211, 218; intensification of, 172, 209–10, 212–20 *passim*; innovations in, 193–94, 197–98, 205; revolution, 206–8

Animals, domestic, 60. *See also* Pigs

Aruní, 31, 39, 41, 123, 137; "world view" of, 66

Bachelors, 23–24, 26–27, 87, 102, 189

Bananas, 39–40 *passim*, 51, 54, 123, 132

"Big-men," 107, 186, 188–92, 217

Cassowaries, 60–61

Casuarina, 40, 41, 54, 76, 90, 139, 193–94; nitrogen fixation by, 143–44

Cattle, 199–200

Central Highlands, 5, 8, 202

Ceremonies. *See* Sadárú; *Tée*

Chimbu, 123, 184, 202, 203, 204, 212–13

Climatic marginality, 9

Coffee, 41, 57, 59, 60, 90, 198

Commercial activities, 199–200. *See also* Coffee; Crops: commercial; *Pyrethrum*

Crops
—"business," 41, 56, 90–91, 198, 199, 205; mentioned, 57, 63
—commercial, 41, 63, 196, 198; adoption of, 58–59, 76, 199; marketing of, 69, 91, 198–99. *See also* Coffee; *Pyrethrum*
—subsistence, 16, 39, 51; segregation of staple from subsidiary, 39, 206, 209; maturation period, 45, 49, 53–54; establishment of, 49, 51, 53; "male" and "female," 51, 53, 100; propagation of, 53; disease, 120; nutritional value of, 123; altitudinal range of, 133; yield, 145. *See also* Bananas; Sweet potato; Taro; Yam

Dani, 202, 203, 207, 211

Death. *See* Health

Demographic pressure. *See* Population

Descent groups, 17, 18, 19, 107, 183–84; and locality, 9, 20, 185–86, 192; political organization, 18, 186; expansion of territories, 72, 74, 186; and residence rules, 188

Diet: eating habits, 121–22; quality of, 122; calorie intake, 123; protein intake, 123, 127; fat intake, 127; introduced foods, 128; purchased foods, 128

251

Population: pressure, 9, 10, 133, 137, 139, 166, 168–70, 173; density, 11, 17, 20, 170–74; growth, 24, 194, 196, 208, 209
Power. *See* "Big-men"
Precipitation, 161–62; seasonality of, 16, 81; intensity of, 81, 142
Prestige, 61, 74, 76, 102–3, 107, 108–12, 200. *See also* "Big-men"
Pyrethrum, 57–58, 59, 197–98

Relations. *See* Intergroup relations; Intragroup relations
Religious affiliation: and residence, 27–30, 38, 197; and house type, 30
Residence: and garden type, 46, 54; change of, 71, 72, 76; predictive model of location of, 178; and terrain type, 180–81. *See also* Minimum energy location

Sabakamádá, 14, 24, 33, 38–39, 67, 137, 149, 173, 181, 191
Sadárú, 16, 86, 87, 108, 109
Settlement pattern: regional variations, 31, 38; stability of, 32, 36, 177, 210; distorted lattice, 36; dispersed, 181, 187; "pulsating," 187; evolution of, 210. *See also* Nearest neighbor analysis
Sex: division of labor by, 22, 27, 98–100, 189, 192; male-female relationships, 22; female pollution, 87, 100
Sirunki, 131, 132, 149, 156, 159
Surplus, agricultural, 110, 112, 113, 117–20, 129
Sweet potato, 10, 39, 50, 88, 100, 120–21, 132–33; propagation of, 45; and pigs, 62; yields, 116; place in diet, 122, 124; introduction of, 206, 208. *See also* Mounds
Soil, 175; types, 44, 134; erosion, 51;

physical and chemical properties, 136, 142, 145, 147, 149, 160; erosion control, 143; aeration, 145–46; organic matter content, 146–47, 167; moisture, 161–66
—fertility: status, 134, 145, 146; maintenance of, 135–36, 141, 144, 146, 159–60, 166; decline, 140, 143, 144, 146

Taro, 39, 51, 63
Tchak Valley, 16, 86, 91, 173, 174, 180
Tée, 60, 69, 86, 108–9, 111, 120, 192, 197, 200
Temperate vegetables. *See* Crops: "business"
Temperature: regimes near the ground, 133–34, 153–56
Terrain types, 14; main range slopes, 14, 208; dissected valley slopes, 16; terrace sections, 16; relationship to garden types, 42, 44, 47–48, 50, 56, 133–35, 202–3, 204; and residence, 180–81
Trade goods, traditional, 108
Trees, economic, 40; and firewood, 90

Unmarried men. *See* Bachelors

Wabag, 156, 168, 175
Wapenamanda, 16, 58, 67, 91, 121, 147–48, 168, 194
Warfare, 37, 111, 168, 185, 186
Widowed men. *See* Bachelors
Work groups, 55, 79–80; defined, 103; size of, 103, 106; composition of, 106

Yam, 39, 51, 53, 80, 106, 116, 123
Yukúsi, 39, 42, 47–48, 56, 137, 166, 167; cultivation cycle, 117